INTENT IN ISLAMIC LAW

INTENT IN ISLAMIC LAW

Motive and Meaning in Medieval Sunnī Fiqh

BY

PAUL R. POWERS

BRILL

LEIDEN • BOSTON
2015

This paperback was originally published in hardback under ISBN 978-90-04-14592-4 as volume 25 in the series *Studies in Islamic Law and Society*.

Cover illustration: Arches of Ahmad Ibn Tulun Mosque in old Cairo, Egypt. © iStock.com/AMA66.

The Library of Congress has cataloged the hardback edition under Library of Congress Control Number 2006272693.

ISBN 978-90-04-29045-7 (paperback)
ISBN 978-90-47-41674-6 (e-book)

For Isaac and Rachel

CONTENTS

LIST OF TABLES

ACKNOWLEDGMENTS

The comprehensive treatment of any significant aspect of Islamic law is a Sisyphean goal. Islamic law is obviously far more than a simple list of rules, and its breadth, richness, and complexity call to mind such evocative phrases as 'an ocean without a shore'. With this in mind, the present work is offered less as a comprehensive presentation of Islamic legal understandings of intent than as a base-line study meant to clarify some important matters and offer a sounding board for future explorations of this and related topics. Despite its monolithic title, then, this book is more a start than an end. I am grateful to any who make use of it.

This book began as my Ph.D. dissertation in the History of Religions at the Divinity School of the University of Chicago, completed in the summer of 2001. I thank A. Kevin Reinhart and Fred Donner for bringing expert knowledge, thoughtful encouragement, and critical insight to bear on my work. I am particularly grateful to Frank Reynolds for his invaluable guidance and friendship. In his spirit, I thank the many colleagues, students, and respondents to papers who helped sharpen my thinking and writing. Wadad al-Qadi, Clarissa Burt, Farouk Mustafa, John Eisele, and Pierre Cachia all helped me learn much of what I needed to ever get this project off the ground. Wendy Donniger, Jonathan Z. Smith, and Joel Kraemer, as well as Eleanor Zelliot, Richard Crouter, and James Laine likewise deserve my thanks.

Marion Katz, Ken Garden, Paul Heck, Rebecca Copenhaver, and Eric Lundgren each provided intellectual conversation and friendship invaluable to sustaining a project of this magnitude. Among my colleagues at Lewis and Clark College, Rob Kugler and Alan Cole deserve special mention for their help and encouragement. James Riley and Joe Haker, both students at Lewis and Clark, served admirably as assistants during various phases of this project, and Joe in particular saved it from many a stylistic infelicity. Bernard Weiss merits singular acknowledgment for his expert attention to and crucial support of this project. I am also grateful to Ruud Peters and Brill for their willingness to publish this book. Trudy Kamperveen and Gera van Bedaf at Brill have been kind and highly professional guides through the publication process.

Portions of chapter 3 previously appeared in the *Journal of the American Academy of Religion* as "Interiors, Intentions, and the 'Spirituality' of Islamic Ritual Practice" (2004). Portions of this book were also presented at conferences, including the 1998 and 1999 Annual Meetings of the American Academy of Religion; the 1998 Middle East History and Theory Conference at the Center for Middle Eastern Studies, The University of Chicago; and the 2003 Northwest Regional Middle East Seminar at Portland State University. The Fulbright Commission awarded me a fellowship whose generous terms allowed me to spend a year studying Islamic law in Jordan. I also thank the Henry Luce Dissertation Fellowship Program for a grant during my final year of dissertation writing, and the members of the Luce Seminar for conversations which invigorated this project. Lewis and Clark College provided funding at several critical points to support various aspects of this project.

Finally, my limitless thanks to my family, especially Rachel and Isaac, for their patience and loving support in all aspects of my life. Words, even an entire book's worth, cannot do them justice.

CHAPTER ONE

INTRODUCTION

> Actions are defined by intentions, and to every person what he intends (*innamā al-a'māl bil-niyyāt wa-innamā li-kull imri'in mā nawā*). So whoever emigrated [participated in the *hijra*] for God and His Messenger, then his emigration was for God and God's Messenger, and whoever emigrated for worldly benefits or for a woman to marry, his emigration was what he emigrated for.[1]

This *ḥadīth* is cited repeatedly in virtually all manuals of Islamic law. It highlights the important role of intent in defining actions and serves as a backdrop for jurists' formulation of the rules of law. Joseph Schacht calls intent nothing less than "a fundamental concept of the whole of Islamic religious law, be it concerned with worship or with law in the narrow sense."[2] Medieval Muslim jurists treat intent as a component of nearly every legally relevant action, from purification and prayer, to sales and divorce, to fornication and murder. In Islamic law, intentions are a constitutive element of human actions, critical to the legal assessment of those actions. Indeed, aside from religious faith itself, intent is arguably the most important subjective or 'internal' component of the actions prescribed, proscribed, and evaluated by Muslim legal scholars.

This is not a situation peculiar to Islamic law. Legal systems, whenever and wherever they are found, often wrestle mightily with the matter of intent. Law, whether secular or religious, by definition seeks to regulate human actions, and for most legal systems, human actions are understood to involve a subjective component, which is at times a mere nuance, at others absolutely definitive. Any American with a television knows at least something about the American legal distinction between first- and second-degree murder, and between murder, manslaughter,

---

[1] This *ḥadīth* is found in most major collections, including al-Bukhārī, Muslim, al-Nisā'ī, al-Tirmidhī, and Ibn Māja, although it is not in Mālik's *al-Muwaṭṭa'*. See A.J. Wensinck, *Concordance et indices de la tradition musulmane* (Leiden: Brill, 1936–1988), s.v. "Niyya." Wensinck cites some 25 *ḥadīth*s employing the term *niyya*. However, the one given here is the only one of these consistently cited in *fiqh* manuals.

[2] Schacht, *An Introduction to Islamic Law* (Oxford: Clarendon, 1964), 116.

and justifiable homicide—distinctions which all hinge on the intent of the killer. In contemporary, secular, Western law intent is generally a critical element, especially of contract and criminal law. The same can be said of Islamic law, which adds a dimension of ritual law not found in Western secular law and where intent is also central.

If intent matters greatly in Islamic law, Islamic law itself matters greatly to Islamic society. While theology, philosophy, mathematics, astronomy, medicine, and so forth all reached impressive heights of sophistication in the medieval Islamicate world, law, the undisputed queen of the sciences in medieval Islam, held a certain pride of place.[3] One reason for, and one dialectical result of, the centrality of Islamic legal discourse is the function it served as a site for theological, ethical, anthropological, sociological, political, and other kinds of reflection (law has been called "theology par excellence in the Islamic tradition"[4]). It may be that the very structure of a monotheistic worldview pushes law to the center of human concern. As Bernard Weiss observes, "Law, it seems, is integral to monotheistic religion. The world's sole creator is necessarily by right its sole ultimate ruler, legislator, and judge. All law worthy of the name must therefore originate with him."[5] When the single, omnipotent and omniscient creator is believed to have specific preferences and requirements for human behavior, and both social order and individual eternal fate rest on adherence to those preferences and requirements, they naturally display an eclipsing brightness.

So intent is a central concern of Islamic law, and law is a central concern of most Muslim societies. A fuller understanding of Islamic societies, then, would be aided by a fuller understanding of the role of intent in Islamic law. The specific understanding of the nature and function of intent varies even within a single legal text, as the author moves from ritual, to economic, family, and penal law. The task at hand is thus to examine each of these legal spheres in turn. The results, it might be hoped, will be more than the sum of the parts, illuminating not only previously unnoticed aspects of Islamic ritual, contracts, family

[3] See G. Makdisi, cited in Bernard Weiss, "Law in Islam and in the West: Some Comparative Observations," in *Islamic Studies Presented to Charles J. Adams*, ed. Wael B. Hallaq and Donald P. Little (Leiden: Brill, 1991), 243.

[4] Weiss, "Law in Islam and in the West," 243.

[5] Weiss, *The Spirit of Islamic Law* (Athens and London: University of Georgia Press, 1998), 1.

structures, and so forth, but the Muslim legal understanding of the nature of human action and agency, the self, and the relation of the self to society and to God.

The overarching arguments of this book are that, in general, Muslim jurists treat intent as definitive of human actions most of the time; that when they do not, they have specific reasons for this; and that the differences among the types of actions with which Islamic law is concerned (such as ritual, contract, family, and penal law) are reflected in different understandings of the nature, role, and terminology of intent. Throughout Islamic law, intent matters because it is partly definitive of many acts; along with certain objective features, *intent makes acts what they are.* Given that Islamic law is manifestly concerned with defining, categorizing, and regulating human actions, anything so central to defining those actions must also be central to the law. Intent partly determines the location of a given action in the legal taxonomy, which in turn determines the legal status of the action, such as prescribed, proscribed, preferred, disliked, and so forth, or any penalties attached to an action. Because intent is subjective—invisible, silent, 'internal'—Muslim jurists must establish some legally-recognized means for discerning it, such as deciding which objective indicants point to which subjective states, and exploring the jurists' efforts in this regard will be another task throughout this book.

An additional broad observation borne out in these pages is that the primary sources of Islamic law present us with no single term for intent. Instead, Muslim jurists draw on a variety of Arabic terms to encompass the conceptual ground covered by the word 'intent' as that term is generally used in English-language sources dealing with law. Of course, English speakers have a variety of terms at their disposal in this regard as well (such as 'goal', 'plan', 'desire', 'will', or 'expectation'), but 'intent' has taken on a technical quality in legal discourse that gives it considerable power and broad scope. The most obvious Arabic candidate for such a term is perhaps *niyya*, and indeed jurists employ this term often in various contexts throughout Islamic law. However, as we will see, *niyya* is joined by several other terms in doing the work often assigned to 'intent' in English. Moreover, the term *niyya* itself is quite malleable, appearing with technical specificity in ritual law, with more generic connotations in family and contract law, and virtually not at all in penal law. This variety of terminology is significant in itself and challenges our tendency to rely too heavily on the single English term 'intent' when talking about Islamic law. Islamic law comprises categories, interests, methods, and historical contexts very different from those reflected in commonplace Western understandings of law, and the Muslim legal approach to intent is just one of the many instances in which 'our' legal language fits 'their' legal discourse only rather loosely.

One important quality of Islamic legal discussions of intent is their pervasive and rich moral overtones. Muslim jurists implicitly establish three broad moral categories of intent, namely positive, neutral, and negative, and they show a strong tendency to use different terms for each moral type. In ritual law—itself a category foreign to contemporary Western notions of law—the jurists employ the term *niyya* almost exclusively and with considerable technical specificity. The exact nature of that technical meaning will be made clear in chapters 2 and 3. For now, it is enough to note that *niyya*, as the intent to perform special acts of religious ritual in obedience to and worship of God, carries strongly positive moral connotations. In what we might call 'civil law', roughly corresponding to Islamic contract and personal status law (discussed in chapters 4 and 5), intent is conceived of as largely morally neutral, the simple intent to act and interact with others in ordinary social intercourse. Here we find the greatest variety of terms, prominently including *qaṣd* and *irāda*, as well as *niyya*, here with only some of the same meaning it carries in ritual law. Finally, in penal contexts—the Western notion of 'criminal law' again fits rather badly the various aspects of Islamic law pertaining to punishments (considered in chapter 6)—these other terms drop away as morally problematic or malicious intent comes predominantly under the rubric of the Arabic term *ʿamd*. *Niyya* and *ʿamd* serve as the book-end terms of the spectrum of moral intent while various, less-precise terms fill out the space between. To be sure, tracking down intent in Islamic law requires more than simply translating a single term. While out of necessity and convenience I will fall back on the English 'intent' throughout this work, this should not obscure the variety and range of the terms and concepts in play in the following pages.

In its various forms and guises, intent is a critical category of Islamic legal discourse, illuminating many wider concerns and commitments of Muslim jurists, but it is not a monolithic entity. I will present no single grand unified theory of intent in Islamic law, for I do not think such a theory is forthcoming. Rather, I find multiple, sometimes overlapping and sometimes divergent, partial explanations that, taken together, suggest how and why the variety of approaches to intent—even within a single legal text—emerge. "Actions are defined by intentions" proclaimed the Prophet. This seemingly simple dictum, however, serves as a prism directing Muslim legal thought in a wide array of directions, reflecting a rich understanding of intentions, actions, and the human agents who produce—and are produced by—them.

Legal History and Sources

This is not a work of legal history as such, being more akin to a history of ideas. But an understanding of the broad outlines of Islamic legal history is necessary for my project. Scholars generally break the history of Islamic law into at least three major eras. The first, 'formative' period begins with the advent of Islam in the early- to mid-first/seventh century and lasts into the mid-fourth/tenth century.[6] This period saw the revelation of the Qur'ān and the prophetic career of Muḥammad, which together provide the foundations for Islamic law. It also saw the rapid spread of Islamic influence outward from the Arabian peninsula west across North Africa and into southwestern Europe, north into the central near East, and northeast and east toward central and south Asia. The new religion of Allāh and Muḥammad, combined with the preexisting societies and legal cultures of the territories brought under Islamic influence (including Jewish, Christian, Roman/Byzantine, Spanish, Berber, Persian, Turkic, Indian, and so forth), provided the raw materials and historical context for the formation of Islamic law.[7] Questions abound about the relative weight of

---

[6] The previous standard dating of this period, established most prominently by Joseph Schacht, placed the end of the formative period about a century earlier. Wael B. Hallaq has recently argued for the later dating adopted here. See his *The Origins and Evolution of Islamic Law* (Cambridge: Cambridge University Press, 2005), esp. 2–7, though recalibrating the dating and clarifying the general dynamics of the formative period constitutes a central theme throughout. Baber Johansen dates the waning of the 'pre-classical' period to the end of the third/ninth century, and dates the 'classical' period to the fourth/tenth-sixth/twelfth centuries, deeming the remainder of the medieval period 'post-classical' ("Casuistry: Between Legal Concept and Social Praxis," *Islamic Law and Society* 2, 2 [1995], 137–138). For an account of the emergence of the *madhhabs*, see Christopher Melchert, *The Formation of the Sunnī Schools of Law, 9th–10th Centuries C.E.* (Leiden: Brill, 1997).

[7] Regarding intent, the influence of Jewish law on Islamic deserves particular attention, though it remains beyond the scope of the present work. See Howard Eilberg-Schwartz, *The Human Will in Judaism: The Mishnah's Philosophy of Intention* (Atlanta: Scholars Press, 1986); Michael Higger, "Intention in Talmudic Law," Ph.D. diss. (Columbia University, 1927); A.J. Wensinck, "De Intentie in Recht, Ethiek en Mystiek der Semietis-

each, and the specific dynamics of development.[8] Scholars in recent decades have made great strides in answering some of them, but for present purposes it is enough to note these general features of this era. Legal doctrines changed significantly over this period as Islamic civilization gave rise to new social, political, and economic patterns, and to new institutions of law. This era gradually ended during the ʿAbbāsid period; by this point the complex creative ferment of the formative period had largely given way to relative uniformity among schools of law (*madhāhib*, sg. *madhhab*) and relative stability in legal doctrine.[9]

I will focus primarily on the 'medieval' or 'classical' period, spanning from around 300/900 to just prior to the rise of the Ottoman Empire, about 800/1400. Some scholars subdivide this long era in various ways, the most prominent being a shift from 'classical' to 'post-classical' by the end of the sixth/twelfth century. In this view, the classical period saw the development of general legal concepts out of the previous era's "simple enumeration of cases and their solutions," and this in turn gave way to the more complex reasoning of Islamic legal theory (*uṣūl al-fiqh*).[10] Certainly Islamic law was hardly uniform and static for all these centuries, and over the vast territories peopled by Muslims during this time.[11] But, as Norman Calder notes (reflecting the earlier dating of the formative period), "the genre of *furūʿ* [positive law] is continuous from the 3rd/9th to the 13th/19th century," and such dynamics took place

---

che Volken," *Verslagen en Mededeelingen der Koninklijke Akademie van Wetenschappen* 5, 4 (1920): 109–140; H.G. Enelow, "Kawwana: The Struggle for Inwardness in Judaism," in *Studies in Jewish Literature*, 82–107 (Berlin: Georg Riemer, 1913).

[8] Wael B. Hallaq argues that Arab culture provided more of the raw material of Islamic law than was previously recognized. This is one of the central themes of his *The Origins and Evolution of Islamic Law*.

[9] As Goldziher and Schacht (who reflect the earlier dating of the formative period) put it, "Until the early ʿAbbāsid period, Islamic jurisprudence had been adaptable and growing, but from then onwards it became increasingly rigid and set in its final mould. This essential rigidity helped it to maintain its stability over the centuries which saw the decay of the political institutions of Islam. As a whole, it reflects and fits the social and economic conditions of the early ʿAbbāsid period. If it grew more and more out of touch with later developments of state and society, in the long run it gained more in power over the minds than it lost in control over the bodies of the Muslims" (Ignaz Goldziher [revised by Joseph Schacht], "Fiḳh," in *Encyclopaedia of Islam*, new ed.). I take this description of the stability of post-formative Islamic law to be overstated, but nonetheless broadly accurate.

[10] Johansen, "Casuistry," 137–138 (and see 138, n. 5).

[11] For one compelling account of change within post-formative Islamic law, see Wael B. Hallaq, *Authority, Continuity and Change in Islamic Law* (Cambridge: Cambridge University Press, 2001).

within broad parameters of doctrine and legal theory that remained remarkably stable.[12] While my study of intent in Islamic law may at times underplay the degree of temporal and regional variation in pursuit of an artificially broad picture of 'the' Islamic legal approach to intent, such an approach is justified by the relative uniformity of relevant legal doctrine in this period, and by pragmatic concerns. Moreover, I will take note of significant juristic disagreements as they arise. Perhaps the best reason to focus on pre-modern law is that this is what most people, Muslim or otherwise, are talking about when they talk about 'Islamic law'.

This relatively stable (not to say static) pre-modern law held sway at least until the emergence of the Turkish-dominated Ottoman empire beginning in the fifteenth century, and in many respects until the large-scale incursion of European colonizers, and concomitant Islamic reform movements, beginning in the early nineteenth century. The upheavals of the colonial era induced changes within legal structures, as Muslim leaders strove to reform Islamic society to stand up to the new challenges, and as European administrators pushed for changes or outright replacement of Islamic law with Western law. This 'modern' era could itself be subdivided severally, most notably between colonial and post-colonial times. The exact, long-term effects of modernization on Islamic law are still very much up in the air. I will touch on modern changes to Islamic law having specifically to do with issues of intent as these matters arise, especially in the concluding chapter. I will not significantly explore issues of social history; no doubt historical contexts did influence the treatment of intentions in classical *fiqh* manuals, but the patterns of such influence are difficult to discern, especially given the efforts of Muslim jurists to make their work appear timeless and universally valid. Perhaps the connections between the law and social history may only fully emerge after the kind of work I undertake here has been done, for we need to know what 'the law' is in order to trace its historical linkages.

While I will draw on a range of primary texts, my principal sources are a variety of *fiqh* manuals drawn from a geographic and temporal range, and while this sample is not exhaustive, it is broadly representative of medieval Islamic law.[13] Texts on which I rely heavily

[12] Calder, "Sharīʿa," in *Encyclopaedia of Islam*, new ed.

[13] I will also draw occasionally on two twentieth-century Arabic-language secondary sources: ʿAbd al-Raḥman al-Jazīrī's *Kitāb al-fiqh ʿalā al-madhāhib al-arbaʿa* (Cairo: Al-

include that of the Persian Abū Isḥāq al-Shīrāzī (d. 476/1083), whose *al-Muhadhdhab fī fiqh al-imām al-Shāfiʿī* is a major manual of the medieval Shāfiʿī *madhhab*;[14] the *Ikhtiyar li-taʿlīl al-mukhtār* of Ibn Mawdūd al-Mūṣilī (d. 683/1284), an Iraqi Ḥanafī;[15] the influential *al-Mughnī* of the Ḥanbalī Ibn Qudāma (d. 620/1223);[16] the *Bidāyat al-mujtahid wa-nihāyat al-muqtaṣid* of the Mālikī Ibn Rushd (d. 595/1198, the famous Averroes) from the Islamic west.[17] These provide representation from each of the four major Sunnī *madhhab*s and were chosen, not because they are somehow unusual or marginal, but rather because they are well known and typical in content. In addition to these *fiqh* manuals, I will also draw on a text titled *al-Umniyya fī idrāk al-niyya*, the author of which was Shihāb al-Dīn al-Qarāfī (d. 684/1285), a Mālikī Berber who became a student and scholar in Cairo.[18] Though it draws primarily on the legal sciences, technically this text is not a *fiqh* manual, but rather a treatise examining the semantic and conceptual field of the term *niyya*. Other primary sources will make occasional appearances as necessary.

Maktaba al-Tijāriyya al-Kubrā, n.d.), and Wahba al-Zuḥaylī's *al-Fiqh al-islāmī wa-adillatuhu* (Beirut: Dār al-Fikr, 1989). These two texts do not take a historical or critical approach to the sources, and they should be taken only as rough guides to tendencies among *madhhab*s.

[14] Abū Isḥāq Ibrāhīm b. ʿAlī al-Shīrāzī, *al-Muhadhdhab fī fiqh al-imām al-Shāfiʿī*, ed. Muḥammad al-Zuḥaylī (Damascus: Dār al-Qalm, 1996). E. Chaumont calls Shīrāzī an "eminent jurist whose work constitutes one of the major reference sources of the S̲h̲āfiʿī school," and notes that the range of his work "extends to all the legal disciplines cultivated in the 5th/11th century, the golden age, in part as a result of his efforts, for those sciences" ("al-S̲h̲īrāzī, al-S̲h̲ayk̲h̲ al-Imām Abū Isḥāḳ Ibrāhīm b. ʿAlī b. Yūsuf al-Fīrūzābādī," in *Encyclopaedia of Islam*, new ed.). Chaumont calls the *Muhadhdhab*, composed between 455/1053 and 469/1076, Shīrāzī's "crowning achievement."

[15] ʿAbd Allāh b. Maḥmūd b. Mawdūd al-Mūṣilī, *al-Ikhtiyār li-taʿlīl al-mukhtār*, ed. Maḥmūd Abū Daqīqa (Beirut: Dār al-Kutub al-ʿIlmiyya, n.d.).

[16] Muwaffaq al-Dīn ʿAbd Allāh b. Aḥmad Ibn Qudāma, *al-Mughnī*, ed ʿAbd Allāh b. ʿAbd al-Muḥsin al-Turkī and ʿAbd al-Fatāḥ Muḥammad al-Ḥilū (Cairo: Hajir, 1992).

[17] Abū al-Walīd Muḥammad b. Aḥmad Ibn Rushd al-Qurṭubī, *Bidāyat al-mujtahid wa-nihāyat al-muqtaṣid* (Beirut: Dār al-Kutub al-ʿIlmiyya, 1988); translated into English as *The Distinguished Jurist's Primer: A Translation of "Bidāyat al-Mujtahid,"* trans. Imran Ahsan Khan Nyazee, The Great Books of Islamic Civilization (Reading: Garnet, 1994). Because this is one of the few *fiqh* manuals available in English translation, I will cite both the Arabic original and the English translation; hereafter I will abbreviate the latter as *DJP*.

[18] Aḥmad b. Idrīs al-Qarāfī, *al-Umniyya fī idrāk al-niyya* (Beirut: Dār al-Kutub al-ʿIlmiyya, 1984). Some sources indicate al-Qarāfī may have died in 682/1283; see Sherman Jackson, *Islamic Law and the State* (Leiden: Brill, 1996), 1, esp. n. 1 and n. 4. On Qarāfī's jurisprudence, see also Sherman Jackson, "The Alchemy of Domination? Some Ashʿarite Responses to Muʿtazilite Ethics," *International Journal of Middle East Studies* 31 (1999): 185–201.

Islamic positive law encompasses two general categories: the *ʿibādāt* (sg. *ʿibāda*), acts of ritual worship, and the *muʿāmalāt* (sg. *muʿāmala*), social interactions. The former are often said to regulate interactions between humans and God, the latter interactions among humans. The *ʿibādāt* include purification, prayer, and almsgiving, while the *muʿāmalāt* include marriage, divorce, inheritance, economic exchange, and injurious actions. Qarāfī gives insight into the role of intentions in the Islamic legal economy when he discusses an aspect of the difference between the *ʿibādāt* and the *muʿāmalāt*. He observes that legal commands are of two types: first, those for which the simple performance of the commanded act achieves the benefit of that act (the *muʿāmalāt*: e.g., payment of a debt, returning entrusted property, and forwarding support payments to a spouse or relative); second, those the external performance of which does not alone achieve the benefit for which God commanded the act (the *ʿibādāt*: e.g., prayer, ritual purification, fasting, the rites of the *ḥajj*).[19] Intention, for Qarāfī, constitutes the distinction: compliance with rules of the first type, regardless of the intention, benefits someone other than the actor immediately and may, if intended as an act of obedience or worship, also bring reward in the afterlife. Compliance with rules of the second type brings benefit to the actor, primarily in the hereafter, and only if intention is present and proper.[20] *Niyya* on this view is that which makes a given action one of obedience and worship, making possible divine reward. The *ʿibādāt* have no other function, while the *muʿāmalāt* do.

Human Will and the Legal Economy

Intent is a subjective, 'internal' phenomenon and as such is closely linked to the human will. Intent might be said to direct the will toward a particular goal, such as the performance of a particular act, or the

[19] Qarāfī, *al-Umniyya*, 27–28. See also Jackson, *Islamic Law and the State*, 201. It is important to note, as Jackson does, that "it is not al-Qarāfī's contention that acts of the first category are not religious acts. On the contrary, these too should be performed with the intention of worshipping God and winning salvation in the Hereafter. His point, however, is that the rules of the first category are designed first and foremost for the benefit of man here and now. As such, whenever they are complied with, man benefits, even if God does not" (201–202).

[20] This insight is drawn from Jackson, *Islamic Law and the State*, 201–202, commenting on Qarāfī, *al-Umniyya*, 27–28.

wider ends that such an act is meant to achieve. Muslims have engaged in major debates over the nature of human will, especially its freedom in a context assuming divine omnipotence. Orthodox Sunnī theology and the creeds it produced profess a belief in predestination (the doctrine of *al-qaḍā' wa-l-qadr*), supplemented by a belief in human responsibility for actions 'acquired' from God (the doctrine of *kasb* or *iktisāb*).[21] The tension between these positions is embraced rather than resolved, in part through reference to divine inscrutability (the doctrine of *bi-lā kayf*). In short, while God is omnipotent and omniscient, humans are fully free and responsible, and the mystery of this paradox only further demonstrates the majesty of the divine.

If Islamic theology holds that divine predestination and human free will coexist, Islamic legal discourse unequivocally operates in the realm of the latter. The economy of Islamic law is one of rules governing rights and duties, obedience and disobedience, worldly benefit and detriment, and reward or punishment in the afterlife. The work of Muslim jurists expresses a belief that God has ordained certain rules of human conduct and holds persons accountable for their obedience to these rules—obedience which is perfectly voluntary. Humans are required by God to do their best to know and obey the rules of the *sharīʿa*—the way God calls them to act—and have the freedom to obey or disobey. Humans do not inherit original sin in the Islamic view, but rather come into the world as 'blank slates', perhaps even

[21] L. Gardet summarizes the 'orthodox' Ashʿarī doctrine on this matter: "God is the creator of human acts, of which man is merely the receiving subject (*maḥall*). But God 'attributes' to a man his acts (the theory of *kasb* or *iktisāb*), and hence are justified both human responsibility and the Judgement promised in the Ḳur'ān." This position emerged in part as a response to Muʿtazilī arguments that man is "'creator of his own acts' by a contingent power (*ḳudra*) which God has created in him, [so] is responsible for what he does, and God is obliged to reward or punish him accordingly" ("ʿIlm al-Kalām," in *Encyclopaedia of Islam*, new ed.). See also George F. Hourani, *Reason and Tradition in Islamic Ethics* (Cambridge: Cambridge University Press, 1985), on debates about the nature of human will and ethical judgment. R. Bell observes that "the Qur'ān as a whole ... maintains human responsibility at the same time as it asserts divine omnipotence ... In the end, then, the Qur'ān simply holds fast to the complementary truths of God's omnipotence and man's responsibility without reconciling them intellectually" (*Introduction to the Qur'ān*, rev. M.W. Watt [Edinburgh: Edinburgh University Press, 1970], 150–152). Bell cites, for example, Qur'ān 6:125, which he translates "If God wills to guide a man, he enlarges his breast for *islām*, surrender (to God), and if he wills to lead a man astray, he makes his breast narrow and contracted," and, in some degree of contrast, 16:104, "Those who do not believe in God's signs, God does not guide."

predisposed to believe and act rightly.[22] Obeying the rules leads to benefits in both this world and the next: in this world, obedience leads to a well-ordered society, in the next, the bliss of heaven. For the theologians, God's judgment is inscrutable, and God is not bound to reward even the most scrupulous pursuit of the *sharīʿa* or, for that matter, to punish the most abject deviance from it. But the jurists assume that obeying the law offers the best means to achieve both worldly order and heavenly reward, and constitutes an unavoidable duty for God's earthly servants.

Whatever else it does, Islamic positive law also produces a sweeping taxonomy of human action. The jurists establish ideal-typical categories of legally defined actions. The place of an actual action in the taxonomy, its correspondence to the ideal-typical form of the action presented by the jurists, determines its religio-legal consequences. But these taxonomizing steps require some definition of an action—what defines the boundaries of a specific, named action, marking it out from

[22] Because free will has been such a vexed issue in the history of Christianity, it is important to delineate how the Muslim view differs. Most importantly, many classical Christian doctrines regarding free will rest on the assumption of original sin and a 'fallen' human nature. Muslims, in contrast, generally view human nature as inherently good, simply because humanity is God's creation. The inherent goodness of creation does not mean people are predisposed to do good (as the Christian Fall is often seen to predispose people to sin); rather, humans begin from a morally neutral standpoint, a 'clean slate', with the ability to do either good or evil. Human action as understood in the law, then, stands on a foundation of free will and moral neutrality. Regarding the moral nature of humanity, Muslims in the early Islamic period debated the meaning of '*fiṭra*', a quranic term (see, e.g., Qur'ān 30:30) for what D.B. MacDonald calls "a kind or way of creating or being created" ("Fiṭra," in *Encyclopaedia of Islam*, new ed.). Muslims disagreed over whether *fiṭra* meant that a child was naturally born a Muslim (and became a Jew or Christian, e.g., only by being perverted by his parents or environment) or rather was born without a religious identity and only acquired one over time and according to the will of God. The Muʿtazilites embraced the former view, while post-Muʿtazilite Sunnīs tended toward the latter. MacDonald notes that the variety of views on *fiṭra* include "that being created according to the *fiṭra* meant only being created in a healthy condition …, with a capacity of either belief or unbelief when the time should come. Another was that that *fiṭra* meant only 'beginning' (*bad'a*). Still another was that it referred to Allāh's creating man with a capacity of either belief or unbelief and then laying on them the covenant of the 'Day of *Alastu*' [Qur'ān 7:171]. Finally that it was that to which Allāh turns round the hearts of men." All of these views agree that humanity is created at least as a neutral moral entity, or is perhaps predisposed toward good or Islam, but is not created predisposed toward evil. On the quranic view of human nature, see Helmut Gätje, *The Qur'ān and Its Exegesis* (Oxford: Oneworld, 1971), 164–170; Kenneth Cragg, ed. and trans., *Readings in the Qur'ān* (London: Collins, 1988), 93–112; and Bell, 124, and also 159–160, where the author notes that the Qur'ān assumes no natural immortality of the soul.

the continuous flow of activity. For Muslim jurists, human actions consist of two dimensions: an outer dimension, which includes the objectively manifest movements, postures, and gestures of the body, including verbal utterances; and an inner dimension, which is the subjective workings of what the jurists predominantly call the heart or mind (*qalb*). Together both dimensions define an action and determine its place in the legal taxonomy.

Islamic law establishes some general parameters for what can count as legally relevant human action, based on a specific basic definition of human agency and concomitant responsibility and obligation. The state of being a legally responsible agent is called *taklīf* (lit., 'being charged or obligated'), and a person of this status is called a *mukallaf*.[23] The *mukallaf* is of sound mind (*ʿāqil*), of majority age (*bāligh*), and Muslim, and thus able and required to adhere to the precepts of Islamic law.[24] The key status that disqualifies an adult Muslim from being *mukallaf* is *majnūn*, meaning 'insane', with connotations of being beset by *jinn*—potentially noxious spirits who can hijack a person's free will. Some situations call for additional qualifications, such as being male, *ʿadl* ('just', with an untarnished reputation), and *mujtahid* (deemed capable of interpreting legal sources). The minimum attainment of *taklīf*, however, makes one subject to the *sharīʿa*.

God's Authorial Intent

An additional aspect of intent in Islamic law should be noted, so as to distinguish it from the object of my study. Because Islamic law is, theoretically speaking, primarily a hermeneutical enterprise devoted to understanding and applying the meaning of a revealed text–or, more accurately, two revealed 'texts', the Qurʾān and the Prophet's *sunna*—the work of the jurists involved a search for the authorial intent of God in producing those texts. While it was certain from the start that God had revealed His will regarding the detailed behavior of humans in

[23] *Mukallaf* beings include the angels, humans, and *jinn* (ʿUmar Sulaymān al-Ashqar, *Maqāṣid al-mukallafīn fīmā yutaʿabbadu bihi li-rabb al-ʿālamīn, aw, "al-Niyyāt fī al-ʿibādāt"* [ʿAmmān: Dār al-Nafāʾis, and Kuwait City: Maktabat al-Falāḥ, 1991], 42).

[24] See al-Ashqar, *Maqāṣid al-mukallafīn*, 42–43. A sleeping person is also excluded from legal responsibility. Children (and the insane) are considered incapable of discernment (*tamyīz*) and understanding (*fahm*).

these texts, their exact meaning was not always obvious. The task, then, was to search diligently for those meanings. Jurists described their work not as legislation but as 'discovery' (*kashf* or *iktishāf*). As Weiss puts it, "God knew best which rule applied in a given case, and it was the toilsome task of the jurist to read the mind of God to the best of his ability."[25] As audacious as it may sound, reading the mind of God was an unavoidable duty and among the highest callings a devout Muslim could answer.

In legal theory, this quest for God's authorial intent crystallized around the Arabic terms *ʿilla* or *sabab*, the 'cause' of a given legal effect. Wael Hallaq calls the *ʿilla* "the relevant similarity which justifies the transference of the judgment from the precedent to the new case"; it is the middle term or bridge in syllogistic, analogical legal reasoning, closely equivalent to what the Common Law calls the *ratio decidendi*.[26] The classic Islamic example is the explicit quranic injunction against consumption of wine. Many jurists extend this prohibition to all intoxicants, based on the argument that the reason or cause for the prohibition is the intoxicating effects of the wine, and not its color or particular ingredients. In this case, intoxication is the *ʿilla*, which is the reason God had in mind, so to speak, when explicitly prohibiting wine in the Qur'ān. While jurists certainly disagreed over the exact structure of proper legal arguments, and the exact *ʿilla* in many specific cases, they agreed on the basic structure of the law and of their work in discovering and interpolating it. The law was whatever God wanted, and deciphering God's desires and directives was their task.

My interest is at least one step removed from this pursuit of God's authorial intent, which I leave to others better suited to the charge. Instead, one of my tasks is to pursue the authorial intent of Muslim jurists as they write the texts of practical jurisprudence. Like most readers of texts, I explore this authorial intent at both the level of the specific wording and the level of oblique intentions looming behind the words. The former task involves translation and basic exposition,

---

[25] Weiss, *Spirit of Islamic Law*, 171; see also the whole of his chapter 3, "The Textualist/Intentionalist Bent."

[26] Hallaq, "Legal Reasoning in Islamic Law and the Common Law: Logic and Method," *Cleveland State Law Review* 34 (1985–1986), 86. See also his "Non-Analogical Arguments in Sunnī Juridical *Qiyās*," *Arabica* 36, 3 (1989), 303; and his *A History of Islamic Legal Theories: An Introduction to Sunnī* Uṣūl al-Fiqh (Cambridge: Cambridge University Press, 1997), 83–95 and *passim*; and Bernard Weiss, *The Search for God's Law* (Salt Lake City: University of Utah Press, 1992), 551–632.

while the latter is more broadly hermeneutical. But the intent I am most interested in—the intent that this book is really about—is that ascribed to ordinary Muslims, or more precisely, the way ordinary Muslim actors and their intentions are envisioned within *fiqh* texts.

Intent and Intentionality: A Philosophical Approach

The work of the contemporary American philosopher John R. Searle in the philosophy of language and mind offers a useful starting point for an analysis of intent. An initial distinction must be made between Intentionality and intention.[27] The former, which Searle distinguishes by capitalization, refers to what he calls "that property of the mind (brain) by which it is able to represent other things."[28] Tim Crane calls this "the mind's capacity to direct itself on things. Mental states like thoughts, beliefs, desires, hopes (and others) exhibit [I]ntentionality in the sense that they are always directed on, or at, something: if you hope, believe, or desire, you must hope, believe, or desire something."[29]

---

[27] These two terms need to be distinguished from a third homonymic term, 'intensionality' ('intensionality-with-an-s', as Searle helpfully, if clumsily, calls it). Searle observes that "intensionality-with-an-s is a property of certain classes of sentences, statements, and other linguistic entities" (*Intentionality: An Essay in the Philosophy of Mind* [New York: Cambridge University Press, 1983], 22–23). This term is usually contrasted with 'extensionality'; Simon Christmas summarizes the distinction succinctly: "The extension of a term is the thing or things it picks out: for instance, the extension of 'the Big Dipper' is the stellar constellation itself. The intension of a term can be thought of as the way in which it picks out its extension. 'The Big Dipper' and 'the Plough' have the same extension—a particular constellation—but pick it out in different ways. The two terms have different intensions. There is much debate about how we should actually understand the notion of an intension" ("Intensionality," in *Routledge Encyclopedia of Philosophy*). Searle observes that "One of the most pervasive confusions in contemporary philosophy is the mistaken belief that there is some close connection … between intensionality-with-an-s and Intentionality-with-a-t. Nothing could be further from the truth … Intentionality-with-a-t is that property of the mind (brain) by which it is able to represent other things; intensionality-with-an-s is the failure of certain sentences, statements, etc., to satisfy certain logical tests for extensionality. The only connection between them is that some sentences about Intentionality-with-a-t are intensional-with-an-s" (24; see also chapter 7, *passim*). 'Intensionality' is employed for logical analysis in the philosophy of language, and is of little concern here.

[28] Searle, *Intentionality*, 24.

[29] Tim Crane, "Intentionality," in *Routledge Encyclopedia of Philosophy*. Crane notes that this is a psychological criterion rather than a logical one. Crane (responding to Brentano) notes that there seem to be mental states "whose nature is not exhausted by their [I]ntentionality," such as "the nagginess of a toothache," and that it is

Such directed mental states are Intentional states; their 'directedness' or 'aboutness' is their Intentionality.

Searle describes several key characteristics of Intentional states, many of which are shared with speech acts. For our concerns, two of these are particularly important: first, Intentional states have what Searle calls 'propositional content' which may be distinguished from illocutionary force. For example, an Intentional state may have the propositional content 'that you will leave the room' or 'that it is raining', while its illocutionary force is determined in part by the specific Intentional state (Searle calls them 'psychological modes'), such as belief, hope, or intention.[30] Second, most Intentional states have 'conditions of satisfaction'.[31] Searle explains that "my belief will be satisfied if and only if things are as I believe them to be, my desires will be satisfied if and only if they are fulfilled, my intentions will be satisfied if and only if they are carried out."[32] Searle stresses that the conditions of satisfaction of the Intentional state are internal to the Intentional state: "part of what makes my wish that it were raining the wish it is, is that certain things will satisfy it and certain other things will not."[33] Together, propositional content and conditions of satisfaction go a long way toward defining a given Intentional state.[34]

---

possible to conceive of things other than mentality that could have intentionality, such as "certain non-mental causal patterns in nature." However, the distance one must go to arrive at such ideas indicates that Intentionality is generally discussed as a quality of mental phenomena—it is this usage which is important for present concerns. Again, there are many philosophical debates about the nuances of Intentionality which need not detain us.

30 Searle, *Intentionality*, 5–7.

31 Ibid., 10–11.

32 Ibid., 10.

33 Ibid., 11.

34 In addition to propositional content and conditions of satisfaction, Searle asserts that Intentional states can have a 'direction of fit', which can be either 'mind-to-world' or 'world-to-mind'. Direction of fit involves what Searle calls 'responsibility for fitting'. For Intentional states, "if my beliefs turn out to be wrong, it is my beliefs and not the world which is at fault,… [for] I can correct the situation simply by changing my beliefs" (ibid., 8). For speech acts, if "the statement is false, it is the fault of the statement (word-to-world direction of fit). If the promise is broken, it is the fault of the promiser (world-to-word direction of fit)" (7). But for an intention or desire, it is "the fault of the world if it fails to match the intention or the desire," and simply saying it was a mistaken intention or desire does not remedy, or even accurately describe, the situation. In short, some Intentional states, such as beliefs (mind-to-world direction of fit) can be true or false. Others, such as desires, and intentions (world-to-mind direction of fit) cannot be true or false—they can be complied with or carried out, or not. It is also possible to have a 'null direction of fit', as with speech acts that insult or congratulate, for example,

Intentionality is a characteristic of all mental states; it is, in Searle's words, "a ground floor property of the mind."[35] The mental state called 'intention', with a lower-case 'i', is simply one among many Intentional states. That is, it is a 'mental' state with Intentionality, the 'intrinsic' quality of 'directedness' or 'aboutness', and each specific instance of intention has propositional content and conditions of satisfaction. For example, one can have an intention with the propositional content 'that I leave the room', and the condition of satisfaction is the act of leaving the room.[36] However, intention has a special status among Intentional states in that it alone has action as its condition of satisfaction. Other Intentional states may lead to actions, but they must do so by means of intentions. To explain the relation between intention and action, Searle begins with the observation that "my intention is satisfied iff [i.e., if and only if] the *action* represented by the [propositional] content of the intention is actually performed," and that "an intentional act is simply the conditions of satisfaction of an intention."[37] In short, "There

---

or Intentional states, such as sorrow or pleasure in certain circumstances (7–9). Additionally, illocutionary acts potentially express an Intentional state with the corresponding propositional content. Searle calls such an Intentional state the 'sincerity condition' of the illocutionary act (9–10). To separate the two is either "logically odd" (to say, for example, "It's snowing but I don't believe it's snowing." Searle also says that while this is "logically odd," it is "not self-contradictory," a distinction he does not explain (9), or is to perform an insincere illocutionary act (a lie). The direction of fit of both is usually the same, and when the illocutionary act has no direction of fit, "the truth of the propositional content is presupposed, and the corresponding Intentional state contains a belief. For example, if I apologize for stepping on your cat, I express remorse for stepping on your cat. Neither the apology nor the remorse has a direction of fit, but the apology presupposes the truth of the proposition that I stepped on your cat, and the remorse contains a belief that I stepped on your cat" (10). A lie, then, is simply an illocutionary act where one does not have the Intentional state one expresses. This is particularly relevant for speech acts, but is equally true of any communicative act.

[35] Ibid., 26.

[36] Searle notes that "even though an event represented in the content of my intention occurs, it isn't necessarily the satisfaction of my intention … it must come about 'in the right way'" (ibid., 82, and see 82–83). That is, if I am carried out of the room by another person, for example, this does not satisfy the intention 'that I leave the room' if I actually intended to walk out of the room.

[37] Ibid., 79–80. Still, intentions do not function as adequate explanations of actions. It sheds little light if, in response to a question about why someone performed a given action, we say, she acted because she intended to perform that action. According to Searle, this is so because by identifying a given action we already identify it in terms of the intention in action (105). To say "he is sharpening the axe because he intends to sharpen the axe" is simply a tautology. An explanation must consist of either other elements of the compound Intentional component, such as "he is preparing to chop down a tree," or at least "he desires a sharper axe" (see 106).

are no actions without intentions."[38] This distinguishes intention from other Intentional states: there can be states of affairs that do not correspond to any beliefs or desires, say—it may be raining while I do not desire this—but there can be no actions without corresponding intentions.[39]

Searle makes a useful distinction between *prior intentions* and *intentions in action*.[40] A prior intention is the intention formed before an action, at some temporal remove and, it seems—though Searle does not use these terms—with some conscious, cognitive separation from the action itself. An intention in action "is the Intentional content of the action," temporally simultaneous with and inseparable from the action, and potentially without conscious cognitive awareness. Not all intentional actions have prior intentions, but they do all have intentions in action.[41] A prior intention is something like a 'plan to act', while an intention-in-action is what we might call 'meaning to act' while acting.

Complex actions have complex intentions, in which cases "the conditions of satisfaction of our intentions go beyond the bodily movements" to include wider meanings and effects. As Searle observes, a complex

---

38 Ibid., 82. Action contains two components: the experience of acting ("which has a form of Intentionality that is both presentational and causal"), and the event. "The experience of acting just is the intention in action" (91). "The experience of acting is a conscious experience with an Intentional content, and the intention in action just is the Intentional component, regardless of whether it is contained in any conscious experience of acting." Thus one can perform an intentional action without necessarily having any consciousness of doing so (91–92).

39 There are such things as unintentional actions (e.g., Oedipus marries his mother) but these must piggy-back on intentional actions (Oedipus marries Jocasta) (ibid., 82). Also see 107: "There are no actions, not even unintentional actions, without intentions, because every action has an intention in action as one of its components." This is, it seems, a stipulative definition of 'action'. Modifying his initial observation that an intention is satisfied iff the action represented by the content is performed, he notes that the conditions of satisfaction of an intention must come about "in the right way" (82). For example, one might intend to kill a man by shooting him, but he shoots at the man but misses, and the shot induces a stampede of pigs which tramples the man to death: "in this case the man's intention has the death of the victim as part of the conditions of satisfaction and the victim dies as a result, but all the same we are reluctant to say it was an intentional killing" (83). For whatever reason, the examples Searle and other philosophers give tend to involve homicide, perhaps simply for the rhetorical weight carried by such a dramatic and morally significant act as killing a person.

40 Ibid., 84–85.

41 As for the relation of prior intention to intention in action, "the prior intention represents the whole action as the rest of its conditions of satisfaction, but the intention in action presents, but does not *re*present, the physical movement and not the whole action as the rest of its conditions of satisfaction" (ibid., 93).

intention has conditions of satisfaction that include "not just a bodily movement *a*" but also "some further components of the action, *b, c, d*,... which we intend to perform by way of ... performing *a, b, c*, ... and the representation of both *a, b, c*,... and the relations among them are included in the content of the complex intention."[42] This possibility to expand true descriptions of actions beyond the basic and immediately obvious components of them is what Searle calls the 'accordion effect'.[43] This phenomenon will be particularly important in our analysis of speech acts in contract and family law. Searle also observes that "for some complex action types we even allow that one can perform an action by getting others to perform it. We say, for example, 'Louis XIV built Versailles', even though the actual construction was not done by him."[44] Ritual acts done by proxy, as discussed in chapter 2 below, provide a case in point.

Intentions are critical to the identity of actions, and thus critical to any effort, such as that manifest in Islamic positive law, to assess and classify actions. As Searle notes, a "whole action is an intention in action plus a bodily movement [or stillness] which is caused by the intention in action and which is the rest of the conditions of satisfaction of that intention in action."[45] The 'boundaries' of actions, the points at which one action ends and another begins, are constituted by intention. These boundaries may be marked in other ways as well, such as by physical movements, verbal utterances, or material conditions, but one essential component of actions—the means by which humans act with

[42] Ibid., 99.

[43] He uses the example of Gavrilo Princip's assassination of Archduke Franz Ferdinand in Sarajevo (ibid., 99–100): "of Princip we say that he: pulled the trigger, fired the gun, shot the Archduke, killed the Archduke, struck a blow against Austria, avenged Serbia." The accordion effect can add to this description components of the action such as "he produced neuron firings in his brain, contracted certain muscles in his hand"; some of these component are more basic than the pulling of the trigger, such as "moved a lot of air molecules," and others are less basic, such as "ruined Lord Grey's summer season," and "started the First World War." But Searle does not consider these to be intentional actions of Princip, or in fact, actions of his at all. He calls them "unintended occurrences that happened as a result of [Princip's] action. As far as *intentional* actions are concerned the boundaries of the accordion [effect] are the boundaries of the complex intention," at least for intentional actions; "but the complex intention does not quite set the boundaries of the action, because of the possibility of unintentional actions" (100).

[44] Ibid., 110.

[45] Ibid., 106. Searle notes that actions may be purely mental, or may be acts of 'refraining', where, for example, a person intends to 'hold still' (see 102–103).

purpose and meaning—consists of intentions. If Islamic positive law is concerned with human actions—as it manifestly is—it must also be concerned with intentions.

Overview of Arguments

The following chapters are tied together by the argument that Muslim jurists often treat intent as part of what defines an action, whether that action be prayer, divorce, sale of goods, or a poke in the eye. Intent helps make these acts what they are and thus helps determine their legal status and consequences. In all these cases, jurists face the issue of access, of knowing another's subjective states. The specific role ascribed to intent in each type of action tells us much about how pre-Modern Muslim jurists understood each of those categories, and it tells us much about how they understood the nature of the law in general.

Chapters Two and Three together examine Islamic ritual law, where the term for intent that the texts employ almost exclusively is '*niyya*'. Chapter Two, "Intent in Islamic Ritual Law," explores the technical details of the usage of *niyya*, showing that *niyya* is widely required as a discrete step in the various religious duties regulated by Islamic law. *Niyya* is an essentially silent, internal phenomenon, done in the 'heart' or 'mind' and at times complemented with a verbal statement of intent. The primary function assigned to *niyya* is definitive: with *niyya*, actors mentally define their actions *as* acts of ritual worship, thus linking them to the legal taxonomy of prescribed actions. *Niyya* turns a given movement or utterance into the named action required by law so that the actor can fulfill his or her duty.

Chapter Three, "Ritual Spirit and Ritual Intent," continues and completes the work begun in Chapter Two, taking up the question of why the law books would insist that an actor intend his actions. Given that ritual acts of worship are manifestly intentional acts, what need is there for a rule insisting that an actor intend to act? I first take up one possible answer pursued by several Western scholars, namely that *niyya* is not merely intent but the spiritual devotion behind a given act, an offering of the act to God. However, I demonstrate that law texts do not treat *niyya* in such spiritual terms, but instead consistently focus on the defining and taxonomizing aspects of *niyya*. They treat *niyya* in quasi-physical terms—as what one does with one's mind while also acting with one's body—while declining to employ the available sophisticated terminology of the soul or spirit. Rather than a 'spiritual' answer, I propose that the peculiar imperative to intend during ritual is best explained using the ritual theory developed by anthropologists Caroline Humphrey and James Laidlaw. They assert that ritual action differs from non-ritual action in that, in the former, actions are at some remove from an actor's intentions. In what they call the 'ritual stance', actions are defined, not by direct intention, but by 'prior ontological stipulation', the rules that name and prescribe the components of a given ritual. A gap thus potentially exists between the actor and his actions, so that one could perform a ritual without intending to do so—it would still 'count' as the ritual. I show that Muslim jurists seem to have a similar view of ritual, and seek to link actors and actions by legal dictate.

Chapter Four, "Intent in Islamic Contract Law," deals with the law of economic exchange, especially contracts of sale. In Islamic law, contracts are primarily oral rather than written, and thus hinge on performative speech acts revolving around verbal offers and acceptances of terms. Intent here matters primarily in terms of sincerity (intending words to mean what they appear to mean) and complexity (intending a speech act to achieve wider goals). The jurists' language of explicit (*ṣarīḥ*) and allusive (*kināya*) speech implicitly produces a three-part typology of speech acts: type 1 consists of unambiguous locutions that are legally binding regardless of sincerity; type 2 consists of ambiguous locutions that are legally effective only if intended to be so; type 3 consists of locutions so ambiguous that they cannot be legally effective regardless of the speaker's intent. In all three cases, the speaker may have complex intentions regarding the wider goals and results of the contract. While jurists widely agree that parties should enter into contracts freely, and thus sincere (intentional) speech is a prerequisite of a valid contract, they differ on the question of the complexity of intent behind a contract. The basic terms of the contract must be legal, but only some jurists hold that a formally correct contract that produces illegal consequences is invalid. For example, producing wine is unlawful for a Muslim, but selling grapes is not, and jurists disagree over whether it is legal to sell grapes knowing that the buyer plans to make wine with them. This disagreement points toward a pattern in conceptualizing the nature and role of Islamic law, at least in the commercial sphere: those for whom intent is minimally significant see the law as providing general parameters within which people have considerable leeway, while those for whom intent is maximally significant conceive of the law in strongly moral terms, as a sweeping yet precise guide to human flourishing. This chapter also demonstrates that in contract law the terminology of intent shifts from an exclusive, technical use of the term *niyya* to a wider range of less technical terms.

Chapter Five "Intent in Islamic Personal Status Law," turns to what is often called 'family law'. Like sales contracts, marriage and divorce both hinge on performative speech acts, and intent matters in terms of what one meant his or her words to mean and accomplish. Muslim jurists take little account of intent in the context of marriage contracts, which are treated formalistically. Jurists largely insist that the marriage be contracted using type 1, unambiguous speech. If such speech is used, the actual intent of the speaker is disregarded. In contrast, intent is a critical and complex aspect of divorce law, in terms of both basic sincerity and complexity. Type 1 speech is generally held binding regardless of sincerity, while other, less explicit speech may depend on intent. Complexity is primarily a matter of the number of divorces enacted toward the three that leave the couple irrevocably divorced. Intent enters into inheritance law in a different fashion. Islamic law contains elaborate, binding provisions for devolvement of property upon death, and a person must dispose of at least two-thirds of his estate according to predetermined rules. Jurists prohibit certain transactions as one nears death, on the assumption that such transactions are intended to circumvent the rules of inheritance. The question of actual intent is made moot by a formal definition of 'death-sickness', so that any illness fitting the legal criteria invalidates otherwise legal selling and gifting. The transactions are retroactively evaluated once the person has died. Thus, the actual intent of the dying person to obey or break the rules matters little, as formal strictures take over. This chapter concludes by exploring a range of analytical frameworks offered by various scholars to help explain the Islamic legal treatment of intent, especially in commercial and family law. While no single framework emerges as a complete theory of intent in Islamic law, taken together several of them greatly illuminate the matter.

In Chapter Six, "Intent in Islamic Penal Law," we see that Muslim jurists typically categorize injurious actions as either intentional, quasi-intentional, or accidental. Intentional acts produce liability for retaliation from the injured party (and/or his kin), although the injured party may choose financial compensation or forgiveness instead. Quasi-intentional and accidental acts produce liability for compensation but no option of retaliation. Jurists disagree about whether acts in any of these categories may also produce liability for a religious expiation, while accidental acts do not. I describe this as an 'intention-based strict liability system', in which any action that harms another produces liability, and attributions of intent determine the exact form of the liability. The texts assess intent based almost exclusively on objective indicants, primarily the means by which the injury is inflicted, the context of the incident, and the prevailing normal expectations regarding each. I then explore the jurisprudence of Ibn Rushd, who asserts that the inherent inaccessibility of others' intentions means that the justice possible in this life is necessarily provisional, as perfect justice, based on perfect knowledge of intent, will only be meted out in the afterlife by the all-knowing God. This highlights the religious nature of Islamic law and the fact that intent is precisely the point at which divine power must be counted on to complement the worldly power of human legal institutions. Throughout this chapter I demonstrate that in cases where Islamic law applies punishments, where the relevant intent is harmful and malicious, the term *'amd* emerges as a technical term for intent. This generates a counterpart for *niyya* in ritual law: *'amd* denotes morally problematic intent, while *niyya* is preserved for morally positive, or at least neutral intent.

Finally, I explore the peculiar Islamic legal category of the *ḥudūd*, a set of actions deemed offenses against 'the rights of God', including fornication, consuming intoxicants, and theft. Intent seems at first glance not to matter at all in such cases, for if one of these offenses occurs, the perpetrator faces a non-negotiable penalty. However, I show that jurists allow for the possibility of unintentional *ḥudūd* offenses, in which case the predetermined penalty is waived, though a lesser penalty may be applied by judicial discretion. Jurists also treat ignorance of the law as an excuse for breaking the *ḥudūd* ordinances, an unusual provision in Islamic law. These allowances regarding intent and ignorance fit a larger pattern of reluctance in applying the heavy *ḥudūd* penalties, a reluctance demonstrated by juristic efforts to define the *ḥudūd* offenses narrowly and to establish exceptionally elaborate rules of evidence in such cases.

The concluding chapter presents a summation of arguments and suggestions for potential further inquiry into intent and related matters in Islamic law. Several anthropologists have taken up the treatment of intent in various contemporary Muslim societies, including Morocco, Yemen, and Indonesia. This work raises the question of the extent to which recent legal practice reflects the normative vision of the classical texts. The cases in question do not provide a single definitive answer, but do highlight the promise of such explorations to better illuminate the simultaneously conservative and dynamic qualities of Islamic legal discourse. We will also briefly consider some potential implications for the treatment of intent as Muslims, whether liberal, conservative, or otherwise, seek to adapt and apply Islamic law in the contemporary world. Changing notions of commerce might require emphasis of some approaches to intent in contracts over other others, and perhaps the modification of notions of *madhhab* adherence, while new approaches to political and social organization, as well as psychology, might alter Islamic legal approaches to penal law and the understanding of intent there.

CHAPTER TWO

INTENT IN ISLAMIC RITUAL LAW

Introduction

Fiqh manuals include a set of materials collectively known as *fiqh al-ʿibādāt*, a term often translated as 'ritual law'. The *ʿibādāt* (sg. *ʿibāda*) include the so-called 'five pillars' of Islam, as well as rules for purification, diet, hunting and ritual slaughter (often treated as a subset of the *ḥajj*), *iʿtikāf* (spiritual retreat to a mosque), and washing and praying for the dead.[1] Jurists treat intent as one of the required (or recommended) elements of these acts; along with various objective features, intent serves to define these actions, marking them out of the general flow of gestures and utterances, making them into the specific named types of actions prescribed by ritual law. As it does elsewhere in the law, then, intent in ritual law fulfills a taxonomic function, locating a given person's actions on the legal map, so to speak. In the next chapter we will explore the wider implications of these facts, first exploring the suggestion that intent constitutes a 'spiritual' element in Islamic ritual practice, and then examining the nature of ritual intent through the lens of ritual theory. First, however, we must establish a basic understanding of the nature and role of intent in *fiqh al-ʿibādāt*.

The principal term for intent in *fiqh al-ʿibādāt* is *niyya*, which is both a generic term for intent and, as we will see, a technical term with connotations peculiar to ritual contexts. Wensinck points out that some members of the Prophet's generation did not consider *niyya* to be an integral part of the *ʿibādāt*. He calls attention to a passage in Shaʿrānī, who notes that Ibn ʿAbbās (d. 68/687) held that "all actions of Islam are

[1] G.-H. Bousquet remarks that "the first 'pillar' of Islam, the *s̲h̲ahāda* ... is so simple a matter that the books of *fiḳh* make no mention of it" ("*ʿIbādāt*," in *Encyclopaedia of Islam*, new ed.). *Fiqh* manuals tend to follow a shared general structural arrangement of topics; this is especially true of sections on ritual law. Bousquet affirms, but does not explain, this general pattern. See also Calder, "S̲h̲arīʿa"; and W. Heffening, "Zum Aufbau der Islamischen Rechtswerke," in *Studien zur Geschichte und Kultur des Nahen und Fernen Ostens*, ed. W. Heffening and W. Kirfel (Leiden: Brill, 1935), 101–118.

included in the intention to embrace Islam (*indirāj furū‘ al-Islām kulluhā fī niyyat al-Islām*)," meaning that "no individual actions of Islam require *niyya* after the person doing the action has chosen to enter into Islam." Wensinck adds that "this means: under the younger *ṣaḥāba* the whole rule of *niyya* was new, and had yet to develop. That Muḥammad had known of it himself and applied it is therefore impossible."[2]

Niyya is, for many later jurists, a necessary part of acts of worship. Oussama Arabi has observed that "in Islamic law the centrality of the inner world of the Muslim subject shows foremost in the law of worship (*‘ibādāt*)."[3] *Niyya* is universally required in prayer, but there is disagreement over the other *‘ibādāt*.[4] Jurists who do not require *niyya*

---

[2] Wensinck, "Intentie in Recht," 114–115, citing Abū al-Mawāhib ‘Abd al-Wahhāb b. Aḥmad b. ‘Alī al-Sha‘rānī, *al-Mīzān al-kubrā* [Cairo, 1279 H], 1:135; in the edition I have used [Cairo: Maktabat Muṣṭafā al-Bābī al-Ḥalabī wa-Awlāduhu], 1:147. Wensinck also attributes this view to Abū Sulaymān al-Dārānī (d. 215/830). Additionally, Wensinck draws attention to the term *‘azm* (resolve): "The period of fasting is from dawn to sunset. Because it is hard to establish precisely the time of dawn, and the fast is not an action which starts at a specific moment, the formulation of *niyya* cannot be immediately followed by the action; one speaks here, when one expresses himself precisely, of *‘azm*; this is not to deny that the term *niyya* is usually used" (110). Wensinck here also cites Ibrāhīm Ibn Muḥammad al-Bayjūrī, who asserts about *niyya* that "its proper time is at the start of the *‘ibādāt*, except in the case of fasting, where it precedes the act because of the difficulty of observing sunrise, and the proper performance that resolve (*‘azm*) takes the place of *niyya*" (Wensinck cites al-Bayjūrī, *Ḥāshiya*, 1:57, without further publication information; in my edition [Beirut: Dār al-Kutub al-‘Ilmiyya, 1994], 1:88). Frederick M. Denny observes that if the *niyya* does not immediately precede the act, "its status is reduced to mere 'decision' (*‘azm*), which would be no more than what precedes ritual *nīya* [=*niyya*]" ("Ethical Dimensions of Islamic Ritual Law," in *Religion and Law: Biblical-Judaic and Islamic Perspectives*, ed. Edwin B. Firmage, Bernard G. Weiss, and John W. Welch [Winona Lake: Eisenbrauns, 1990], 209). These references seem to treat *niyya* and *‘azm* as distinct terms and concepts. However, Ibn Qudāma uses the term *‘azm* when discussing the timing of *niyya* for fasting, effectively treating *‘azm* and *niyya* as synonymous in this context: "The meaning of the *niyya* is the aim (*al-qaṣd*), and this is the settling of the *qalb* to do something, and one's resolve about it (*‘azmuhu ‘alayhi*) without wavering" (*al-Mughnī*, 4:337). Further: "if one begins prayer with a *niyya* wavering between completeness and interruption (*mutaraddada bayna itmāmihā wa-qaṭ‘ihā*) the prayer is invalid, because *niyya* is firm resolve (*al-niyya ‘azmu jāzimu*)" (2:133); he gives a similar definition of *niyya* when he first discusses it at length (1:156). It seems that the precise relationship between *niyya* and *‘azm* is not made clear, or entirely agreed upon, in *fiqh* texts.

[3] Oussama Arabi, "Intention and Method in Sanhūrī's *Fiqh*: Cause as Ulterior Motive," *Islamic Law and Society* 4, 2 (1997): 211. Arabi begins his article with a similar observation: "The weight of intention in Islamic law is unevenly distributed between ritual law (*‘ibādāt*) and the law of worldly transactions (*mu‘āmalāt*)," and is more prominent in the former (200).

[4] This is confirmed by Wensinck, "Niyya," in *Encyclopaedia of Islam*, new ed.

in a given *'ibāda*, however, generally do treat it as recommended (often calling it *sunna*). Many jurists insist on *niyya* as a part of *wuḍū'* (ritual ablution) and *tayammum* (ablution without water), and, less universally, as a part of *ghusl* (bathing). It is usually listed among the preliminary steps for prayer, along with purification, facing the *qibla*, and properly covering the body. *Niyya* may be part of both the washing of the dead and prayer for the dead. Payment of *zakāt* is to be accompanied by *niyya* (as discussed below, this is complicated by the case of payment by proxy). Fasting in Ramaḍān (or in fulfillment of a vow) includes *niyya*, as does *i'tikāf* (spiritual retreat to a mosque, often done during Ramaḍān). The *ḥajj* formally begins with, among other things, formulation of *niyya*, and some of the subsets of the *ḥajj*, such as circumambulating the Ka'ba and slaughtering an animal, have their own *niyya*. When *niyya* is required, its omission invalidates the act of worship, and even uncertainty over having formulated *niyya*, like uncertainty over any other required part of an *'ibāda*, invalidates the act.[5]

As we will see below, jurists identify the location (*maḥal*) of *niyya* as the 'heart' (*qalb*), which was understood to be the locus of the 'mind' or 'rational faculty' (*'aql*). As a function of the heart/mind, *niyya* has no necessary external expression; some jurists indicate that a verbal expression of one's *niyya* might be considered *sunna*, but they do not require it. In general, *niyya* is to be formulated at the beginning of an act of worship and maintained for the duration of the act. *Niyya* may be 'lost' or variously invalidated, thereby invalidating the act of worship and necessitating re-performance.

The Arabic root from which '*'ibāda*' is derived (*'-b-d*) carries connotations of both worship and service, even servitude. The noun *'abd* (pl. *'abīd*, *'ubdān*, *'ibdān*) is a common term for servant or slave, and is also commonly used in the term (widely used as a proper name) *'abd Allāh*, 'servant of God'.[6] The *'ibādāt* are those things properly done by ser-

[5] See, for example, Shīrāzī, *al-Muhadhdhab*, 1:236: "If one enters *iḥrām* (purity for prayer) then is uncertain (*shakka*) whether he formulated his intention, then remembers that he did so, and if this was before doing any of the acts of prayer, this fulfills the obligation, but if one remembers after doing some of [the acts of prayer] then the prayer is invalidated, because he [prayed] while uncertain about [the status of] his prayer." Also note that, here and throughout, my translation in the imperfect tense reflects the imperative sense of the text, rather than the literal perfect tense of the Arabic.

[6] Many scholars translate *'abd* as 'slave'; see, for example, Talal Asad, *Genealogies of Religion* (Baltimore: Johns Hopkins, 1993), 221–222. Such a translation is technically correct, but I think it is often chosen for shock value and does a disservice. The implied

vants of God (i.e., all Muslims), acts of worship and obedient service in accord with the *sharīʿa*. Alms and fasting are thus as much a part of the *ʿibādāt* as are prayer and pilgrimage. (While retaining the commonplace 'ritual law' to translate *fiqh al-ʿibādāt*, I will refer to the specific *ʿibādāt* as 'acts of worship'.[7]) 'Ritual' and 'worship' are not elements of most modern secular conceptions of law.[8] But ritual law is situated squarely within the religo-legal discourses of medieval Islam. Not only are the *ʿibādāt* discussed in the same texts, by the same authors, as other categories of Islamic positive law (i.e., the *muʿāmalāt*), but by the classical period the *ʿibādāt* come first sequentially in the texts.[9] If the various subgenres of Islamic law are connected by the basic notion of obedience to God, the *ʿibādāt* are the most basic and universal expressions of this obedience. Further, the *ʿibādāt* are, in many ways, conceptually prior to

comparison of Islamic worship to 'slavery' (an English term with specific historical connotations) misleadingly taints the Arabic terminology of worship.

[7] The boundaries of the category *ʿibādāt* are not perfectly clear. A central connotation of the term *ʿibāda* is 'duty' or 'obedience', and thus all acts treated by *fiqh* carry this connotation to some degree. That is, following the rules of *fiqh* is itself an act of obedience, an *ʿibāda*. As will be seen below, some jurists clarify this boundary by discussing whether a given rule in *fiqh* has a 'rational' meaning or function, or is purely an act of obedient worship. Jurists also employ the term *qurba* when discussing the acts included among the *ʿibādāt*. *Qurba* is derived from a root (*q-r-b*) denoting 'drawing near' and 'approaching', as well as 'being related to', as in kinship. In its technical usage in *fiqh*, *qurba* refers to 'acts defining the relationship of humans to God'; thus *qurba* is effectively synonymous with *ʿibāda*, and is often used interchangeably. However, *qurba* also carries a slightly different connotation than *ʿibāda*; beyond simply 'acts defining the relationship of humans to God', *qurba* also suggests 'acts which draw one closer to God'. While these nuances are not developed explicitly in *fiqh* manuals, at times *qurba* seems to be chosen over *ʿibāda* to emphasize the unique experience of acts of worship.

[8] Perhaps for this reason, the *ʿibādāt* are somewhat overlooked by Western scholars of Islamic law in favor of *uṣūl al-fiqh* (legal theory) and the *muʿāmalāt*. Both Schacht (*Introduction*) and N.J. Coulson (*A History of Islamic Law* [Edinburgh: Edinburgh University Press, 1964]), for example, give the *ʿibādāt* short shrift in their well-known introductions to Islamic law. Many academic introductions to Islam treat ritual practices as largely separate from 'the law'; see, for example, Frederick M. Denny, *An Introduction to Islam*, 2d ed. (New York: Macmillan, 1994). David Waines (*An Introduction to Islam*. [Cambridge: Cambridge University Press, 1995]) better integrates ritual law with the rest of the law, reflecting the close interconnection in the original sources. On the usefulness of studying ritual law for insight into broader religious, legal, and socio-cultural aspects of Islam, see, for example, Marion Katz, *Body of Text: The Emergence of the Sunnī Law of Ritual Purity* (Albany: State University of New York Press, 2002); A. Kevin Reinhart, "Impurity/No Danger," *History of Religions* 30, 1 (1990): 1–24; and Denny, "Ethical Dimensions."

[9] Calder, "Sharīʿa."

the *muʿāmalāt*. Numerous fundamental concepts such as legal competence (*taklīf*) and duty (*farḍ/wājib*) receive extensive attention in *ʿibādāt* sections of *fiqh* manuals.

Fiqh al-ʿibādāt illuminates many aspects of pre-modern Islamic thought, including aspects of theology, ethics, anthropology, and history. Commenting on the role of ritual law in Judaism, Jacob Neusner asserts that "the Mishnaic rabbis express their primary cognitive statements, their judgments upon large matters, through ritual law, not through myth or theology. Indeed we observe a curious disjuncture between ritual laws and theological sayings concerned with the *heilsgeschichtliche* meanings of the laws."[10] Similarly, Muslim religious scholars gravitated toward law, especially ritual law, to express their understanding of many weighty matters. Theology, while important, has received less elaboration than law in Islamicate civilization, and moreover, the relation between theological doctrines and the law is often opaque, the latter having a greater impact on daily life. Ritual law in Judaism, according to Neusner, functions much like myth in other religio-cultural contexts: "so far as the laws describe a ritual, the ritual itself is myth … While lacking in mythic articulation, the ritual expresses important ideas and points of view on the structure of reality."[11] Similarly, in Islam *fiqh al-ʿibādāt* establishes and expresses the basic nature of the relationship of humanity to God and the fundamental religio-legal economy of deontology, obedience, and reward.

Intentions in Fiqh al-ʿIbādāt: *An Overview*

As previously noted, the key term for intention in the *ʿibādāt* is *niyya*. The root of this term, *n-w-y*, appears only once in the Qurʾān, in *sūrat al-Anʿām*, 6:95. Here the root is used in the word *al-nawā*, meaning fruit or date pit. This highlights an etymological aspect of the root, illustrating its connotation of seed, kernel, core, or central inner element.

[10] Jacob Neusner, "Ritual Without Myth: The Use of Legal Materials for the Study of Religions," *Religion* 5, 2 (1975): 99. Neusner makes the essential point that "the laws, it is clear, do not contain explanations" (98). Ritual laws often do not interpret themselves in any wider functional, socio-cultural, or historical ways; instead they simply describe the proper behavior.

[11] Ibid., 91. Neusner's corollary point, that the ritual was not carried out in the Jewish context, does not apply, but this does not undermine the relevance of the rest of his argument.

However, no nominal or verbal form of the root appears in the Qur'ān with the meaning 'intention'. The term does appear in several widely accepted *ḥadīth*s, where it displays the general meaning of intention, but not the technical sense found in works of *fiqh*.[12] The most important, and most commonly cited in *fiqh* manuals, of these *ḥadīth*s is the following (which was cited above):

> Actions are defined by intentions, and to every person what he intends (*innamā al-a'māl bil-niyyāt wa-innamā li-kull imri'in mā nawā*). So whoever emigrated [participated in the *hijra*] for God and His Messenger, then his emigration was for God and God's Messenger, and whoever emigrated for worldly benefits or for a woman to marry, his emigration was what he emigrated for.[13]

This *ḥadīth* is cited—in full, or often only in part (often the equivalent of the first sentence in the English)—in virtually all *fiqh* manuals, and in most it is the only *ḥadīth* cited in regard to *niyya*. Given this fact, it is striking that it sheds so little light on the legal meaning of *niyya*. The *ḥadīth* is vague in its usage of the term *niyya*—here it has very general connotations of plan or purpose. It says nothing of acts of worship, or of requiring or recommending *niyya* as an element of any action. Rather, it seems to suggest that *niyya* is a pervasive fact of human life, the motive behind action. The *ḥadīth* has a vaguely moralistic tone, as the Prophet calls for honesty and piety in behavior and implies that God knows the motives behind actions and judges accordingly. In short, neither the Qur'ān nor *ḥadīth* tells us much about the specific meanings of *niyya* in *fiqh*. Thus the reason for including *niyya* as an element of the *'ibādāt* is not that the Qur'ān or Prophet have called for this, and instead we must search elsewhere for our understanding of the meaning and role of intention in ritual law, namely in the texts of *fiqh al-'ibādāt* themselves.

Regarding the legal language of intent in the formative period, A.J. Wensinck observes that in early sources "in some instances [the term] *adjma'a* is used, where the later language has *nawā* (e.g., al-Nasā'ī, *Ṣiyām*, *bāb* 68; al-Tirmidhī, *Ṣawm*, *bāb* 33)."[14] In post-formative sources, the most common verbs used to indicate the act of formulating or having *niyya* are simply verbal forms of the root *n-w-y*, from which the noun *niyya* is derived. *Nawā* (in the third person masculine per-

---

[12] Wensinck asserts that the term *niyya* "is found in canonical *ḥadīth*, but the passages show that it has not yet acquired in this literature the technical meaning and limitation" found in *fiqh* ("Niyya").

[13] See above, chapter 1, n. 1.

[14] Wensinck, "Niyya."

fect) and *yanwī* (in the third person masculine imperfect) are the base verb forms—it is these terms that I have translated as derivations of 'to intend'. There are some instances in *fiqh* manuals of other verbs being used to express the act of formulating or having *niyya*. At one point Shīrāzī uses the verb *ḥaḍara* in the phrase "if one ... does not formulate/maintain (*lam yaḥḍar*) the *niyya* of *wuḍū*'"; this term carries connotations of being present or in attendance.[15] And Muḥammad b. Idrīs Shāfiʿī (d. 204/820) at several points uses the verb *ḥadatha*, for example: "... and then one formulates (*ḥadatha*) the *niyya* of *tayammum*."[16] The root of this verb (*ḥ-d-th*) produces a wide array of important terms, including *ḥadīth* (a report of the Prophet's words and deeds) and *ḥadath* (minor impurity), but its basic connotation is of occurrence, happening, taking place; in this instance, it may mean 'to say'. It is tempting to speculate about these terms, exploring the implications of such usage for the definition of *niyya*. However, given the rarity of these usages and the fact that the authors in question give few clues regarding such implications, it seems more prudent to simply note their occurrence.

The *ʿibādāt* consist of a set of actions which include movements of the body and often involve some speech. The texts give rules for these actions, imperatives for how and when the body should be moved and what formulas must be uttered. But the jurists do not treat the *ʿibādāt* as exhausted by these external components alone; rather, most consider the *ʿibādāt* to also include an internal, subjective component: *niyya*. Jurists, however, do not give simple and direct answers regarding just what *niyya* is, how it is done or what its doing accomplishes. Moreover, they disagree over many specific aspects of the nature and function of *niyya*. Most discuss *niyya* in some way for each of the *ʿibādāt*, but the exact role of *niyya* in each varies both within a given text due to the differing nature of the actions in question, and between texts, reflecting different opinions on the matter.

An important aspect of the meaning and role of *niyya* emerges if we consider the general type of rules found in *fiqh al-ʿibādāt*. The *ʿibādāt* consist mainly of constitutive rules, creating or defining new forms of behavior (i.e., the acts of worship) rather than governing existing forms of behavior as do the rules of the *muʿāmalāt*. That is, the *ʿibādāt*, unlike economic exchange or family relations, for instance, would not exist without the rules of *fiqh al-ʿibādāt* to define them. For many jurists, the

---

[15] Shīrāzī, *al-Muhadhdhab*, 1:71.

[16] Shāfiʿī, *al-Umm* (Beirut: Dār al-Fikr, 1990), 1:63.

rules of the *ʿibādāt* include *niyya*, so *niyya*, among other things, especially bodily movements in particular times and places, constitutes the acts.

Qarāfī gives further insight into the nature and role of intentions when he discusses another kind of difference between the *ʿibādāt* and the *muʿāmalāt*. As noted above, he observes that legal commands are of two types: first, those for which the simple performance of the act achieves the benefit of that act (this is characteristic of the the *muʿāmalāt*); second, those the external performance of which does not alone achieve the benefit for which God commanded them (characteristic of the *ʿibādāt*).[17] *Niyya* plays a key role in Qarāfī's distinction: compliance with rules of the first type, regardless of the intention, generates immediate worldly benefits and may also bring reward in the afterlife, while compliance with rules of the second type brings benefit to the actor, primarily in the hereafter, and only if *niyya* is present and proper. In this view *niyya* is a definitive element of the *ʿibādāt*—acts performed for the sake of obedience and heavenly reward, and which have no other function.

Ibn Rushd pursues a line of thought similar to Qarāfī's in discussing whether *niyya* is required in acts of worship. In *fiqh al-ʿibādāt*, a principal question is whether *niyya* is a necessary component of a given act of worship. In a rich passage about *wuḍūʾ* that contains his first remarks about *niyya*, Ibn Rushd addresses this question explicitly:

> The *ʿulamāʾ* of the cities (*amṣār*) disagree as to whether *niyya* is a requirement for valid *wuḍūʾ* or not, despite their agreement on the stipulation of *niyya* in the *ʿibādāt* according to what [God] Almighty said, "And they have been commanded no more than this: to worship Allāh, offering Him sincere devotion,"[18] and according to what [the Prophet Muḥammad] said, "*innamā al-aʿmāl bil-niyyāt*," the famous *ḥadīth*... The reason (*sabab*) for their disagreement is uncertainty (*taraddud*) over whether *wuḍūʾ* is a pure act of worship (*ʿibāda maḥḍa*).[19]

---

[17] Qarāfī, *al-Umniyya*, 27–28. See also Sherman Jackson, *Islamic Law and the State*, 201–202; it is important to note, as Jackson does here, that "it is not Qarāfī's contention that acts of the first category are not religious acts. On the contrary, these too should be performed with the intention of worshipping God and winning salvation in the Hereafter. His point, however, is that the rules of the first category are designed first and foremost for the benefit of man here and now. As such, whenever they are complied with, man benefits, even if God does not."

[18] Qurʾān 98:5. Unless otherwise noted, my translations of the Qurʾān here and throughout are my own, but are based in part on the translation by ʿAbdullah Yūsuf ʿAlī, *The Meaning of the Holy Qurʾān* (Brentwood, Md.: Amana, 1991).

[19] Ibn Rushd, *Bidāyat al-mujtahid*, 1:8; *DJP*, 1:3.

We will return in the next chapter to Ibn Rushd's citation of the Qur'ān. For the moment, the last sentence is key, implying that every 'pure act of worship' (*ʿibāda maḥḍa*) requires *niyya* in order to be valid, and that for some jurists *wuḍū'* does not require *niyya* because it is not a 'pure act of worship'. He explains:

> By this [i.e., *ʿibāda maḥḍa*] I mean [an act] which has no rational meaning (*ghayr maʿqūlat al-maʿnā*), and what is meant by it is *only* an act of worship (*al-qurba*), like prayer and the like, as distinguished from an act of worship with rational meaning (*ʿibāda maʿqūlat al-maʿnā*), such as washing off major impurity (*ghusl al-najāsa*).[20]

In other words, a 'pure act of worship' is an act with no other purpose—there is no rational justification for prayer beyond its being a religious duty and devotional action. Some acts categorized as acts of worship, however, do have other purposes: *ghusl*, for example, physically removes unclean substances. In effect, this establishes a three-fold classification of acts governed by *fiqh*: pure acts of worship (*ʿibāda maḥḍa*, synonymous with *ghayr maʿqūlat al-maʿnā*), actions which combine worship with material or instrumental ends (*ʿibāda maʿqūlat al-maʿnā*, or, as below, *al-ʿibāda al-mafhūma al-maʿnā*), and acts with purely material or instrumental ends. Ibn Rushd continues: "There is no disagreement that a pure *ʿibāda* requires *niyya*, and that an *ʿibāda* with a rational meaning (*al-ʿibāda al-mafhūma al-maʿnā*) does not [necessarily] require *niyya*" (the third category, purely instrumental acts, implicitly does not require *niyya*).[21] Ibn Rushd uses this same basic formula each time he introduces a different *ʿibāda*.[22] Though not universal, this language of 'pure acts of worship' is also not unique to Ibn Rushd.[23]

---

[20] Ibid., emphasis added. Tim Crane notes that *muʿqūl* and *maʿnā* are the terms used by al-Fārābī and Ibn Sīnā, respectively, to translate the Greek term 'noema', the historical origin of the term 'intentionality' (Searle's 'Intentionality'), which Crane calls "concepts, notions, or whatever it is which is before the mind in thought" (Crane, "Intentionality"). But here Ibn Rushd, although he is among the most prominent of the Islamicate philosophers, is using the terms differently, as I show below.

[21] Ibn Rushd, *Bidāyat al-mujtahid*, 1:8–9; *DJP*, 1:3–4; *wuḍū'*, he notes, has characteristics of each category, combining the effects of cleansing with fulfilling a devotional duty, and jurists must try to determine which characteristic they deem stronger.

[22] Ibn Rushd applies this schema throughout his discussion of the *ʿibādāt*. For example, in a section addressing the requirements (*shurūṭ*) of *tayammum*, he observes that "the majority [of jurists] hold that *niyya* is a requirement for [*tayammum*] because it is an act of worship with no rational meaning (*ʿibāda ghayr maʿqūlat al-maʿnā*)" (*Bidāyat al-mujtahid*, 1:67; *DJP*, 1:71).

[23] Shīrāzī for example employs this distinction throughout his discussion of the *ʿibādāt*: *al-Muhadhdhab*, 1:69, 236; 2:598, 642, 698.

Niyya, then, is a definitive element of pure acts of worship, acts with no rational functions or explanations, only 'religious' ones—these are acts done simply because one is commanded to do them. Without *niyya*, such acts would simply not occur. *Niyya* gives a defining purpose or goal—that is, to be acts of worship—to acts with no other purpose. While this does not go very far in clarifying just what *niyya* is or how one does it, it does indicate that *niyya* is, at least in part, a specific kind of intention with a special role in acts of obedient worship. Whatever else it is or does, *niyya* helps make ritual acts what they are.

Niyya *as an 'Internal', Silent Phenomenon*

Turning to the specific nature and function ascribed to *niyya*, we see that *niyya* is (1) an 'internal' action or state arising and existing in the 'heart' (*qalb*), which may be accompanied by a verbal pronouncement, and (2) an action or state which differentiates otherwise indistinguishable acts, effectively defining the action. Beginning with the first premise, we can establish that *niyya* is depicted as essentially silent and invisible, with no necessary objectively observable components. Thus it is not available for objective evaluation, and it is not readily proved or disproved by any tangible phenomena. According to some jurists, *niyya* may, or should at times, be simultaneous with a particular verbal pronouncement; however, this is a separate accompaniment to the *niyya*, which remains in essence an 'internal' phenomenon.

By unanimous consent, the principal 'organ' of *niyya* is the *qalb* (literally, 'heart'). Many *fiqh* manuals include a subsection dealing with "the location (*maḥāll*) of *niyya*." In many texts, locating *niyya* in the *qalb* is simply a matter of assertion. For example, Mūṣilī says "*niyya* is done in the *qalb* because it is an action of the *qalb* (*'amal al-qalb*)."[24] However, determining the implications of so locating *niyya* is more complex. The legal texts do not explicitly discuss this question, as most are content to simply assert that *niyya* is located in the *qalb*. But the texts reflect the belief prevailing in medieval Islamicate lands that the *qalb* (known to be an organ located in the chest[25]) was the seat of the intellect, the *'aql* (mind

---

[24] Mūṣilī, *al-Ikhtiyār*, 1:47–48. See also Shīrāzī, *al-Muhadhdhab*, 1:69, 236; Ibn Qudāma, *al-Mughnī*, 2:132.

[25] L. Massignon, *La passion d'al-Ḥallādj* (Paris, 1922), 468; in L. Gardet, "Ḳalb," in *Encyclopaedia of Islam*, new ed.

or rational faculty).[26] The *qalb* was not seen as either simply a blood-pumping organ or as the seat of the emotions, but as what Wensinck calls the "the central organ of intellect and attention."[27] Contrary to contemporary Western folk understandings, the 'heart' was not seen as the locus of bodily lusts, which were taken to come from the liver and bile.[28] This was not only in keeping with the antecedent Semitic understandings of the 'heart', it was unequivocally endorsed by the Qur'ān.[29] Prior to the Islamicate adoption of Galenic medicine, which held the brain (Arabic: *dimāgh*) to be the organ of perception and intellection, this view held sway. In fact, this position was widely held until long after the Greek medical system was circulating in Arabic; Greek thought in general took greater hold among the Islamicate philosophers than among the jurists or the general population.[30] Classical *fiqh* texts reflect this understanding of the 'heart' as the seat of the intellect,[31] and even

[26] See Qarāfī, *al-Umniyya*, 17–18.

[27] Wensinck, "Niyya." See also L. Massignon, *Essay on the Origins of the Technical Language of Islamic Mysticism*, trans. Benjamin Clark (Notre Dame: University of Notre Dame Press, 1977), esp. 198–199.

[28] Massignon, *La passion*, 489, n. 7; in Gardet, "Ḳalb."

[29] See Gardet, "Ḳalb." He cites, for example, Qur'ān 7:101, 179; 22:46; 26:89; 30:59; and 39:45.

[30] The Ṣūfīs in particular focused on the heart as not only the seat of intellectual apprehension, but the organ of awareness of God, and what Massignon calls "the secret and hidden (*sirr*) home of the conscience, whose secrets (*nadjwā*) will be revealed on Judgement Day" (Massignon, *La passion*, 478; in Gardet, "Ḳalb").

[31] At least one prominent legal scholar, Qarāfī, reflected on the relationship of the heart (*qalb*), mind (*'aql*), brain (*dimāgh*), and soul (*nafs*). Qarāfī discusses the nature of the heart explicitly, giving further insight into the legal understanding of *niyya*, stating that *niyya*, along with all other aspects of the will, as well as knowledge, speculation, fear, hope and "all actions that are related (*yansibu*) to the heart are seated in the soul (*al-nafs*)" (*al-Umniyya*, 17). Here Qarāfī takes as given that the location of *niyya* is the heart (*qalb*). He then enters into an implicit debate regarding the relationship of heart, mind/rational faculty (*'aql*), brain (*dimāgh*), and soul. He first observes that "most jurists and a few philosophers say that the rational faculty (*al-'aql*) is seated in the heart, while most philosophers and a few jurists say it is seated in the brain (*al-dimāgh*), their argument being that if injury befalls the brain, the rational faculty is corrupted, and [likewise all] the capacities (*aḥwāl*) of the soul [are corrupted]" (17). Unlike "the philosophers," Qarāfī professes the priority of revelation over reason, arguing that since several passages in the Qur'ān locate the *'aql* in the heart, and not the brain, the *'aql* must reside in the heart, though he admits that a sound brain is also necessary for its functioning (17; he cites Qur'ān 22:46, 50:37, 58:22, and 39:22). Qarāfī takes the occasion to reflect on the nature of the soul. He asserts that if the *'aql* is seated in the heart, so too must be the soul, for "everything related to the *'aql* such as thought and knowledge and the like are properties (*ṣifāt*) of the soul" (18). In other words, the *'aql* is presumed to be an aspect of the soul, and the Qur'ān establishes that the *'aql* is seated in the heart, so the soul is seated in the heart (18). He adds, "these three

many modern legal scholars retain it.[32] In the legal texts, the *qalb* is an organ of thought, and *niyya*, as a function of that organ, is a rational mental phenomenon. (Loose translation of *qalb* as 'heart' may itself support romantic misreadings of *niyya* in *fiqh*, so I will use the Arabic, or the translations 'mind' or 'heart/mind' instead.)

Jurists consistently identify *niyya*'s location as being the *qalb*, but, again, they do little to either prove this or explore its implications. The primary goal of jurists seems not to be the finer philosophical or physiological implications of locating *niyya* in the *qalb*, but rather establishing *niyya*'s 'interiority'. That is, whatever else it may mean that *niyya* is 'an action of the *qalb*', it means that *niyya* is a subjective phenomenon that has essential characteristics which we might deem 'mental', but not essential characteristics which are 'external' and objectively observable.[33]

Niyya is essentially silent, for although jurists observe that *niyya* might be verbalized, they insist that this is, at most, a complement or ampli-

---

names (*ruḥ*, *'aql*, *nafs*) express three qualities but share one characteristic, which is that they are located in the heart," and, "The soul is a subtle body dwelling transparently within the physical ['heavy', *kathīf*] body, from which it is distinguished like a fetus. And it is the nature of the soul to give rise to knowledge and thought, and it this that is called *'aql*, the rational faculty." It seems that Qarāfī was somewhat familiar with Islamicate philosophy, but his discussion of the nature of the soul is both brief and rather unclear, and certainly appears unsophisticated in comparison with the *falāsifa*. He goes on: "If the soul is located in the heart, so is *niyya*, and the will, and all types of knowledge, and all other aspects of the soul (*aḥwāl al-nafs*) are located in the heart" (18). Qarāfī's logic is not entirely clear: systematic arguments (e.g., an argument from quranic authority that the *'aql* resides in the heart) are mingled with unargued assertions (e.g., the connection of *niyya* to *'aql*). But the end result is that, for Qarāfī, *niyya* is an aspect of both mind/rational faculty and soul, and as such is located in the heart. We will return to this topic in detail in the next chapter.

32 See, for example, al-Ashqar, *Maqāṣid al-mukallafīn*, 115–117. His explanation is much like Qarāfī's: *niyya* is related to *'aql*, and the Qur'ān locates *'aql* in the *qalb*, so *niyya* is in the *qalb*. A similar approach is also found in the modern source Muḥammad 'Abd al-Ra'ūf Bahnasī, *al-Niyya fī al-sharī'a al-islāmiyya* (Cairo: Dār al-Qawmiyya al-'Arabiyya lil-Ṭibā'a, n.d.), 6–8.

33 The link of *niyya* to *'aql* and *qalb*, and the apparent subjectivity and interiority of all three, suggest that *niyya* is at least somewhat analogous to what Searle calls a 'mental' phenomenon. Searle argues that "mental states have an irreducibly subjective ontology;" that is, while it is difficult to find out about others' subjective states (how to find out about such things is an epistemological question), that does not mean that their ontology must be reduced to objective behavior, or, even that they do not exist (both positions having adherents in the philosophy of mind) (John R. Searle, *Rediscovery of the Mind* [Cambridge, Mass.: MIT Press, 1992], 19–23; quote is from 19). It appears certain that medieval Muslim jurists likewise held that certain mental phenomena (including *niyya*) are real, even if intrinsically subjective.

fication. Shīrāzī, for example, insists that "if one expresses with the tongue while 'intending' (*qaṣada*) with the *qalb*, this is most certain (*ākid*)."[34] Ibn Qudāma similarly holds that "If one verbalizes (*lafaẓa*) what he intends, this is by way of emphasis (*ta'kīdan*)."[35] Mūṣilī states that "it is required that *niyya* be done with the *qalb*, and it is recommended (*sunna*) to pronounce it with the tongue, and doing both together is preferred (*afḍal*)."[36] In short, *niyya* must be done by the *qalb*, as an essentially interior, subjective, nonverbal ('mental') act, and it may at times also be accompanied by verbal pronouncement.[37] Regardless of the position taken on verbalization, no *fiqh* manual I have yet read cites a particular statement to be made aloud if one decides to do so.[38]

---

34 Shīrāzī, *al-Muhadhdhab*, 1:69; see also 1:236: "The location of *niyya* is the *qalb*, and if one intends with his *qalb* without his tongue, it is valid, and one of our companions says: 'intend by the *qalb* and pronounce it on the tongue; it is of no consequence, because *niyya* is the *qaṣd* of the *qalb*'."

35 Ibn Qudāma, *al-Mughnī*, 2:132.

36 Mūṣilī, *al-Ikhtiyār*, 1:47–48 (referring, without specific citation, to Muḥammad b. al-Ḥassan al-Shaybānī). Wensinck states that "The jurists say … that the seat [*maḥall*] of the *niyya* is the heart, which does not diminish the fact that one likes to express it with the lips and thus 'let the tongue help the heart' [citing al-Bayjūrī, *Ḥāshiya*, 1:57, without citation of the edition used; in my edition this is found on 1:88]; this is the ritual in its most perfect form [citing al-Sha'rānī, *al-Mīzān al-kubrā* (Cairo, 1279 H), 1:136]. Only Mālik is different here from the consensus: he does not like to see the pronunciation of the *niyya* [citing ibid.]. But the other schools do not insist that it be pronounced. The meaning and intention of the *niyya* are shown very well by Sha'rānī's remark concerning this point: the imāms agree in this, that the *niyya* for ritual washing, formulated with the heart though not pronounced, gives juridical force to the action; and that the *niyya*, pronounced though not formulated with the heart, does not give juridical power to the action [citing ibid., 1:135]" ("Intentie in Recht," 111).

37 In her study of popular modern devotional manuals, Constance E. Padwick devotes a chapter to the role of intention in the *'ibadat*. She finds that these texts, largely aimed at teaching Muslim children the proper performance of acts of worship, present the formulation of *niyya* as a verbal act: "If you desire to make your ablution, say: 'I make the intention of legal purification,' then wash" (*Muslim Devotions: A Study of Prayer-Manuals in Common Use* [London: S.P.C.K., 1961], 48, citing the devotional manual *Durūsu 'd-dīni 'l-islāmī*, Book I, 29). Padwick refers to such pronunciation of *niyya* as "a universal custom of worship in Islam" (49). However, she cites no medieval *fiqh* manuals (her further comments on *niyya* in ritual contexts include comments on *ḥadīth* and on Ṣūfī texts), and so her conclusions are based on a very different set of sources, from a different genre and time period. Padwick observes that legal texts do not endorse verbalization, but asserts that the devotional manuals she studies show a tendency to treat *niyya* as part of a 'spiritual discipline' (49–50). See also Denny, *Introduction*, where he indicates that "*niyya* [is] uttered before the observance begins" (118).

38 According to al-Jazīrī, none of the four Sunnī *madhhab*s requires verbalization of *niyya*, but all consider verbalization to be recommended ('*sunna*' for most *madhhabs*) in purification (*Kitāb al-fiqh 'alā al-madhāhib al-arba'a*, 1:53–73). In prayer, Shāfi'īs

There is no established verbal formula, so it is not entirely clear what 'pronouncing *niyya*' would entail.[39]

While many jurists are not opposed to verbalizing *niyya*, and seem indifferent to or mildly in favor of the practice, this issue vexes other scholars. In particular, the Ḥanbalī iconoclast Ibn Taymiyya (d. 728/1328) argues strenuously that *niyya* should not be verbalized, that verbal pronouncement is innovation (*bid'a*): "It is enough that *niyya* is in the *qalb*," he says, "and God knows what is in the *qalb*."[40] For Ibn Taymiyya, the proof is that the Prophet explicitly said that one begins prayer by saying the *takbīr* ('*Allāhu akbar*', 'God is most great'), and said nothing about pronouncing *niyya* in prayer or any of the other *'ibādāt*, therefore doing so is innovation.[41] Ibn Taymiyya goes on at length on this issue, but he is clearly concerned less with the verbalization of *niyya* than with questions of religious authority and innovation. His reformist agenda was focused on returning to the 'original' sources of Islamic belief and practice, rooting out such 'innovations' as Ṣūfī saint veneration.[42] His opposition to the verbalization of *niyya* reflects his desire to adhere to the *sunna* of the Prophet, and as he finds no evidence that the Prophet verbalized his *niyya*, he takes this as proof that such verbal-

and Ḥanbalīs consider verbalization of *niyya* to be *sunna*, while Mālikīs and Ḥanafīs reportedly stand against any verbalization of *niyya* in prayer; Jazīrī asserts that Mālikīs allow whispering of a pronunciation of *niyya* if one whispers all the verbal formulas of prayer, while Ḥanafīs consider verbalization of *niyya* in prayer to be *bid'a* (heretical innovation), and prefer that one avoid whispering while praying (1:214–215). Jazīrī's summary regarding prayer is confirmed by Zuḥaylī, *al-Fiqh al-islāmī wa-adillatuhu*, 1:615–621, although the latter omits reference to the Ḥanafīs in regard to prayer.

39 Jazīrī gives several examples of possible verbal phrases in the case of *wuḍū'* for prayer, including "I intend (*nawaytu*) to perform *wuḍū'* for prayer, drawing toward God Almighty," "I intend removal of *ḥadath*," and "I intend that my prayer be acceptable (*nawaytu istibāḥat al-ṣalāt*)" (*Kitāb al-fiqh 'alā al-madhāhib al-arba'a*, 1:67). In *ṣalāt*, Jazīrī recommends the phrase "I pray the required noon prayer," for example; for Shāfi'īs and Ḥanbalīs, there is no problem if one intends the proper prayer in the heart, but verbally pronounces the wrong prayer when doing so (e.g., intending the noon prayer at the right time, but saying "*al-'aṣr*" [i.e., the mid-afternoon prayer]) (1:214). Neither these nor any other phrases are indicated in the medieval *fiqh* manuals I consulted, however.

40 Aḥmad Ibn Taymiyya, *Majmū' al-fatāwā* (Riyāḍ: Maṭābi' Riyāḍ, 1381–1386 H), 22:219.

41 Ibid., 221.

42 On the complexities of Ibn Taymiyya's religious identity and reformist agenda, see George Makdisi, "Ibn Taymīya: A Ṣūfī of the Qādiriya Order," *American Journal of Arabic Studies* 1 (1974): 118–129, reprinted in *Religion, Law and Learning in Classical Islam* (Hampshire, U.K.: Variorum, 1991) (reprint retains original pagination).

ization is illegitimate innovation.[43] Though Ibn Taymiyya here shows little interest in any other aspects of *niyya*, he demonstrates that one can make a pointed argument against verbalization of *niyya*.

In *fiqh al-ʿibādāt* there are three apparent potential exceptions to the dissociation of *niyya* from verbalization: the association of *niyya* with the *basmalah* (saying 'In the name of God …') in ritual purification, with the *takbīr* (saying 'God is most great') in prayer, and with the *talbiyya* (saying 'Here I am, O Lord …') in the *ḥajj*. However, on close inspection, the sources reveal that *niyya* is an action separate from, even if simultaneous with, these prescribed verbal invocations. Beginning with the relation of *niyya* to the *basmalah* in purification, we see an association of the two acts, but not an identity.[44] Ibn Qudāma indicates that the *niyya* must be the first step in any act of purification, calling *niyya* a "foundation" or "precondition" (*sharṭ*) of *ṭahāra*.[45] The *basmalah* (he uses the synonym "*al-tasmiya*") comes "after the *niyya*, before all the actions of purification."[46] Shīrāzī, commenting on *tayammum*, reverses the order but maintains the separation: "The proper way to do *tayammum* is to first say the *basmalah*,… then intend, then strike the hands against the dust."[47]

Similar to the relation of *niyya* to the *basmalah* in purity, jurists give *niyya* a range of temporal proximity to the *takbīr* in *ṣalāt*. Mūṣilī, for example, locates *niyya* before prayer: "There are six required [preliminaries to prayer]: purity of the body from major and minor impurities, purity of the clothing, purity of the place, proper covering of the body, locating of the *qibla*, and *niyya*."[48] The prayer itself begins with the *takbīr*, clearly separated from the formulation of *niyya*. However, Shīrāzī voices the more common opinion, that the *niyya* is formed at the same time as the *takbīr*, with these two actions simultaneously constituting the first act of prayer proper: "It is necessary that the *niyya* be simultaneous with

---

43 This interpretation of Ibn Taymiyya is supported by his broader discussion, in this same section of *Majmūʿ al-fatāwā*, regarding the difference between 'good innovation' (that of the Prophet's 'Companions' and the 'Successors', i.e., the Prophet's generation and the following generation, respectively) and 'bad innovation' (any significant changes introduced after the generation of the 'Successors').

44 According to Jazīrī, Mālikīs, Ḥanbalīs, and Shāfiʿīs agree that *niyya* (in the *qalb*) is required in *wuḍūʾ*, while Ḥanafīs say it is only *sunna* (*Kitāb al-fiqh ʿalā al-madhāhib al-arbaʿa*, 1:63). However, as noted above, none of the *madhhab*s requires verbalization, though all consider verbalization recommended, or at least allowed.

45 Ibn Qudāma, *al-Mughnī*, 1:159.

46 Ibid., 1:146.

47 Shīrāzī, *al-Muhadhdhab*, 1:128.

48 Mūṣilī, *al-Ikhtiyār*, 1:45.

the *takbīr* (*muqārina bil-takbīr*), because this is the first requirement of the prayer so it is necessary that the *niyya* be simultaneous with it."[49] Insisting on simultaneity only makes sense if the two items are distinct and potentially separable. Ibn Qudāma, implicitly endorsing a preference that *niyya* and *takbīr* occur simultaneously, asserts that in prayer, "it is permitted for the *niyya* to precede the *takbīr* by a brief interval, but if this interval is extended, or the *niyya* is invalidated (*fasakha*), then it is not permitted."[50] In short, while closely linked, the *niyya* and *takbīr* are clearly distinct, the former remaining interior and subjective regardless of its proximity to the verbalized *takbīr*.[51]

As for the *talbiyya* in the *ḥajj*, Mūṣilī observes, "[the pilgrim] prays two *rakʿa*s and says: 'O God, I desire to perform the *ḥajj*, so make my way easy and accept it from me', and if he intends in his *qalb*, this [makes the *ḥajj*] lawful." He adds, "[one enters *iḥrām*] when he intends and calls out the *talbiyya*."[52] For his part, Shīrāzī asserts that "one says the *talbiyya* to emulate [the first generations of Muslims], but if one restricts oneself to the *niyya*, and does not say the *talbiyya*, it is valid."[53] Again, while the *niyya* and the verbalized *talbiyya* are closely linked, they are also clearly distinct, and the *niyya* without the *talbiyya* is valid (implicitly, the reverse would be invalid). The verbalization of the *talbiyya*, as with the other two invocations, is presented as being ancillary to the existence and validity of *niyya*.[54] *Niyya* is essentially an act of the *qalb* and verbalization may accompany, express, and perhaps objectively confirm the *niyya*.

---

[49] Shīrāzī, *al-Muhadhdhab*, 1:236.

[50] Ibn Qudāma, *al-Mughnī*, 2:136.

[51] Zuḥaylī confirms that none of the *madhhab*s requires a verbal pronunciation of *niyya* in *ṣalāt*, and that all "prefer" (*yandūb*), but do not require, that the *niyya* be simultaneous (*muqārinan*) with the *takbīr* (*al-Fiqh al-islāmī wa-adillatuhu*, 1:614–615).

[52] Mūṣilī, *al-Ikhtiyār*, 1:143–144.

[53] Shīrāzī, *al-Muhadhdhab*, 2:698–699.

[54] Zuḥaylī asserts that "*Iḥrām* is not valid without *niyya*, for the Prophet ... said [the *ḥadīth*], and because [*iḥrām*] is a pure *ʿibāda* (*ʿibāda maḥḍa*) which is not valid without *niyya*, like fasting and prayer. The location of *niyya* is the heart, and for *iḥrām niyya* is in the heart, but according to most scholars it is preferred (*al-afḍal*) that one pronounce what one intends." Zuḥaylī notes that this is because people heard the Prophet pronounce the *talbiyya* when on *ḥajj* and *ʿumra*. Zuḥaylī adds that one should pronounce one's *niyya* in this case "because pronouncing it keeps one farthest from inattentiveness." However, Zuḥaylī then indicates that the verbalization of *niyya* is distinct from the *talbiyya*, for he offers the following as examples of how one pronounces the *niyya* of *ḥajj*: "I intend (*nuwaytu*) the *ḥajj* or *ʿumra*, and I have entered *iḥrām* for it for God Almighty," and "O God, I intend (*urīdu*) the *ḥajj* or *ʿumra*, so make my way easy and accept it from me." These are all distinct from the formula of the *talbiyya*. He notes

Niyya, then, is in essence an internal, silent, mental act. If it is verbalized, as some recommend (but none require), or linked to a required or customary verbal formula (like the *basmalah*), *niyya* nonetheless remains a discrete step in the performance of an act of worship. It is not simply the internal component of a verbal act, the Intentionality (i.e., 'aboutness') of a speech act, but rather is itself something one does as part of the compound actions of purification, prayer, pilgrimage, and the rest of the *ʿibādāt*. The mental act of formulating an intention is itself a separate step in the performance of an act of worship, and *niyya* is not reducible to these or any other verbal formulas.

The nature of *niyya* as an internal mental action is further illuminated by discussions of the loss or invalidation of *niyya*. Once formed, *niyya* can simply 'slip' and be lost without a different mental state or event taking its place. Shīrāzī discusses this possibility, observing first that "it is preferred (*al-afḍal*) that one intend from the start of *wuḍū'* until the completion of *wuḍū'* and that one continue the *niyya* [throughout]."[55] Thus, *niyya* is to be present throughout the action—although he

---

that "most jurists prefer that one say the *talbiyya* after entering *iḥrām*, meaning [that one should say the *talbiyya*] along with *niyya*" (*al-Fiqh al-islāmī wa-adillatuhu*, 3:123).

[55] Shīrāzī, *al-Muhadhdhab*, 1:69. Most jurists agree that *niyya* must be formulated at the start of, and endure throughout, acts of worship. However, for some acts, this raises the issue of just when the act occurs. As noted above, Wensinck asserts regarding fasting in Ramaḍān that "The period of fasting is from dawn to sunset. Because it is hard to establish precisely the time of dawn, and the fast is not an action which starts at a specific moment, the formulation of *niyya* cannot be immediately followed by the action; one speaks here, when one expresses himself precisely, of *ʿazm* [resolve]; this is not to deny that the term *niyya* is usually used" ("Intentie in Recht," 110). Wensinck here cites al-Bayjūrī, who asserts about *niyya* that "its proper time is at the start of the *ʿibādāt*, except in the case of fasting, where it precedes the act because of the difficulty of observing sunrise, and the proper performance that resolve (*ʿazm*) takes the place of *niyya*" (Wensinck cites al-Bayjūrī 1:57, again without further publication information; this passage is found on 1:88 of my edition). Timing is also a complex issue in the *ḥajj*. Wensinck remarks that "the intention for the pilgrimage for the Muslim jurists has been a difficult point. One would expect that the pilgrim at the entry into the sacred area would formulate his *niyya* in the usual precise manner that he intended to do the major or minor pilgrimage, and for this would take on the consecrated status [i.e., *iḥrām*]. And thus he can do. But because [*iḥrām*] imposes duties of abstinence and many pilgrims arrive in Mecca long before the start of the pilgrimage period, one is permitted to enter *iḥrām* for the minor pilgrimage and to put it off after the performance of the mandatory duties, until the start of the major pilgrimage. In such a case one thus pronounces his *niyya*, that he wants to perform the minor pilgrimage, although he has traveled to Mecca before the *ḥajj*. No one would in this case consider the *niyya* to have great value, and Shāfiʿī therefore allows, at the formulation of the *niyya* for the *iḥrām*, to omit the mentioning of major or minor

calls this "preferred," not required. However, "If one formulates intention at the point of washing the face, and then the *niyya* slips [from one's mind] (*'azabat*), it [the washing] is valid, because [the washing of the face] is the first of the obligatory actions."[56] Here the *niyya* is envisioned as simply 'slipping [from the mind]' (*'azaba*), ceasing to exist, thereby invalidating the act it accompanies. Nothing displaces the *niyya*, and no outward sign accompanies this slip.

Niyya for an act of worship can also be displaced by an incompatible intention:

> If one intends breaking off (*al-khurūj*) from prayer or intends that he will break off [in the future] or doubts whether he broke off or not, the prayer is invalidated, because *niyya* is required throughout the prayer, and he has already cut it off (*qad qaṭa'a*) by so doing and thus invalidated the prayer, as purity [is removed] if it is cut off by minor impurity.[57]

In addition to reinforcing the point that *niyya* must persist throughout the prayer, this passage introduces a new prospect, namely that one might intend the ending of, or exiting from, prayer. This passage presents the actor as changing the *niyya* from '*niyya* to pray' to '*niyya* to break off from prayer', with the implication that one can only have a single *niyya* at a time. In short, changing *niyya* is like 'changing one's mind'. Here Shīrāzī's treatment of *niyya* elides a purely technical usage of *niyya*—*niyya* as the intention to perform an act of worship—to a non-technical usage—*niyya* as the intention to perform any act (including the act of ending prayer). Further, Shīrāzī gives *niyya* something of a magical character: he does not describe a person necessarily acting on the intention to cease praying, but simply formulating such an intention, thereby invalidating the prayer. Or, more to the point, forming the *niyya* to break off the prayer *is* the act of breaking off the prayer—as much or more than any outward indication, such as ceasing the bodily movements of prayer.

Shīrāzī further considers the possibility of changing one's *niyya*: "If one enters into noon prayer then changes the *niyya* to the mid-afternoon prayer this invalidates the noon prayer, because it interrupts (*qaṭa'a*) the *niyya*, and the mid-afternoon prayer is not valid because he

---

pilgrimage; this is actually in conflict with provisions concerning *niyya*" (113–114, citing al-Shāfi'ī, *Kitāb al-umm* [Cairo 1321–1325 H], 2:132). On the term *'azm*, see n. 2 above.

[56] Shīrāzī, *al-Muhadhdhab*, 1:69–70.

[57] Ibid., 1:237.

did not intend this at the point of [entering] *iḥrām*."[58] Once prayer has been begun with the proper *niyya*, changing or 'interrupting' the *niyya* invalidates the prayer.[59] Further, *niyya* alone does not define the act, for one can intend to perform an obligatory prayer, but if one acts before the proper prayer time, the prayer only counts as a supererogatory prayer. The act is not totally vacated, but the *niyya* cannot overcome certain objective limitations; subjective and objective criteria come together in defining the act.

These discussions of the loss and invalidation of *niyya* highlight the fact that *niyya* itself is a part of the ritual. *Niyya* is not, however, an utterance, though it may be temporally linked to—and made more certain or emphatic by—certain utterances. While the texts at times employ the term to refer to a general intention, more frequently they present *niyya* as a technical term unique to ritual. *Niyya* is, in effect, what one does with one's mind while performing ritual actions, while moving one's body in certain ways and making certain utterances. I think we are not far off to understand *niyya* in such physical-sounding terms, as part of the embodied practices of the *'ibādāt*.

Niyya *as Definitive of Actions*

Niyya, then, is a silent, internal, mental phenomenon. What *niyya* does is to help define actions—mentally marking out the boundaries of a given action and differentiating otherwise indistinguishable acts—effectively giving acts of worship their specific identity. *Niyya* thus serves a crucial taxonomic purpose, linking actual human actions to the ideal-typical actions defined by the texts of ritual law. *Niyya* turns the undifferentiated flow of human gestures and movements into *particular named actions*, especially the actions required by God and regulated by *fiqh*. In this way

[58] Ibid.

[59] Similarly, Ibn Qudāma remarks: "If one enters *iḥrām* for a religious duty (*farīḍa*) then intends to change (*nawā naqlahā*) to another duty, the first duty is cancelled (*baṭalat*), because the *niyya* is interrupted (*qaṭ'a*), and the second act is invalid because he did not intend it from the start" (*al-Mughnī*, 2:135). Ibn Qudāma goes farther, suggesting not only the binary possibilities of '*niyya*/not-*niyya*', but also an extant but insufficiently firm *niyya*: "if one begins prayer with a *niyya* wavering between completeness and interruptedness (*mutaraddada bayna itmāmihā wa-qaṭ'ihā*), the prayer is invalid, because *niyya* is absolute certainty (*al-niyya 'azmu jāzimu*)" (2:133). *Niyya* must remain firmly in place throughout the act.

niyya may also serve a psychological purpose, allowing a person some degree of knowledge and confidence that he has fulfilled his religious duties.

Searle's approach may help illustrate how intentions are definitive of actions. As discussed above, Searle says an action consists of two components: Intentional content (expressed linguistically as a proposition) and the conditions of satisfaction (an action brought about in the right way, and 'caused' by the intention). Thus it is intention that gives Intentional definition to an action. This is perhaps most clearly illustrated by the case of 'refraining': intention is the difference between sitting still to 'listen quietly' on the one hand, and to 'obey an order to be still' on the other, or simply sitting still absent-mindedly (which may still be intentional).[60] Each instance of 'sitting still' may appear objectively identical, yet each is a different kind of action due to the Intentional content of the intention.

Qarāfī explicitly asserts that *niyya* is that which defines a particular act of worship, distinguishing it from other actions: "The rationale for the requirement [of *niyya*] is distinguishing (*tamyīz*) acts of worship (*al-ʿibādāt*) from ordinary actions (*al-ʿādāt*), and distinguishing among levels of acts of worship."[61] The term *tamyīz*, 'distinguishing' or 'isolating', is central to Qarāfī's definition of *niyya*. For Qarāfī, as summarized by Jackson, "the role of intention [is] to isolate (*yumayyiz*) the specific objective for which a willful act is performed."[62] Further, Qarāfī asserts:

> [*Niyya*] distinguishes that which is for God from that which is not ... For example, bathing (*ghusl*) may accomplish cooling off and cleaning up, but can also fulfill a commanded act of worship ... In the absence of *niyya* ... fasting (*al-ṣawm*) is [merely] lack of nourishment.[63]

---

60 Searle, *Intentionality*, 102–103.

61 Qarāfī, *al-Umniyya*, 20; see also 9–10.

62 Jackson, *Islamic Law and the State*, 200.

63 Qarāfī, *al-Umniyya*, 20. Cf. Shāfiʿī: "If one is immersed in flowing or still water in which there is no impurity, and the immersion reaches all the limbs [that one must purify in] *wuḍū*', [and while doing this] one intends purification, it is permitted. Likewise, if one sits under a water tap, or a flow of rain water, or rain [directly], intending by this [to achieve] purity, [purity] is achieved for all the limbs [that one must purify in] *wuḍū*'; provided nothing is omitted, it is permitted" (*al-Umm* [Beirut: Dār al-Fikr, 1990], 1:44). For Shāfiʿī, then, the *niyya* for purification allows one to achieve purity under a variety of circumstances, including immersion in moving or still water, using water from a tap, or being struck by rainwater. *Niyya*, in short, turns otherwise generic contact with water (within certain broad parameters) into an act of ritual purification.

Echoing Shīrāzī's discussion of multiple compatible goals, Qarāfī emphasizes that it is *niyya* that makes the difference between objectively identical actions. Further, Qarāfī indicates that *niyya* distinguishes levels of *'ibādāt* such as required prayer from supererogatory prayer.[64] Again, *niyya* distinguishes among acts whose outward form is identical, giving these acts their identity. *Niyya* is what differentiates performing *wuḍū'* from simply washing up or cooling off (even if, like Shīrāzī, one considers these compatible additional goals); *niyya* is what differentiates one prayer from another, or *ṣalāt* from calisthenics. One must also perform the actions correctly, but without *niyya*, a set of movements, no matter how precisely performed, is not an *'ibāda*. (We will revisit the potentially 'spiritual' connotations of Qarāfī's statements in the next chapter.)

Attestations to this definitive and taxonomic function of *niyya* abound in *fiqh* texts. For example, Shīrāzī says of *niyya* in prayer that "If the prayer is a required one, one must have specific *niyya*, intending the noon prayer or the evening prayer to distinguish (*li-tatamayyaz*) it from other [prayers]."[65] *Niyya* also distinguishes a required prayer from a recommended additional (*sunna*) prayer.[66] Similarly, *niyya*, alongside certain objective indicants, determines the specific identity of actions in the context of group prayer. The law establishes that whenever two or more Muslims pray together, one must be the leader, the *imām* (here having the general meaning of 'prayer leader'), and the others must take their cues from him or her.[67] Shīrāzī reflects on the critical role *niyya* plays in the designation of prayer leader:

> Group prayer is not valid unless the follower (*al-ma'mūm*, the member of the prayer congregation) intends [to be among the congregation in] the group prayer, because one means (*yurīdu*) to follow another [person], so

[64] Qarāfī, *al-Umniyya*, 20. He also indicates that *niyya* distinguishes a required (*farḍ*) action from one that is merely recommended (*mandūb*).

[65] Shīrāzī, *al-Muhadhdhab*, 1:236.

[66] Shīrāzī adds: "If the prayer is a [recommended, but not required prayer] (*sunna rātiba*), like *witr*, and like *sunna* of *fajr*, it is not valid unless one specifies the *niyya* (*yu'ayyinu al-niyya*) to distinguish it from anything else" (*al-Muhadhdhab*, 1:236). Here the literal reading is "specify the *niyya*," rather than "specify by *niyya*;" however, the sense of the passage is clearly that *niyya* is the means (not the object) of specification. Muḥammad 'Alī b. 'Alī b. Muḥammad al-Tahānawī's technical dictionary defines the recommended prayers called *rawātib* (sg. *rātib*) as *sunna* prayers that are subsequent to required prayers (*farā'iḍ*) (*Kashshāf iṣṭilāḥāt al-funūn* [Beirut: Dār al-Kutub al-'Ilmiyya, 1998], 2:177).

[67] In general, a woman may lead other women, children of either gender, or anyone not of sound mind. Usually, it is preferred that the eldest male lead, and the followers are arranged by descending age to his right and/or behind him. Adult males come first, then either male children or women and then children.

> it is necessary to [have] the *niyya* of following. If two men decide to pray individually and [a third person] intends to follow the two, his prayer is not valid, because it is not possible for him to emulate the two at one time, and if he intends emulation of one of the two, without specifying (*'ayyin*) [which one], his prayer is not valid, because if he does not specify it is not possible to emulate [one of them].[68]

When two or more people pray together, each must have the appropriate *niyya* to lead or follow. Standing in the leader's position does not alone make one the leader, nor does temporal priority—*niyya* is a critical ingredient—and given that few Muslims really need a leader's cues in order to pray properly, *niyya* constitutes perhaps the key difference between leader and follower. Every follower must specify by *niyya* which person he is following, for he can only follow one leader, and must not follow another follower (i.e., one without the *niyya* to lead). If two people praying together both have the *niyya* to lead, the prayers of each are valid (so a group of two does not require that one lead the other); if both intend to follow, both prayers are invalid.[69] In all these cases, *niyya* defines the action taking place and in turn defines the status of the actor. Moreover, one person's *niyya* can also have implications for the validity of others' acts: the prayer of the would-be follower depends on the *niyya* of the putative leader.

Niyya also plays a definitive role in the case of abbreviated prayer. In some instances, such as when traveling, ill, or at war, a Muslim is permitted to perform an abbreviated version of the daily prayers. The goal of the *niyya* must be not simply to pray, but to pray an abbreviated prayer, and this must be established prior to the start of the prayer.

[68] Shīrāzī, *al-Muhadhdhab*, 1:310. Ibn Rushd recounts a disagreement among jurists on this issue: "[The *'ulamā'*] disagree about whether it is required that the *niyya* of the follower agree with the *niyya* of the leader in specification (*ta'yīn*) of the prayer and its necessary steps (*al-wujūb* [i.e., the outer form]), that he is not permitted to pray the noon prayer behind a leader who is praying the mid-afternoon prayer, or to pray a supererogatory prayer when the follower prays a required prayer. Mālik and Abū Ḥanifa hold that it is necessary that the *niyya* of the follower agree with that of the leader, while al-Shāfi'ī holds that this is not necessary" (*Bidāyat al-mujtahid*, 1:120; *DJP*, 1:132).

[69] The passage continues, demonstrating how fine the distinctions effected by *niyya* can get: "If one of the two was praying [following] the other and he [the third party] intends to emulate the one of the two who is following, his prayer is not valid, because he follows the other [the one who is himself following], and it is not permitted to follow [the non-leader]. If two men pray and each of them intends to be the leader, this does not invalidate the prayer, because each one [effectively] prays by himself, but if each one intends to follow the other, neither prays a valid prayer, because each follows one who is not leading" (Shīrāzī, *al-Muhadhdhab*, 1:310).

Doing so establishes which prayer (full or abbreviated) the ensuing bodily actions constitute.[70] If one should perform the movements of full prayer, but with the *niyya* of abbreviation, the action would be counted as abbreviated prayer. It is also *niyya* which distinguishes one who is traveling (and thus may abbreviate the prayer) from one who is stationary:

> If one who is traveling intends (*nawā*) to stay for four days, excluding the day he arrives and the day he leaves, he is considered (*ṣār*, lit., becomes) stationary (*muqīman*), and his license (*rukhaṣ*) [to perform the abbreviated practices] of travel is invalidated … If one intends to stay four days during time of war, two things may be said: one, he abbreviates his prayer; … two, he does not abbreviate, because he intends to stay for four days without traveling and so does not abbreviate, as when one intends to stay when there is no war.[71]

The issue is not staying in one place, but intending to do so, and once one has this intent, one shifts from being a traveler to being a stationary person. One does not wait until he or she has actually stayed the requisite number of days, but begins full prayer when the *niyya* to stay for that long is formed. Jurists may disagree over how many days one must have in mind to be considered stationary, but they agree that *niyya* is the central issue.[72] *Niyya* here defines the action, the legal status of the actor, and the prescriptions incumbent upon him or her. As with the intent to cease praying, we again see a shift from a technical usage of *niyya* specifically as part of an act of worship to a non-technical usage. *Niyya* here is not the intention to perform an *ʿibāda*, but rather is simply the intention to act in a certain way, namely, to stay put.

In Searlean terms, the prior intent to stay obligates one to perform full prayers at that point, and effectively collapses into an intention-in-action with the propositional content 'that I am staying (now)'. If one originally had the *niyya* to stay and then circumstances changed so that one did not actually stay the requisite number of days, it would still be

[70] See, for example, Shīrāzī: "Abbreviation (*qaṣr*) is not permitted unless one intends abbreviation at the point of entering into the prayer state (*iḥrām*), because the norm (*al-aṣl*) is the complete version [i.e., the default mode is full prayer unless otherwise specified by *niyya*]; so if one did not intend abbreviation while establishing his purity, he is obligated [to perform] a full prayer, and is not permitted to abbreviate, as is the case for one who is not traveling" (*al-Muhadhdhab*, 1:338).

[71] Ibid., 1:339–340.

[72] Ḥanafīs usually put the number of intended stationary days at fifteen. See Mūṣilī, *al-Ikhtiyār*, 1:79; and Abū Bakr b. Masʿūd al-Kāsānī, *Kitāb badāʾiʿ al-ṣanāʾiʿ fī tartīb al-sharāʾiʿ* (Beirut: Dār al-Kitāb al-ʿArabī, 1974), 1:97.

incumbent on him to pray the full prayer up to that point when circumstances changed. That the conditions of satisfaction that one stay *x* days are actually not met only comes into play at the point of the change of circumstances, which would, of course, involve a change of intention from staying to leaving. Up to that point, the intention to stay is definitive, establishing the place of the action within the legal taxonomy.

Niyya is required in fasting, whether that fasting is for Ramaḍān, in fulfillment of an oath, as an expiation (*kaffāra*), or as supererogatory devotional act. In fact, *niyya* is a crucial element constituting both a fast per se (as opposed to simply not eating at a given moment) and the difference among fasts.[73] This is demonstrated by Ibn Qudāma: "one must specify the *niyya* for each required fast, such as whether the next day's fast is for Ramaḍān, or for making up a previous broken fast, or as an expiation, or [in fulfillment of] an oath."[74] Ibn Qudāma, like many jurists, enters a debate over just when the *niyya* is to be formed, particularly whether it must be formed before sunrise on the day of fasting, or whether it can validly be formed after that (among the major *madhhab*s, the Ḥanafīs are alone in generally supporting the latter idea).[75] For example, Ibn Qudāma asserts that it is not acceptable to form the *niyya* a day ahead, "unless one maintain it into part of the night," so that there is *niyya* the night immediately preceding the day of fasting.[76] He further discusses a debate regarding whether one must re-formulate the *niyya* each night of Ramaḍān, or one may form it once for the whole month (three *madhhab*s say the former, while Ḥanafīs say the latter[77]). Another aspect of Ramaḍān, 'retreat to the mosque' (*i'tikāf*, the supererogatory act of spending time, usually in the evening, and sometimes even overnight, in a mosque) also requires or is recommended to have *niyya*. *Niyya* is the intention that a given stretch of time spent in a mosque count as the *fiqh*-defined action *i'tikāf*, thus distinguishing the act from the outwardly identical act of simply spending time in a mosque.[78]

[73] Ibn Qudāma, *al-Mughnī*, 4:333–334.

[74] Ibid., 4:338; he notes, however, that jurists disagree about this, with some allowing less specificity about the fast when formulating *niyya* (see 4:338–339).

[75] See Mūṣilī, *al-Ikhtiyār*, 1:26.

[76] Ibn Qudāma, *al-Mughnī*, 4:336.

[77] See Ibn Rushd, *Bidāyat al-mujtahid*, 1:292ff.; *DJP*, 1:341ff.; Abū Zakariyyā Muḥyī al-Dīn b. Sharaf al-Nawawī, *Kitāb al-majmū': sharḥ al-muhadhdhab lil-Shīrāzī* (Cairo: Dār Iḥyā' al-Turāth al-'Arabī, 1995), 6:266ff.

[78] See for example Mūṣilī, *al-Ikhtiyār*, 1:136–138.

The payment of *zakāt* (mandatory alms) is made valid with *niyya*. For example, Mūṣilī observes simply that "He who pays alms on all his wealth fails if he does not intend."[79] The *niyya* is what makes a given transfer of wealth into *zakāt*, as distinguished from other forms of voluntary charity or gifting. The *niyya* of *zakāt* is made more complicated by the possibility of paying through a proxy, as will be discussed below. The remaining major Islamic ritual is the *ḥajj*, the pilgrimage to Mecca required once in the lifetime of every physically and financially able Muslim. This is a complex activity, with numerous sub-elements governed by a detailed array of rules. *Niyya* appears at several points along the way, first as the *niyya* of the overall performance of the *ḥajj* (or *ʿumra*, the supererogatory 'lesser pilgrimage'), and later for several separate constituent elements. The pilgrimage proper begins when the pilgrim reaches one of the several approved entry sites into the precincts of Mecca. At this point the pilgrim must be in the state of *iḥrām* (purity, inviolability), which includes wearing a special seamless garment. Mūṣilī observes, "[the pilgrim] prays two *rakʿa*s and says: 'O God, I desire to perform the *ḥajj*, so make my way easy and accept it from me,' and if he intends (*nawā*) in his *qalb*, this [makes the *ḥajj*] lawful," and he adds, "[one enters *iḥrām*] when he intends (*nawā*) and calls out the *talbiyya* [i.e., calling out 'here I am, O Lord …,' a standardized invocation]."[80] Shīrāzī (and his commentator al-Nawawī) asserts that *niyya* determines the taxonomy of the act, whether it counts as *ḥajj* or *ʿumra*: "One should specify [with *niyya*] whether one is preparing for the *ḥajj* or the *ʿumra*."[81]

Acts Not Requiring Niyya

That *niyya* functions to differentiate and define actions is further indicated by jurists' discussion of a class of actions that do not require *niyya*. Such actions have in common that they cannot be, or be mistaken for, any other actions, and thus do not need *niyya* to provide their identity or place in the legal taxonomy. Qarāfī, for example, discusses religious acts in which *niyya* has no place. *Niyya* is not necessary for acts that are inherently directed toward God, which he calls "acts of worship (*al-*

---

[79] Ibid., 1:101.
[80] Ibid., 1:143–144; cf. Shīrāzī, *al-Muhadhdhab*, 2:698–699.
[81] Al-Nawawī, *Kitāb al-majmūʿ*, 7:237; see also 7:235–239 *passim*.

qurbāt) about which there is no confusion,"[82] and "actions of the *qalb* devoted (*muta'alliqa*) to God Almighty."[83] These include:

> believing in God, affirming [God's] greatness and majesty, fearing His punishment, hoping for His reward, depending on His mercy, humility before His splendor, adoration of His wondrousness, awe before His authority, and likewise pronouncing the *tasbīḥ* and the *tahlīl* (common invocations of God's glory and unity, respectively), recitation of the Qur'ān, and engaging in *dhikr* (recalling and/or reciting the name[s] of God).[84]

These are mostly actions that are 'internal' states in and of themselves. These acts also all have in common that their object is effectively defined by the act itself—one cannot believe in and fear God without the act being 'for God'. As Qarāfī puts it, "these are distinguished (*mutamayyiza*) by being for the honor of [God] Almighty, and thus the *niyya* is directed (*munṣarifa*) to God Almighty by their very form (*bi-ṣūratihā*). Thus there is no harm done if [these acts] have no additional *niyya*."[85] In other words, it is not that these acts do not involve any *niyya*; rather the acts in Qarāfī's list have an intrinsic *niyya* with its object being the glorification of God. Here the form of the act defines the *niyya*. The act is what matters, and while *niyya* makes some acts into the correct acts as required by *sharī'a*, it is superfluous for those that "by their very form" are "for God."

In Searle's terms, some of these acts are subjective Intentional states akin to belief, fear, desire, hope, and so forth. As such, they have 'directedness' or 'aboutness' intrinsic to themselves, and do not have actions as their conditions of satisfaction. Thus they do not involve either prior intention or intention-in-action. In these cases, Searle's 'Intentionality' and Qarāfī's '*niyya*' seem to overlap: *niyya* here is the 'directedness' of these mental states, rather than a mental state with action as its condition of satisfaction. However, some items on Qarāfī's list—Qur'ān recitation and *dhikr*—are 'external' or objective bodily actions, and thus for Searle necessarily have intention as a component. Qarāfī includes them in his list without making any explicit distinction between these and the purely subjective states. The fact that these objective, external acts are said not to require *niyya* indicates that there

---

82 Qarāfī, *al-Umniyya*, 21.
83 Ibid., 34.
84 Ibid., 21; see also 34.
85 Ibid., 21.

is a limit to the overlap between '*niyya*' and 'intention' and also that Qarāfī is perhaps not fully consistent in his usage of '*niyya*'. That is, these are certainly intentional acts, and if they can be done without *niyya*, then *niyya* here does not simply mean 'intention'.

At the same time, *niyya* is not necessary for avoidance of evil. For Qarāfī, one need not have *niyya* to avoid committing an offense.[86] If one is going about his or her business and not doing anything illicit, one need not have *niyya* with the goal 'that the actions not be illicit'.[87] Such actions, of course, still involve actors' intentions. *Niyya* in this context takes on the implication of being needed only for acts involved in becoming or being elevated above the norm; *niyya* is perhaps the special form of intent for acts of worship. *Niyya* is parallel in a way to ritual purity (*ṭahāra*)—it is necessary for elevation above the norm in acts of worship, but is not needed for ordinary actions. Qarāfī's comments here reinforce the impression that the term *niyya* is generally reserved for intentions with positive moral valences.

Two Special Cases

A. Niyya *in Purification (*Ṭahāra*)*

Fiqh al-ʿibādāt includes two special cases of *niyya* defining the action it accompanies, and each deserves a brief excursus. Each case demonstrates that even in particularly complex situations, when intention and action seem to be somewhat removed from one another, *niyya* still retains its role as definer of actions. The first special case of *niyya* pro-

[86] Qarāfī uses the term "*mulābasat al-khubth*," which can mean 'unlawful sexual intercourse' or more general 'wicked behavior' (*al-Umniyya*, 28).

[87] Shīrāzī, discussing the difference between *najas* and *ḥadath* (major and minor impurity, respectively), remarks that "*niyya* is not necessary for purity from *najas*, because *najas* is to be avoided, like the avoidance of fornication, drinking wine, [etc.]" (*al-Muhadhdhab*, 1:69). *Ḥadath*, in contrast, occurs from such lawful and even unavoidable actions as urination, defecation, and sleeping, among other things. In this way, the state of minor impurity might be described as 'normal', and purity from *ḥadath* is an elevation above the normal state for the sake of performing acts of worship. Major impurity is a reduction below normalcy, as it were, and purification from this is needed simply to 'become normal'. This picture is complicated by the inclusion of menstruation among the causes of major impurity, belying a distinct gender bias to these implicit ideas of 'normalcy'. On the matter of impurity as the 'normal' state, see Reinhart, "Impurity/No Danger."

viding the identity of an act of worship arises in the case of purification (*ṭahāra*). The fact that purification is done as a necessary preparation for other acts of worship (especially prayer) creates a situation unique in *fiqh al-ʿibādāt*, in that no other *ʿibāda* consists of preparation for another *ʿibāda*—all the others are ends in themselves. As a result, the *niyya* for acts of purification has a unique character: it can be intention either for the act of purification itself or for the subsequent act for which one is purifying.[88] More specifically, the *niyya* of purification may be an intention either to remove impurity or to achieve purity (negative or positive formulations of the same goal), or, as a more specific version of the latter, to purify in order to perform an action which requires purity (e.g., while performing *wuḍūʾ*, one might form the *niyya* to purify for prayer). These three possibilities are often presented as equally valid options.[89] Finally, in some cases, one cannot intend purity at all, but can

[88] Shīrāzī illustrates how *niyya* in *ṭahāra* raises peculiar issues: "The characteristic nature (*ṣifa*) of *niyya* is intending the removal of minor impurity (*ḥadath*) or [intending] purity (*ṭahāra*) from minor impurity, and either is valid, because one intends the goal (*al-maqṣūd*), and this removes the minor impurity. Intending purity without qualification (*al-ṭahāra al-muṭlaqa*) is not valid because the purity could be purity from minor or major impurity, so it is not valid to have an unspecified *niyya*" (*al-Muhadhdhab*, 1:70). So one may formulate the *niyya* negatively, intending the absence (removal) of impurity, or positively, intending the presence of purity; Shīrāzī sees these as equivalent. (In Searlean terms, the propositional Intentional content of the intention can be either 'that impurity is removed' or 'that purity is established'.) For Shīrāzī, whether understood negatively or positively, one must also specify by *niyya* whether the impurity is major or minor.

[89] See, for example, Shīrāzī: "If one intends purity for prayer, or an act (*ʿamr*) that is not permitted except in a state of purity, such as touching a *muṣḥaf* [copy of the Qurʾān] and the like, it is permitted, because [such an act] is not permitted in a state of impurity, so if one intends purity for such a thing, the *niyya* encompasses (*taḍammanat*) the removal of impurity" (*al-Muhadhdhab*, 1:70). When purifying for a duty that requires purity, Shīrāzī allows for having the goal of the intention to be positively defined as 'purity for the act (which requires purity)' (as opposed to 'absence of impurity', a negative formulation). In his discussion of *niyya* in *tayammum*, Shīrāzī further considers the object or goal of the *niyya*: "*Tayammum* is not valid without *niyya*, as we said about *wuḍūʾ*, and one intends by *tayammum* the licitness (*istibāḥa*) of the prayer, for if one intends by [*tayammum*] the removal of *ḥadath*, there are two possible opinions: one, it is not valid, because [*tayammum*] does not remove the *ḥadath*; two, it is valid, because the *niyya* for removal of *ḥadath* encompasses the licitness (*istibāḥa*) of prayer" (1:127). Shīrāzī thus indicates that it is valid for one to intend the prayer while performing *tayammum*, rather than intend the removal of impurity. However, if one does intend the latter, there is a difference of opinion, and Shīrāzī does not indicate which of the two options he endorses. Shīrāzī's editor notes that al-Nawawī, in his commentary on the *Muhadhdhab*, endorses this opinion (1:70, n. 2, citing an unspecified edition of Nawawī's *Kitāb al-majmūʿ*, 1:374; this is found on 1:366–367 of the edition I consulted [Cairo: Dār Iḥyāʾ al-Turāth al-ʿArabī, 1995]). For Shīrāzī (like many jurists), *tayammum* does not truly

only intend the performance of the *ʿibāda* for which one is preparing (e.g., obligatory prayer). This holds in cases where impurity cannot actually be removed, at least in an enduring way, such as in cases of chronic impure discharge, and, for most jurists, in the case of *tayammum*, which many hold does not remove impurity.[90]

Another unusual aspect of purification is that it can potentially have effects or functions other than simply fulfilling a religio-legal duty. In spite of the fact, noted above, that Shīrāzī considers *wuḍū'* a 'pure act of worship' (*ʿibāda maḥḍa*),[91] here he depicts the effects of *wuḍū'* as potentially extending beyond obedient worship:

> If one intends by his purification the removal of *ḥadath* and also cooling off and getting physically clean (*tanaẓẓaf*), the *wuḍū'* is valid … because one thus intends removal of *ḥadath* and combines (*ḍamma*) it with things that are not incompatible with it, [although] there are those among our colleagues who say: "Such *wuḍū'* is not valid because it combines (*ashrak*) in the *niyya* [both] an act of worship and something else."[92]

---

eliminate impurity, but only establishes a state of quasi-purity, enabling one to perform a single act of ritual worship, but not establishing a state of full and enduring purity. Thus one must intend the ritual act (e.g., prayer) rather than the act of removing *ḥadath*.

90 As for acts that do not require purity, but for which purity is recommended, Shīrāzī notes a difference of opinion: "If one intends purity for reciting the Qur'ān or sitting in a mosque and similar acts for which it is preferred [but not required] that one be pure, there are two possible positions: One, it is not permitted, because these acts are allowed without being in a state of purity … [Shīrāzī remarks (tongue in cheek?) that this would be 'the same as if one did *wuḍū'* to wear clothing']. Two, it is permitted, because it is preferred that one not do these acts if one is impure, so if one intends purity thus, his *niyya* encompasses the removal of impurity" (*al-Muhadhdhab*, 1:70). In other words, if one is preparing to do an act for which purity is merely preferred, one opinion is that such an act is not a proper goal of the *niyya* while purifying, because one could do the act without being pure (the goal is too weak, so to speak, to provide the content of the *niyya* during purification). In such a case one must intend purification itself, rather than purity for the act for which one is purifying. The other opinion is the opposite: since purity is preferred in such cases, having such a goal as the object of one's *niyya* 'encompasses', or is strong enough, so to speak, to effect the removal of impurity. Shīrāzī does not endorse either opinion.

91 Ibid., 1:69; Ibn Rushd, also as noted above, asserts that a 'pure *ʿibāda*' "is only an act of worship (*al-qurba*)" with no meaning beyond fulfilling a religio-legal obligation. He classifies washing off major impurity (*ghusl al-najāsa*) as an act that combines both worship and material or instrumental ends (*Bidāyat al-mujtahid*, 1:8; *DJP*, 1:3–4). Ibn Rushd notes that jurists who distinguish between rational and non-rational acts of worship consider removal of major impurity (*najas*) to be a rational act, one which removes actual (physical) filth, and consider removal of minor impurity (*ḥadath*) to be non-rational, or non-functional act (1:75–76; *DJP*, 1:81).

92 Shīrāzī, *al-Muhadhdhab*, 1:70; c.f., Shāfiʿī, *al-Umm*, 1:44. Note that *wuḍū'* is not itself seen as being done for cleanliness (*tanaẓẓaf*), but is done to achieve ritual purity (*ṭahāra*),

In Shīrāzī's opinion, multiple 'compatible' goals are acceptable in *wuḍū'*, although some jurists disagree.[93] Note that cooling and cleaning are not presented here as unintentional consequences of the action, but part of the object of the *niyya*.[94] Shīrāzī allows adding additional compatible goals, provided the initial goal is maintained undisrupted and unchanged.[95]

Finally, *tayammum* represents a special subset of purification.[96] Jurists agree that *tayammum* does not actually remove major or minor impurity, but simply makes valid a particular performance of an *'ibāda* for which one must be pure. Unlike *wuḍū'*, which puts one in a state of purity that endures until broken, *tayammum* must be repeated before each performance of an *'ibāda*.[97] This raises the question of just what one

---

and to obey the command to do so and prepare for doing other commanded acts, such as prayer; on this, see Reinhart, "Impurity/No Danger."

93 Shīrāzī goes on to consider another aspect of the same issue, the division of the goal of the *niyya*: "If one becomes impure with multiple impurities, and then intends to remove [a single] one of them, there are three possible positions: One, the *wuḍū'* is valid, because the impurities are intermingled (*tatadākhkhal*) and eliminating one eliminates them all; two, it is not valid, because one did not intend the removal of all impurities; three, if one intends the removal of the first impurity (*al-ḥadath al-awwal*), it is valid, and if one intends the removal of additional [impurities] (*mā ba'dahu*), it is not sound [and only the first impurity is actually removed], because what is required is purification from the first, not the others. The first [opinion] is most correct" (*al-Muhadhdhab*, 1:70–71). Shīrāzī endorses the first ruling, that intending removal of one impurity effects the removal of all impurities. The third opinion seems to be simply a clarification of the first opinion. If the object of the *niyya* is only some of the impurities, it must include the 'first' of them, in which case the others are encompassed. Otherwise the *niyya* is invalid. The nature of the distinction between 'first' and 'additional' impurities is not explained.

94 As noted above, Searle calls such compound Intentional content the 'accordion effect', where the conditions of satisfaction include a multiplicity of components; for example, one may intend to raise one's arm and by so doing to cast a vote (*Intentionality*, 98–100).

95 Shīrāzī notes: "If one intends a valid *niyya* then changes (*ghayyara*) the *niyya* regarding some of the limbs, so that he intends [rather] washing the legs for cooling off or cleaning, and does not produce (*lam yaḥḍar*) the *niyya* of *wuḍū'*, then the washing for cooling off or cleansing is not valid [as *wuḍū'*]. If one produced the *niyya* of *wuḍū'* and added to it the *niyya* to cool off, it is as I previously mentioned [i.e., the *wuḍū'* is valid because the goals are not incompatible]—[although there are] disagreements [over this]" (*al-Muhadhdhab*, 1:71).

96 *Tayammum* is generally done when plentiful, suitable water is not available; See Ibn Rushd, *Bidāyat al-mujtahid*, 1:63–68; *DJP*, 1:67–71 for a discussion of the details of the conditions under which one may resort to *tayammum*.

97 Most jurists hold that one may not perform more than one required prayer after a single *tayammum*, but one may perform a required prayer and a supererogatory prayer (provided the required prayer is done first); according to Ibn Rushd, Abū Ḥanīfa allows

can intend while formulating the *niyya* of *tayammum* (which most jurists agree one must do[98]). Given that *tayammum* does not actually remove impurity, many jurists hold that the *niyya* of *tayammum* cannot be *niyya* to become pure (as it can for *wuḍūʾ*), or simply intention to perform *tayammum*, but rather can only be intention to perform the *ʿibāda* for which one is preparing.[99]

B. *Performing* ʿIbādāt *by Proxy*

The second type of special case of *niyya* providing the identity of an act of worship arises in the case of acts carried out by proxy. As a general rule, each person must perform her or his own acts of worship. However, there are two specific exceptions, namely the payment of *zakāt* by proxy and the performance of *ḥajj* by proxy, in both of which the *ʿibāda* is enacted bodily by someone other than the person fulfilling the duty and seeking the benefit. The direct connection of agent-intention-action is thus severed. However, the agency as well as the religio-legal 'credit' and religious benefit or reward still accrue to the 'actor' rather than the proxy. Under scrutiny, these two cases of action by proxy prove not to undermine the characterization of *niyya* developed above, but, in fact, to emphasize the role *niyya* plays in determining the identity of actions.

The payment of *zakāt*, like the other *ʿibādāt*, requires *niyya* at the time of performance. However, the jurists readily envision a case in which the person paying the *zakāt* does not directly (bodily) transport the payment to the recipient, but rather the transaction involves a third party acting on behalf of the payer. In discussing the "timing of the *niyya*," Shīrāzī addresses the complications caused by the possibility of paying the *zakāt* by proxy:

---

two required prayers after a single *tayammum* (*Bidāyat al-mujtahid*, 1:73–74; *DJP*, 1:78–79). Mālik reportedly held that the intention (*irāda*) to perform two required prayers while performing *tayammum* invalidates the *tayammum* altogether, even for the first prayer (1:72; *DJP*, 1:77).

[98] Ibn Rushd, *Bidāyat al-mujtahid*, 1:67; *DJP*, 1:71.

[99] See, for example, Aḥmad Ibn Naqīb al-Miṣrī, *ʿUmdat al-sālik wa-ʿuddat al-nāsik*, ed. and trans. Nūḥ Ḥā Mīm Keller, *Reliance of the Traveller: A Classic Manual of Islamic Sacred Law* (Beltsville, Md.: Ammana, 1994), 90–91; and Shīrāzī, *al-Muhadhdhab*, 1:127, where he recounts disagreements among jurists over the details of *niyya* in *tayammum*. Both Ibn Naqīb and Shīrāzī, for example, use the phrase "intend the permissibility of the prayer" (*yanwī istibāḥat farḍ al-ṣalāt* [Ibn Naqīb, 90]; *yanwī bil-tayammum istibāḥat al-ṣalāt* [Shīrāzī, 1:127]).

> Regarding the timing of the *niyya*, there are two opinions: one, one must intend the situation of payment (*ḥāl al-dafʿ*) because entering into the action is an *ʿibāda*, so it is necessary to intend at the beginning like in prayer; two, it is permitted that the *niyya* precede [the payment] because delegating authority (*tawkīl*) is permitted for [*zakāt*], and *niyya* is not simultaneous with the fulfillment [of the duty] by the delegate, so it is permitted that the *niyya* precede the action, unlike in the case of prayer.[100]

Shīrāzī does not explicitly endorse a position, but his commentator al-Nawawī holds the second to be preferred.[101] In this case, the action ('paying *zakāt*') can, in a sense, be dissociated from the actor, and the action is compound and temporally extended. The *niyya* may be formed at one point in the compound action and still cover the rest of the action, so that the actual paying may be done at some temporal (and spatial) remove, by someone other than the one fulfilling the duty of *zakāt*. This solves the problem of how to fulfill the duty of almsgiving in a realistic and practical way while still retaining the necessity of *niyya*. However, this solution gives rise to a conceptual dilemma regarding the relationship of intention to action. One might think of intention and action being necessarily simultaneous, and this is how Shīrāzī treats the *niyya* of purification and prayer, but this connection is disrupted in the case of action done by proxy.

Searle's idea of prior intention is useful here: the *niyya* of *zakāt* by proxy is akin to a prior intention to pay *zakāt*. 'Payment of *zakāt*' is the compound action of calculating and collecting the payment, on the one hand, and delivering it to the proper recipient, on the other. There is, it seems, a prior intention representing the entire compound action, and intentions-in-action presenting the various component actions that make up the compound action. In the case of payment by proxy, there would be an intention-in-action for the action of giving the payment to the proxy, but the payer of *zakāt* would have no intention-in-action for the actual delivery of the payment to the recipient—only the proxy would have this. Searle considers action by proxy intentional action, provided the conditions of satisfaction (re)presented by the intention are fulfilled 'in the right way'.[102] The action of the payer of *zakāt*, in

[100] Shīrāzī, *al-Muhadhdhab*, 1:560.

[101] Ibid., n. 4, citing an unspecified edition of Nawawī's *Kitāb al-majmūʿ*, 6:187 (6:156–158 in my edition).

[102] Searle, *Intentionality*, 82. He elaborates: "Suppose that unknown to me my arm is rigged up so that whenever I try to raise it, somebody else causes it to go up, then the action is not mine, even though I had the intention in action of raising my arm and in

these terms, is 'getting the other agent to pay it', not simply 'paying it'. The requisite *niyya* in this case need not be simultaneous with the actual transfer of payment (i.e., an intention-in-action), but can instead be a prior and complex intention.

A somewhat different scenario arises in the case of *ḥajj* performed by proxy. Most jurists allow the *ḥajj* or *ʿumra*, whether obligatory or non-obligatory, to be performed on behalf of another person who, for valid reasons (primarily physical inability), is unable to undertake the journey himself.[103] The pilgrimage, then, is the one exception to the rule that no one may perform an *ʿibāda* on behalf of another. The person on whose behalf the pilgrimage is performed may, but need not necessarily, pay the traveling expenses of the proxy (jurists disagree over whether a proxy may profit from his or her efforts).[104] Most jurists hold that the proxy must already have performed his or her own obligatory *ḥajj*, and one may not perform the *ḥajj* for more than one person at a time, including oneself.[105] The proxy performs all the obligatory acts of the *ḥajj*, and the key element in making the *ḥajj* count on behalf of another is the proxy's *niyya*. Jurists depict this as a case where one makes

---

some sense that intention caused my arm to go up … [But] suppose I know how my arm is rigged up and I want it to go up. My intention in action then is *getting the other agent to raise it*, not *raising it*. *My* action is getting him to raise it, *his* action is raising it … And indeed for some complex action types we even allow that one can perform an action by getting others to perform it. We say, for example, 'Louis XIV built Versailles', even though the actual construction was not done by him" (110).

[103] Ibn Rushd notes that Mālikīs disagree among themselves over whether one can perform a *ḥajj* on behalf of an infant. According to Ibn Rushd, Mālik and Abū Ḥanīfa agree that if one is unable to go oneself, this lifts the obligation to perform *ḥajj*; one may have a proxy perform on his or her behalf, but is not obligated to do so. Shāfiʿī does consider this an obligation—if a person cannot go himself, but can afford to pay someone else's way, he is obligated to do so. Some Shāfiʿīs further hold that if a person dies without having performed the *ḥajj*, it is binding on his heirs to set aside something from the estate with which someone can perform the pilgrimage on his behalf (*Bidāyat al-mujtahid*, 1:319–320; *DJP*, 1:375–376). The jurists disagreed over many details about this matter, such as exactly what constitutes an inability to perform the *ḥajj* oneself. Mālik, for instance, is reported to have held that *ḥajj* cannot be done for a living person, since that person may yet be able to do it himself. See also Shīrāzī, *al-Muhadhdhab*, 2:674–676, 700; Mūṣilī, *al-Ikhtiyār*, 1:170–172.

[104] Ibn Rushd, *Bidāyat al-mujtahid*, 1:321; *DJP*, 1:377. He notes that Mālik and Shāfiʿī allow a person to offer himself for a wage for performing *ḥajj* on another's behalf, but they disapprove of it, while Abū Ḥanīfa does not allow it.

[105] According to Ibn Rushd (*Bidāyat al-mujtahid*, 1:320; *DJP*, 1:376–377), Mālik is the only jurist who did not require the proxy to have completed her or his own *ḥajj* first, and only allowed this for *ḥajj* on behalf of a deceased person, and he preferred even in this case that the proxy perform his own *ḥajj* first. See also Ibn Naqīb, 304–306.

a verbal pronouncement of the fact that the pilgrimage is being done on behalf of another person, who is specifically named; however, like the *talbiyya*, this pronouncement is linked to, but not identical with, the *niyya*. For example, according to Mūṣilī, "Whoever performs the *ḥajj* on behalf of another intends (*yanwī*) the *ḥajj* for that person, while saying 'I am at your service, O Lord, on behalf of so-and-so'."[106] Here the *niyya* in effect turns one person's bodily actions into the acts of another person, or at least into acts the legal obligation and religious value of which accrue to another.

Conclusion

The materials examined in this chapter make apparent that Islamic ritual law, while dealing extensively with setting out the details of the objective acts considered incumbent upon Muslims, also recognizes a subjective element as essential to those acts. The treatment of *niyya* by the jurists demonstrates that they are not strict behaviorists in defining and assessing actions. The outward, objective form of actions certainly matters, but the subjective element is also critical. Jurists weigh in on exactly when and how *niyya* must be formed, the implications of not having or maintaining it, how it might be lost or invalidated, and many other technical details.

As a silent and internal phenomenon, this subjective element is, by definition, unavailable for objective evaluation. One possible implication of this fact is reflected by Qarāfī, who argues on this basis that the *ʿibādāt* are not the business of the government. As Jackson shows, Qarāfī's view of *niyya* as a necessary and irreducibly subjective element of the *ʿibādāt* serves his wider effort to establish the limits of legitimate state interference in religious practice.[107] According to Jackson's compelling interpretation of Qarāfī, the reach of the 'law' in the sense of an embodied regulating agency (i.e., 'the state' and 'the judiciary') reaches it limits at the body of the legal subject. In short, *niyya* occupies

---

[106] Mūṣilī, *al-Ikhtiyār*, 1:170–171. See also Shīrāzī, *al-Muhadhdhab*, 2:700, where he indicates that one performing the *ḥajj* on behalf of another should say "I make this offering as the offering of so-and-so." Wensinck observes that "One can perform the major pilgrimage as a proxy (*plaatsvervanger*). The principal [i.e., the one on whose behalf the proxy acts] is the one who benefits, but the *niyya* is pronounced by the proxy" ("Intentie in Recht," 114).

[107] Jackson, *Islamic Law and the State*, 203. This included the prosecution of apostasy.

a space not open to external evaluation or governance, and so practices dependent on it, especially the *ʿibādāt*, cannot be regulated by the government. This point is generally supported by Brinkley Messick's comments on the prospects of discerning "an historically specific form of 'inwardness'" in Muslim legal discussions of intent.[108] He observes that

> The relevant metaphor of the human interior in this legal discourse locates processes of intent formation specifically in the human "heart," which is part of the larger interior realm of the "self," the *nafs*, with the overarching construct being the *sharʿī* subject … These legal analyses of intent are … cross-cut by another set of categories which also are applied to the relations between the outward or manifest as opposed to the inward or concealed. The terms in question are *ẓāhir* and *bāṭin* and, in the legal domain, a fundamental principle holds that analyses are to be conducted at the level of the outward or manifest, the *ẓāhir*, and not on that of the *bāṭin*.[109]

Given the general treatment of *niyya* in the *ʿibādāt* as having no necessary connection to any outward, manifest indicants, it is simply not available for objective analysis. Messick asserts that "in the Islamic tradition there was no legal psychology; the classic expert called to court was the physiognomist, the specialist in reading outward physical signs as indications."[110] Such an expert would have little to say about *niyya* in acts of worship, a fact which adds weight to Qarāfī's call to keep the judiciary away from such matters. The jurists (*fuqahāʾ*), according to Qarāfī, should be left to argue over and comment on such matters.[111] But this view seems to overestimate the extent to which even the *fuqahāʾ* can be said to govern the *ʿibādāt*, for our discussion of *niyya* in the *ʿibādāt* indicates that the jurists recognize the limits of their own ability to know the subjective states of others. In the end, intent in the *ʿibādāt* seems to be governed more by conscience than by legal scholars or judges.

We have seen that a primary function assigned to *niyya* in *fiqh al-ʿibādāt* is definitive and taxonomic. *Niyya* helps make acts of worship what they are, and allows an actor to locate his actual actions on the map of ideal-typical actions laid out in the law texts. In this regard, ritual intent seems rather like any other intent, for, as the work of Searle

---

108 Brinkley Messick, "Indexing the Self: Intent and Expression in Islamic Legal Acts," *Islamic Law and Society* 8, 2 (2001): 176.

109 Ibid., 176–177.

110 Ibid., 177.

111 Jackson, *Islamic Law and the State*, 203.

helps show, such definitive functions are themselves partly constitutive of intent: intent is the Intentional state accompanying an action and giving it a crucial part of its identity. However, we are still faced with limits in fully understanding the role of intent in Islamic ritual law. Most notably, we must yet address the fact that in *fiqh al-ʿibādāt*, jurists do something altogether odd with intent, namely insisting that one intend while acting. If *niyya* is simply ordinary intent, and ritual actions are simply ordinary actions, then it makes little sense to do this. That is, if the actions governed by *fiqh al-ʿibādāt* are intentional actions, as they manifestly are, then they are by definition accompanied by intent to act. It would sound quite odd, for example, to tell someone to 'stand up' and then add to this command, 'and intend to stand up while you do it'. Barring very strange and probably artificial circumstances (such as being attached to a machine that makes one stand against one's will), one cannot stand up without intending to (and we would probably not say of the person attached to the standing machine that 'he stood up intentionally').

So why tell someone to 'perform prayers, and intend to do so while you do it'? The definitive and taxonomic functions we have observed *niyya* performing do not explain this, for those same functions would be fulfilled if the jurists simply assumed actors to have intentions and then queried them regarding exactly what intention they had, allowing the answer to help legally define the action (this is exactly what jurists do with intent in non-ritual contexts, as we will see later). Thus, it seems that there is indeed something peculiar about ritual intent. In the next chapter, we will explore the two most promising explanations of this peculiarity: first, that ritual intent is not simple intent to act, but a spiritual dedication of the act, and second, that specifically ritual action differs somehow from non-ritual action, especially in terms of the relationship between intention and action.

CHAPTER THREE

RITUAL SPIRIT AND RITUAL INTENT

Introduction

The previous chapter explored the technical details of the nature and role of intention in Islamic ritual law, and while that exploration answered a number of questions, it also raised several others. Many of these can be subsumed under the simple question of 'why': Why insist on having the intention to perform acts of worship? Intentional actions must, by definition, be intended by the actor. If acts of worship are intentional actions—which they patently are—then what sense does it make to insist that one intend them while acting? How could one do otherwise? No one could accidentally perform all the detailed movements and utterances of *ṣalāt*, or trip over his shoelace and end up performing a *ḥajj*. In the other legal spheres discussed in the following chapters, it is assumed that actors have intentions and that they need not be told to have them; the question is how to know and assess them. Insisting that one have *niyya* during acts of worship implies that one might act without *niyya*, and in fact, the jurists are explicit that this could happen and that it should not. So it seems that there is something peculiar about either this kind of intention, the context in which it operates, or both.

One potential solution to this mystery readily presents itself, namely that *niyya* is some sort of 'spiritual' phenomenon. The *'ibādāt* are obviously religious acts, directed at obeying and worshiping God. They clearly include objective bodily postures, movements, and verbal utterances, but we have seen that they also include a subjective, internal, silent component. Perhaps this subjective component is a spiritual action, a link between the individual soul and God. Rather than 'intention' in the terms employed by philosophers of action, language, and mind, perhaps *niyya* is an 'opening of the heart' to God, a spiritual communion undergirding mere bodily postures and verbal utterances. If so, then the imperative to 'have *niyya*' could be read as the insistence that one be properly pious, focused on the spiritual communing with the divine that the *ʿibādāt* occasion, and spiritually offering his or her actions to God.

In fact, numerous Western scholars have read *niyya* this way. In addition to solving the specific mystery of why jurists insist on intending an intentional act, several secondary studies also see *niyya* as the solution to the wider 'problem' of a perceived lack of spirituality in Islamic ritual. That is, Islamic religious ritual can appear to non-Muslim observers as overly concerned with physical, bodily matters, such as the minutia of movement, and not sufficiently concerned with the more important matter of spiritual disposition. *Niyya* comes to the rescue by providing that missing link, the spark that turns rote repetition into spiritual reverie. As a silent, internal action of the 'heart', integral to acts of worship, it seems to fit this spiritual description.

This explanation founders, however, on the straightforward meaning of the legal texts. The first part of this chapter will explore arguments in favor of a spiritual reading of *niyya* in *fiqh al-ʿibādāt*, and refute them based largely on evidence already presented in the previous chapter. Muslim jurists simply do not treat *niyya* as the spiritual component of acts of worship and, moreover, do not share the assumption of the secondary sources that there is something missing from Islamic religious ritual, some spiritual gap that *niyya* would bridge. Certainly, some Muslims do treat *niyya* as spiritual, but the classic works of *fiqh* do not.

If this spiritual response to the question 'Why *niyya*?' falls short, we are not without other options. The second part of this chapter will argue that a better explanation can be found by looking at the nature of ritual action as a peculiar species of human activity. Caroline Humphrey and James Laidlaw have proposed a theory of ritual that helps explain the Muslim jurists' odd insistence that people intend to act when acting out ritual acts of worship. Humphrey and Laidlaw argue that ritual action differs fundamentally from non-ritual action in that ritual action is not directly governed by intention the way non-ritual action is. Thus, Islamic ritual law's call to intend one's ritual actions reflects a recognition that one might do otherwise, and that a gap potentially exists between ritual actor and action. What looks to others like a valid ritual action might well be performed without attentiveness or intent. The '*niyya* imperative' serves to bridge this 'ritual intent gap', defining valid ritual actions only as those done with direct intent.

Part 1. *Niyya as the 'Spirit' of Islamic Ritual?*

As I have argued elsewhere, it is often said that Islam is more a religion of orthopraxy than of orthodoxy, focused more on ritual practices and proper comportment than on theological doctrines and philosophical reflection.[1] Many observers see in Islam an emphasis on law over theology or philosophy, and they see in law an emphasis on acting correctly.[2] Certainly Muslims have reached impressive heights of theological and philosophical sophistication, but many scholars recognize a certain pride of place Islamic societies have often given to proper comportment and to the efforts to determine the rules of such comportment. This view of Islam as praxis-oriented reflects a welcome modification of much previous Western scholarship that saw Islam as mechanically ritualistic and thus ethically superficial. In 1878, for example, Robert Durie Osborn said of Islam "there is no [other] creed the inner life of which has been so completely crushed under an inexorable weight of ritual"; Muslims' distant view of God "empties all religious acts of spiritual life and meaning and reduces them to rites and ceremonies."[3] William Tisdall in 1910 claimed that "the stress which [Islam] lays upon ceremonial observances, such as fasting,... the recitation of fixed prayers at stated hours, the proper mode of prostration, etc., *tends* to make the great mass of Muḥammadans mere formalists"; thus "it will be evident that purity of heart is neither considered necessary nor desirable: in fact it would be hardly too much to say that it is *impossible* for a Muslim."[4] In 1951 Gustave E. von Grunebaum remarked that Islam, its prayer marked by a "peculiar formalism," "left the believer

---

[1] See Paul R. Powers, "Interiors, Intentions, and the 'Spirituality' of Islamic Ritual Practice," *Journal of the American Academy of Religion* 72, 2 (June 2004): 425–459.

[2] For example, Frederick Denny notes that in Islam "Belief, interestingly, is perfected and proved in service to God, service that includes worship acts performed according to strict rules and procedures" (*Introduction to Islam*, 112; see also 113, 174; cf. H.A.R. Gibb, *Mohammedanism* [Oxford: Oxford University Press 1970], 60). A. Kevin Reinhart finds that "Islamic morality is a morality of action ... Only God knows hearts, say the legal sources, so one must judge by actions. Right action is thus presumptive evidence of inward virtue" ("Transcendence and Social Practice: *Muftīs* and *Qāḍīs* as Religious Interpreters," *Annales Islamologiques* 27 [1993]: 24).

[3] Osborn, *Islam under the Khalīfs of Baghdād* (London: Seeley, Jackson, & Halliday, 1878), 4; in William St. Clair Tisdall, *The Religion of the Crescent*, 3rd ed. (London: Society for Promoting Christian Knowledge, 1910), 57.

[4] Tisdall, *Religion of the Crescent*, 80, 88; emphasis in original. The latter phrase [taken from the 1906 second edition, with the same page number] is cited in Ignaz Goldziher, *Introduction to Islamic Theology and Law*, trans. Andras Hamori and Ruth

satisfied with an arid, if physically exacting liturgy."[5] Islamic law itself has been seen by some as the convoluted result of an overemphasis on the outward forms of action. N.J. Coulson has argued that by the fifth century of Islam jurists were so focused on elaborating the minutiae of right action that the law they generated "could not be supported by society in practice ... Their fundamental concern was the study and development of 'law' for its own sake. Practical considerations were only employed where this could be done without infringement of any theoretical principle."[6] For many observers, Islamic law suffers from obsessive-compulsive worry over the infinite potential forms of action, ironically so focused on praxis as to be impractical. Thus, even when Muslim concern with right action has been recognized, it has often been denigrated.

The newer standard of seeking a neutral description of Islam as praxis-centered is an advance in both accuracy and attitude, reflecting a general increase in academic comfort with ritual and the body. Some scholars, perhaps attempting to atone for the sins of previous generations, have sought to show that both Islamic ritual and praxis in general are not just 'empty ritualism' and cynical 'letter of the law' compliance but rather the surface of a deeply spiritual experience. In their efforts, some such scholars have focused on the treatment of *niyya* in Islamic ritual law. As a pervasive, subjective, individual, and 'internal' component of ritual, *niyya* seems to be a good place to look for a 'deep' or spiritual component of ritual.

However, as we have already begun to see, such a spiritual treatment of *niyya* is more than the legal sources will bear. Muslim jurists often treat *niyya* as one formal step in the process of performing acts of ritual worship; *niyya* is a focusing of the mind on the act of worship. The 'right *niyya*' for a given act is simply the '*niyya* to do that act'. While the effort to thrust *niyya* into a spiritual role is part of a wider effort to defend Islam from charges of 'empty ritualism', this move in fact subtly reinforces the characterization of Islam as superficial and legalistic. Much scholarship on *niyya* belies the scholars' own *a priori* definition of 'proper

---

Hamori (Princeton: Princeton University Press, 1981), originally published as *Vorlesungen über den Islam* (Heidelberg, 1910), 19.

[5] Gustave E. von Grunebaum, *Muhammadan Festivals* (New York: Schuman, 1951; reprint, London: Curzon, 1992), 13, 3.

[6] N.J. Coulson, "Doctrine and Practice in Islamic Law: One Aspect of the Problem," *Bulletin of the School of Oriental and African Studies* 18, 2 (1956): 222–223.

religion' as 'spiritual', revolving around an inner, individual, private, non-material, eternal (and thus preemptively important) dimension of the self, the 'true self' beneath an ephemeral surface. To be sure, Islam encompasses some aspects that can accurately be described as spiritual, but also some aspects that are decidedly exoteric, materialist, and 'this-worldly', treating the temporal and bodily as the locus of the most important religious activity. *Niyya* in ritual law is a part of this embodied dimension of religion.

Rather than recognizing the value some Muslims sometimes ascribe to 'this world', and seeing such value as properly religious, scholars have sought to make *niyya* the solution to a problem of their own making. Moreover, the apologetic effort to spiritualize Islamic ritual by spiritualizing *niyya* participates in the troubled enterprise of seeking a sweeping, holistic characterization of 'Islam', merely substituting an ostensibly favorable characterization ('deep/profound') for a negative one ('superficial/legalistic'). In short, *niyya* does not serve the spiritual purposes attributed to it and, moreover, these mischaracterizations of *niyya* reflect a misguided effort to show that Islam really is, in spite of itself, deep and spiritual.

Ignaz Goldziher, in his 1910 *Introduction to Islamic Theology and Law*, strives to demonstrate that Islam is more than law and the performance of ceremonial acts. He declares that in the Qur'ān, "the intention behind an act is the criterion for the religious value of the act,"[7] and that "the highest value is ascribed to *ikhlāṣ*, unclouded purity of heart (40:14); *taqwā al-qulūb*, 'piety of heart' (22:32); [and] *qalb salīm*, 'a whole heart' (26:89)." He concludes that,

> Such are the criteria by which the believer's religious worth is assessed … They are extended over the entire range of religious life by the doctrine that *nīya* [=*niyya*], the disposition or intention behind a religious act, serves to gauge the value of that act. According to this doctrine, a tincture of selfish or hypocritical motive deprives any good work of its value.[8]

[7] Goldziher, *Introduction*, 18. He cites Qur'ān 2:177 and 22:34, 37.

[8] Goldziher, *Introduction*, 18–19. Goldziher uses this observation explicitly to refute William Tisdall's condemnation of Islam as rigidly legalistic, quoted above. Goldziher remarks: "Thus no unprejudiced observer will accept the Reverend Tisdall's dictum that 'it will be evident that purity of heart is neither considered necessary nor desirable: in fact it would be hardly too much to say that it is impossible for a Muslim'" (19, citing Tisdall, *Religion of the Crescent*, 88). As I show, however, Goldziher seeks only to salvage a putative "original ethical vision" of Islam that he finds lacking in most of Islamic history.

For Goldziher, such emphasis on the "disposition or intention behind a religious act" is clearly a good thing, the mark of a religion with the proper values and priorities, and he lauds the centrality of such concerns in Islam:

> The value of works is determined according to the intention that prompts them: this is one of the supreme principles of religious life in Islam. One may infer the importance of this principle for the Muslim from the fact that a statement of it is inscribed over one of the main entrances of al-Azhar, the mosque in Cairo that is the much-visited center of theological learning in Islam. It reminds all who enter, whether their mind is set on study or devotion: "Deeds are judged according to intentions; each man's accounts are drawn up according to his intentions." This hadith rose to be the guiding thought of all religious action in Islam.[9]

Here Goldziher cites the key *ḥadīth* passage already cited above that is the proof text Muslim jurists most often employ regarding intent.[10] Without citing any Muslim commentary on the topic, aside from noting the al-Azhar epigram, Goldziher presents *niyya* as nothing less than a "supreme principle" and "the guiding thought of all religious action in Islam."

From this properly spiritual early phase, Goldziher depicts Islam on a trajectory of decline, from the early period's high ethical standards centered on internal dispositions and intentions, toward a later, degraded religious sense dominated by legalistic concerns for outward practice. Goldziher pulls no punches when discussing classical Islamic law:

> This cultivation of jurisprudence, which reached its prime as early as the second Islamic century, contributed a new element to the intellectual world of Islam: *fiqh*, the science of religious law, a science which, perverted by casuistry, was soon to become disastrous for religious life and religious learning.[11]

This 'disaster' was precipitated by the establishment of consensus (*ijmāʿ*) as a "doctrine of the infallibility of the *consensus ecclesiae*" and the attendant emergence of a class of legal experts with inordinate control over

---

[9] Goldziher, *Introduction*, 42.

[10] Goldziher cites several other *ḥadīth*s that seem to fit his characterization (see ibid., 41–43); these are not common in *fiqh* texts. Goldziher presents decontextualized Qur'ān and *ḥadīth* passages together with his own exegesis, without exploring whether Muslim commentators agree.

[11] Ibid., 44.

the form Islam would take.[12] These developments led to the adulteration of the Qur'ān's and the Prophet's ethical vision, for even if "the scholars of *fiqh* did not intend to embitter the life of the Muslim by imprisoning him in a stockade of legal restraints,"[13] their work led Islam into "soul-destroying pedantry."[14] The profound, interioristic religion of the Prophet gave way to excessive legalism as the "theological spirit was trained to … quibbling discriminations … that proved detrimental to the inwardness of religion,"[15] undermining "true piety, the devotion of the heart" in "perversion of the religious ideal."[16] Fortunately (in Goldziher's eyes), the Ṣūfīs, especially al-Ghazālī (d. 505/1111), "worked hard to rescue the inwardness of religion from the clutches of quibbling religious lawyers"[17] and restored "inward religiosity" to Islam by rejecting legalistic casuistry and "the hairsplitting of the dogmatics of the *kalām* (dialectical theology)."[18]

It could hardly be clearer that Goldziher harbors an *a priori* definition of 'good religion' against which various aspects of Islam are to be measured.[19] For Goldziher, religion with a proper 'theological spirit' is 'inward' and thus 'truly pious'. *Niyya*, elevated by Goldziher to the level of 'supreme principle', both constitutes and demonstrates this spiritual piety. Straining to find the good in it, Goldziher reasons that Islam must have had a proper spirit at one point, but it slipped away in a wash of legalism and distracted theologizing, only to be partly salvaged by Ṣūfism. For all his historical-critical insight (he was one of the pioneers of Western *ḥadīth* criticism), he is wedded to a contrived vision of the golden age of the Prophet, against which later Islam largely pales.

---

[12] Ibid., 50. Goldziher admits, however, that *ijmāʿ* "provides Islam with a potential for freedom of movement and a capacity for evolution" that explains the impressive "adaptability of Islam" (52).

[13] Ibid., 55.

[14] Ibid., 62.

[15] Ibid., 63.

[16] Ibid., 66.

[17] Ibid.

[18] Ibid., 158–159. My point is not that al-Ghazālī did not make these arguments but rather that they are not, from a scholarly point of view, the restoration of the true and proper form of religion that Goldziher wants them to be. Neither al-Ghazālī's work nor anything else licenses Goldziher's sweeping claim that "Amid this hairsplitting struggle over formulas and definitions, Sufism alone harbored a tolerant spirit" (165).

[19] For an interesting study of Goldziher's personal views, see Raphael Patai, *Ignaz Goldziher and His Oriental Diary: A Translation and Psychological Portrait* (Detroit: Wayne State University Press, 1987). Patai is generally sympathetic toward Goldziher, yet he documents Goldziher's distaste for much of the contemporary Islamic world, his

If Goldziher's work is a *locus classicus* of this view of *niyya* as the 'heart of Islam', it is hardly alone. This same set of views is reflected in A.J. Wensinck's brief but dense entry on "*Niyya*" in the influential *Encyclopaedia of Islam*. Wensinck asserts that in the canonical *ḥadīth*, "which, generally speaking, reflects the state of things up to the middle of the 2nd/8th century," *niyya* "has not yet acquired in this literature the technical meaning and limitation" that it displays in *fiqh* works; instead *niyya* here has "the common meaning of intention."[20] Wensinck then recapitulates Goldziher's treatment of *niyya* as an inner, profound matter:

> In this [common, non-technical] sense, [*niyya*] is of great importance. Al-Bukhārī opens his collection with a tradition, which in this place is apparently meant as a motto. It runs: "Works are only rendered efficacious by their intention" ... This tradition occurs frequently in the canonical collections. *It constitutes a religious and moral criterion superior to that of the law.* The value of an *ʿibāda*, even if performed in complete accordance with the precepts of the law, depends upon the intention of the performer, and *if this intention should be sinful, the work would be valueless.* "For," adds the tradition just mentioned, "every man receives only what he has intended"; or "his wages shall be in accordance with his intention."[21]

Wensinck here, like Goldziher, gives his own exegesis of the *ḥadīth*, not that of Muslim sources. Having just indicated that the relevant *ḥadīth* predates the technical developments of *fiqh*, Wensinck nonetheless claims that the meaning of *niyya* in those *ḥadīth* "constitutes a religious and moral criterion superior to that of the law," and then applies this 'prior' usage to *fiqh al-ʿibādāt*. *Niyya* certainly carries a less technical meaning in the cited *ḥadīth* than in *fiqh*, yet Wensinck arbitrarily holds the former superior and measures the latter against it. For Wensinck, errant *niyya* is 'sinful', a moral interpretation he does not support with evidence. He then notes that both some *ḥadīth*s and some later sources, such as *Lisān al-ʿArab* and al-Ghazālī's *Iḥyāʾ ʿulūm al-dīn*, indicate that "the intention of the faithful is better than his work,"[22]

"disdain for foreigners" (70–71, and, e.g., 90), and his preference for spiritual mystery over embodied practice. See, for example, the remarkable entry of October 1, 1873, recounting a visit to an Istanbul synagogue (99–100).

[20] Wensinck, "Niyya."

[21] Ibid., emphasis added. Wensinck cites one other *ḥadīth*: "There is no hidjra after the capture of Mecca, only holy war and intention." This is the only other *ḥadīth* about *niyya* to appear regularly in *fiqh*, though much less frequently than the other one we have noted.

[22] Ibid.

thus suggesting that at least some Muslims returned to this prior, 'superior', antinomian sensibility. Wensinck follows Goldziher in seeing a trajectory from *ḥadīth*, the high point of religious depth, so to speak, downward/outward into *fiqh*, and then back upward/inward through al-Ghazālī and Ṣūfism.

Wensinck's *Encyclopaedia of Islam* entry is essentially a condensed version of portions of an earlier and largely overlooked Dutch article, his 1920 "De Intentie in Recht, Ethiek en Mystiek der Semietische Volken." This article covers both Islamic and Jewish treatments of intention in a range of textual genres, especially ritual law and 'mystical' writings. It is careful and thorough within its limits, and it is unfortunate that it has not, to my knowledge, been translated into a more-widely read language. Moreover, the *Encyclopaedia of Islam* entry loses much of the article's subtlety. For his Islamic sources, Wensinck first focuses on the term *niyya* in *fiqh al-ʿibādāt*, recounting basic technical details, such as the timing and 'location' of *niyya*. Here Wensinck is accurate and clearheaded about the formalism of the sources, noting for example, the jurists' insistence that *niyya* correspond closely to the ritual action it accompanies—for instance, the noon prayer must include *niyya* for that prayer, not the evening prayer.[23] Wensick then goes on to explore ethical and Ṣūfī materials, especially al-Ghazālī's mystical/ethical treatise, *Iḥyāʾ ʿulūm al-dīn*, and again provides a responsible account of his sources.[24] Unlike in his encyclopedia entry, Wensinck here keeps his genres distinct, allowing *fiqh* materials their independent due, even if his agenda is disconcertingly broad—pursuing a holistic account of intentions in "the two Semitic monotheisms."

Joseph Schacht's seminal 1964 *Introduction to Islamic Law* includes a chapter on "General Concepts" which gives primacy of place to *niyya*: "a fundamental concept of the whole of Islamic religious law, be it concerned with worship or with law in the narrow sense, is the *niyya* (intent)."[25] Characteristically terse, Schacht asserts a historical trajectory that is already becoming familiar:

> [*Niyya*] applied originally to acts of worship; the religious obligation is discharged not by outward performance as such but only if it is done

---

23 Wensinck, "Intentie in Recht," 112. My access to this Dutch text is limited to a partial translation that I personally commissioned; my thanks to Alex van der Haven for his invaluable assistance.

24 Ibid., 121–138.

25 Schacht, *Introduction*, 116.

> with a *pious intent. But Islamic orthodoxy insisted on the performance*, and *niyya*, from being a state of mind, became an act of will directed towards performing a religious duty; it must, as a rule, be explicitly formulated, at least mentally. An act of worship without *niyya* is invalid, and so is the *niyya* without the act.[26]

Schacht's observations about technical details are correct, as is his observation of a shift from a general to a technical meaning specific to ritual contexts—a development we have seen asserted by Wensinck. However, Schacht subtly suggests a devolution from *niyya* as "pious" to *niyya* as mere "will" directing mechanical, "orthodox" performance of ritual duties.

By now a picture is emerging of *niyya* as a spiritual component of Islamic ritual, one that was endorsed as such by the Prophet himself, fell out of favor with the jurists, and re-emerged with the rise of Ṣūfism. Goldziher, Wensinck, and Schacht share the idea that in its early usage, *niyya* was an 'ethical' matter before law made Islam into a legalistic religion. Wensick and Schacht grudgingly recognize that medieval *fiqh* treats *niyya* formalistically. Goldziher and Wensinck restlessly yearn for Ṣūfism to (re)inspire the faith, while Schacht simply watches it ossify.

Among the most significant recent studies of *niyya* in Islamic ritual is a 1990 article by Frederick Denny, which treats *niyya* as the ethical and spiritual core of Islamic ritual practice, and forcefully asserts that

> *Nīya* is believed to emanate from the worshiper's innermost being. It safeguards the sincerity (*ikhlāṣ*) of the ritual performance … Only by a sort of descent into the self's core before resurfacing with correct intention in the presence of one's creator may the Muslim truly commune with God. There is thus an ethical relationship between worshipper and Lord … [*N*]*īya* ensures spiritual spontaneity as well as integrity in worship.[27]

Denny gives little evidence to support such strong claims, and he provides no citations, though he implies that his inspiration here is al-Ghazālī. The effect is that he appears to be trying to characterize all of 'Islam'. Denny's project, exploring the "ethical dimensions of Islamic ritual law," strikes me as a good one, and the technical aspects of *niyya* that Denny does discuss are accurate as far as they go.[28] But from this

---

[26] Ibid., emphasis added.

[27] Denny, "Ethical Dimensions," 209.

[28] For example, he rightly notes the requirement that *niyya* immediately precede and endure throughout most acts of worship, though he mistakenly indicates that *niyya* must be verbalized (jurists disagree about this). Additionally, he notes without elaboration

starting point, he runs quickly into territory uncharted by Islamic ritual law. In a passage reminiscent of Goldziher, Denny comments on 'the' *ḥadīth*:

> "Works are in the intentions" ... is a frequently cited *ḥadīth*. This saying is encountered in many contexts—ritual, legal, and others—and *serves as a universal ethical principle among Muslims.* In the case of ritual, there is a kind of dialectic between *nīya* and the performance of the various acts of worship ... Individual and personal moral responsibility are required for *nīya* and *without it the act would be devoid of ethical meaning.*[29]

Nīyya here "emanate[s] from the worshiper's innermost being," and "serves as a universal ethical principle among Muslims," giving ritual practice its "ethical meaning." This ethical meaning Denny defines as a "communing with God," for *niyya* puts one "in the presence of one's creator." In short, *niyya* is again placed by a scholar at the heart of Muslim spirituality; the acts of Islamic ritual law have no value save the spiritual one they supposedly get from *niyya.*

Denny goes on to argue a point seemingly similar to that which I am making myself: that Islamic ritual practice has often been central to Muslim religious life, and that this praxis-centered quality is easily misunderstood and debased by outside observers—especially those accustomed to certain Christian antinomian attitudes.[30] However, Denny does not accept this praxis-orientation as properly religious but rather seeks to defend Islam against charges of legalism by asserting that 'authentic' Islam *really is* spiritual, and *niyya* is central to his argument. My point here is subtle but crucial, so I will quote Denny at length:

> It appears that ritual acts are at the heart of Islamic ethics, and in fact are their source and ground to the extent that they function as a means of drawing near to God in a predictable pattern. This supremely valuable relationship must, then, be hedged about with the protection and minute regulation of law. *Nīya is the basic moral act involved in ritual.* The *nīya* ensures the validity of the specific ritual to be performed, and the performance itself reinforces the integrity of both the individual and her or his "moral community," to adapt Durkheim's phrase ... When *nīya* and the core meaning of *akhlāq* [i.e., Islamic ethics] are considered,

that "*nīya* is itself a ritual act, of course, and as such it is defined and explicated in the *fiqh* books" (ibid., 209).

29 Ibid., emphasis added.

30 Denny observes that "Christian thinkers at least since the Apostle Paul have denounced legalism in relations between humankind and God. The history of Christian liturgy, however, displays much concern for regulation and decorum, although there has never been a universally uniform cultus since the primitive church" (ibid., 210).

> along with the flexible "five principles [i.e., required, recommended, permitted, detested, and forbidden—the possible assessments in Islamic law]," Islamic ritual may be understood to be *anything but legalistic in its authentic form*. Many western critics of Islam who have sometimes decried what they have perceived to be rote repetition in Islamic worship have known little about the inner dimensions of Muslim piety, whose patterns and habits in and outside the mosque are informed and energized by religion as a complete way of life. The legal elements are strong and determinative, not because they are the possession of a legalistic people, but because they safeguard the spiritual path of a serious people ... [W]e need to be sensitively aware of the intimate relationship between ritual, legal, and ethical norms in the Islamic scheme of things. This relationship derives from the common Semitic ethical monotheism that Jews, Christians, and Muslims share, and that at its most authentic always bases itself on God as the sole source of value.[31]

Denny recognizes both the centrality of ritual praxis and that Islamic ritual takes place in a social, embodied context. I welcome his observation that Muslim rituals are potentially interwoven with serious ethical reflection and, yes, spiritual concerns. But Denny does not assert that one ought simply to accept the possibility that Muslim ritual practice might place a strong emphasis on form, bodily posture, verbal utterance, and simple mental focus; rather he seeks to erase this formalism with a *niyya*-based spirituality. I take issue with his implicit claim that to be properly moral and religious means to be inwardly focused, and especially that *niyya*, as "the basic moral act involved in ritual," is what makes Muslims' praxis properly moral and religious. Denny seems to be trying to save Islam from itself. No doubt his heart is in the right place, perhaps a significant improvement over Goldziher, but he still produces a profound, if subtle, distortion.

In sum, much of what has been written by western scholars on the topic of *niyya* in Islamic ritual law tends to devalue the physical, bodily, praxis-oriented qualities so central to Islamic ritual law and practice. Even when they seek to defend and not denigrate, as with Denny, they imply that Islamic approaches to ritual are defective to the extent that they really are temporal, bodily, and this-worldly. Earlier generations of scholars perhaps reflected the colonialist and missionary biases of their times, while the more recent work is surely politically more benign, with an honest goal of achieving greater understanding. But the later work retains a surprising level of antinomian, anti-ritual animus. If we are

[31] Ibid., 209–210, emphasis added.

spared a view of "Muḥammadan mere formalism" with its "inner life completely crushed under an inexorable weight of ritual," it is in part because *niyya* has been transformed by scholarly alchemy into the lever that pries open the spiritual heart of Islam.

As we have already seen in the previous chapter, however, *niyya* in *fiqh al-ʿibādāt* is not the spiritual phenomenon it has been made out to be. Rather, *niyya* is one step among several in the proper performance of an act of ritual worship. It is, in short, what one does with one's mind while performing ritual actions. One might say that the jurists treat the *qalb* as coextensive with the body, subject to the will, and required to be in proper alignment for the act of worship to be proper and valid. *Niyya* is the mental state accompanying an act of worship, the intention 'that I perform this act'. As such, *niyya* defines a given action as a particular *kind* of action, a specific, named type of action, so that it can be located in the legal taxonomy of actions; *niyya* 'to pray', for example, helps make a given set of words and gestures into prayer. The function medieval jurists assign to *niyya* is not vaguely spiritual, but explicitly taxonomic.[32]

Niyya in the legal sources is indeed subjective, 'internal', individual, done by the *qalb*, and unavailable for direct assessment by anyone other than the actor himself. But it is not "the supreme principle of religious life in Islam" emanating from "the worshiper's innermost being," or a "descent into the self's core" placing one "in the presence of one's creator." As I will note below, some Muslim sources do treat *niyya* in this spiritual fashion, but since a central strand of Islamic normative discourse does not, we cannot simply characterize *niyya* as spiritual, nor can we in turn use *niyya* to characterize 'all Islam', as the secondary scholarship has too often done. In demonstrating this point I will elaborate on what has already been said in the previous chapter. That chapter showed that the overarching function of *niyya* in *fiqh al-ʿibādāt* is definitive and taxonomic, allowing actors to locate their actions on the map of ideal-typical actions laid out in the works of *fiqh*. *Niyya* is understood as a discreet act, at a discreet moment in time, done silently in the *qalb* to license those ritual actions that accompany or follow it. It

32 We can speculate that *niyya* also serves an emotional and epistemological function, by allowing the ritual actor the knowledge that a given action is the legally stipulated one, that one has fulfilled his or her duty, but this is still not the spiritual function presented in the secondary sources explored here.

is lost by 'slipping from the mind', not by 'sin'. The object of *niyya*, what is intended while intending, is simply the act itself.

These findings should instill some doubt that *niyya* refers to a state of spiritual reverie and communion with the divine. It first appears as one step among many in the specific formal procedures of the *'ibādāt*. *Niyya* connects the mind to the outward actions, not the spirit to God and the heavens. We have already seen that jurists identify the location of *niyya* as the *qalb*, understood as the principle organ of the intellect. Medieval Muslim jurists had at their disposal a well-developed vocabulary for dealing with the 'spirit', and we have to assume that they deliberately chose not to use it when discussing *niyya*. Classical Arabic religious and legal texts generally employ a sophisticated terminology for various aspects of the self, including *rūḥ* (soul, spirit), *nafs* (spirit, self), *irāda* (will), *fikr* (thought), *'ilm* (knowledge, understanding), the various emotions, and so forth.[33] The terms *rūḥ* and *nafs* are largely interchangeable, and in what Calverley calls "the dominant Muslim doctrine," the spirit/soul is seen as corporeal, "different in quiddity (*al-māhiyya*) from [the] sensible body, of the nature of light, high, light in weight, living, moving, interpenetrating the bodily members as water in the rose."[34] Created to be eternal, it leaves the body temporarily in sleep, and leaves again to undergo the first judgment after death. It then normally returns to the body to await resurrection during the Last Days. Thus, the spirit in much Islamic thought is itself seen in corporeal terms, capable of sensations and actions, and closely linked to the physical body. The Aristotelian notion of an incorporeal spirit did find a niche in Islamic thought, especially via al-Ghazālī and theistic philosophy, but as Calverley notes, "it has never dominated Islam" as has the corporeal view.[35]

Most jurists say nothing about the *nafs* or *rūḥ* when discussing *niyya*. Instead, they simply assert that *niyya* is located in the *qalb*.[36] In his trea-

---

[33] See E.E. Calverley, "Nafs," in *Encyclopaedia of Islam*, new ed.; Louis Massignon, *Essay on the Origins of the Technical Language of Islamic Mysticism*, trans. Benjamin Clark (Notre Dame: University of Notre Dame Press, 1997), esp. 29, 55, 65, 154, 195–196, 204; Jane H. Smith and Yvonne Y. Haddad, *The Islamic Understanding of Death and Resurrection* (Albany: State University of New York Press, 1981), esp. 17–21, 36–37, 56–59, 121–125; Qarāfī, *al-Umniyya*, 7–16.

[34] Calverley, "Nafs."

[35] Ibid.

[36] As noted above, Brinkley Messick has observed that in Islamic legal discourses, the *qalb* is "part of the larger interior realm of the 'self', the *nafs*, with the overarching construct being the *shar'ī* subject" ("Indexing the Self," 176–177).

tise on *niyya*, al-Qarāfī holds that *niyya* is indeed an aspect or function (*ḥāl*) of the soul (*nafs*), at least indirectly, because *niyya* is a function of the mind (*ʿaql*), which in turn is among the properties (*ṣifāt, aḥwāl*) of the soul. In discussing the location of *niyya*, al-Qarāfī asserts that *niyya* is a part or type (*nawʿ*) of the will (*irāda*) and a function of the mind (*ʿaql*).[37] Since the Qurʾān establishes that the *ʿaql* is seated in the *qalb*, so too is the *niyya*. Moreover, "if it is established that the *ʿaql* is in the *qalb*, it must be among our axioms that the *nafs* is in the *qalb*, because everything related to the *ʿaql* such as thought and knowledge and the like are properties (*ṣifāt*) of the *nafs*," and further, "it is the nature of the soul to give rise to knowledge and thought, and it this that is called *ʿaql*".[38] So *niyya*, being related to the *ʿaql*, is a "property of the soul." However, this does not lead al-Qarāfī into a discussion of *niyya* as the spiritual conduit between humans and God, in part because he clearly holds the dominant corporeal view of the soul: "The soul (*al-nafs*)," he says, "is a subtle ['light', *laṭīf*] body dwelling transparently within the physical ['heavy', *kathīf*] body, from which it is distinguished like a fetus."[39] The soul does not appear here as the unfathomable inner depths of the self but as a corporeal entity with a place in the body. Al-Qarāfī is primarily concerned to show that *niyya* is located in the *qalb*. He ends up demonstrating the indirect link of *niyya* to the soul, but shows no interest in the spiritual implications of this fact.

As we have seen, al-Qarāfī explicitly asserts that *niyya* is that which defines a particular act of worship, distinguishing it from other actions: "The rationale for the requirement [of *niyya*] is distinguishing (*tamyīz*) acts of worship (*al-ʿibādāt*) from ordinary actions (*al-ʿādāt*), and distinguishing among levels of acts of worship."[40] Further, al-Qarāfī asserts:

> [*Niyya*] distinguishes that which is for God from that which is not, so the action is fit for glorification (*fayaṣluḥu al-fiʿl lil-taʿẓīm*). For example, bathing (*ghusl*) may accomplish cooling off and cleaning up, but can also accomplish a commanded act of worship (*ʿibāda*). If one intends specifically that the act is for God, the person accomplishes the glorification of the Lord with this bathing (*fayaqaʿu taʿẓīm al-ʿabd lil-rabb bidhālika al-ghusl*). In the absence of *niyya* … fasting (*al-ṣawm*) is [merely] lack of nourishment.[41]

37 Qarāfī, *al-Umniyya*, 17. See also chapter 2, n. 31 above.
38 Qarāfī, *al-Umniyya*, 18.
39 Ibid.
40 Ibid., 20; cf. 9–10.
41 Ibid., 20.

Niyya not only defines an act, but also allows certain acts to accomplish "the glorification of the Lord" and the fulfillment of divine commands. It does this, not by moral soul-searching or vague 'spiritualization', but by making a given action into an *'ibāda*—an act that glorifies God by its very nature. It is through *purification* and not through *niyya* that a person 'glorifies the Lord'; *niyya* makes washing into *wuḍū'* or *ghusl*, abstaining from food into *ṣawm*, and *those acts* glorify God. The point of *niyya* is to define a given action as the particular action called for by the *sharī'a*—an action that in itself accomplishes the religious goals of worship and glorification of God. These acts are religious, even spiritual in a sense, but not because *niyya* makes them so. *Niyya* does not make just any act into a religious one; it would not make sleeping or turning summer-saults into spiritual offerings to God. *Niyya* makes certain movements, such as rinsing with water in a certain fashion, into the stipulated acts of *fiqh al-'ibādāt* (e.g., *wuḍū'*), acts that are religious *because they are stipulated by religious law*, not because they are accompanied by *niyya*.

Niyya is a prominent element of *ṣalāt*, a case which deserves special attention here. Prayer in many religious traditions involves some kind of interacting between the human/natural and divine/supernatural realms, and is widely treated as an arena of spirituality. *Niyya* is a prominent element of Islamic *ṣalāt* and seems to lend itself handily to interpretation as a spiritual phenomenon. But a survey of the sources only further proves that, however spiritual *ṣalāt* may be, *niyya* in medieval *fiqh* is largely a formal, bodily, and mindful matter. *Ṣalāt* as described in medieval *fiqh al-'ibādāt* is an act of obedient worship, not a 'conversation with God', and does not properly include personalized entreaties to God or petitions for specific blessings or rewards. Islamic law and popular practice do provide for such activities, but these are distinct from the obligatory *ṣalāt*. *Ṣalāt* is a set of prescribed bodily postures and verbal pronouncements, to be done in the prescribed time and place. *Niyya* is a prescribed mental component that accompanies the outward, bodily forms and completes them as *ṣalāt*.

Mūṣilī provides a typical example of the general role given to *niyya* in *ṣalāt*: "There are six required [preliminaries to *ṣalāt*]: purity of the body from major and minor impurities, purity of the clothing, purity of the place, proper covering of the body, locating of the *qibla* [i.e., the direction of Mecca], and *niyya*."[42] This account puts *niyya* on the

[42] Mūṣilī, *al-Ikhtiyār*, 1:45.

level of the formal, physical alignment of body and space prior to *ṣalāt* proper. In *ṣalāt*, the object of *niyya* must be the specific type of *ṣalāt* to be performed. As Shīrāzī's asserts, "If the prayer is a required one, one must have specific (*taʿyīn*) *niyya*, intending the noon prayer or the evening prayer to distinguish (*li-tatamayyaz*) it from other [prayers]."[43] Again *niyya* defines the act of worship that it accompanies. Shīrāzī considers the possibility of changing one's *niyya*: "If one enters into noon prayer then changes the *niyya* to the mid-afternoon prayer this invalidates the noon prayer, because it interrupts (*qaṭaʿa*) the *niyya*, and the mid-afternoon prayer is not valid because he did not intend this at the point of [entering] *iḥrām*."[44] Once prayer has been initiated with the proper *niyya*, 'changing' or 'interrupting' the *niyya* (again, not 'sin') invalidates the prayer.[45] And one's *niyya* can be wrong, causing the act to fail. The act is central, and *niyya* again does not make just any act into an offering to God; rather, if put in the right 'place', it makes an act the one called for by the *sharīʿa*. *Niyya* alone, however, does not define the act, for if one intends to perform an obligatory prayer, for example, but begins before the proper prayer time, the prayer only counts as a supererogatory prayer. The *niyya* cannot overcome certain objective limitations; subjective and objective criteria both matter in defining the act.

Muslim jurists' discussion of *niyya* in *ṣalāt* clearly produces a great deal of casuistic detail, and *niyya* appears at several specific points in this complex set of rules. Through all this, *niyya* operates as a basic focusing of the mind on the act at hand, paying attention to the movements of *ṣalāt* and, as it were, putting the mind in the right 'place' while simultaneously putting the hands, head, and feet in the right places. We are perhaps not far off base here to suggest that *niyya* is akin to a bodily posture, the posture of the *qalb*. Further, *niyya* partly constitutes the distinction between outwardly identical acts. As such, *niyya* helps locate a given action in the taxonomy of Islamic law, linking a given action

---

43 Shīrāzī, *al-Muhadhdhab*, 1:236.

44 Ibid., 1:237.

45 Ibn Qudāma remarks: "If one enters *iḥrām* for a religious duty (*farīḍa*) then intends to change (*nawā naqlahā*) to another duty, the first duty is invalid because the *niyya* is interrupted (*qaṭʿa*), and the second duty is invalid because he did not intend it from the start" (*al-Mughnī*, 2:135). He goes beyond the binary possibilities of '*niyya*/not-*niyya*', suggesting the possibility of insufficiently firm *niyya*: "if one begins prayer with a *niyya* wavering between completeness and interruptedness (*mutaraddada bayna itmāmihā wa-qaṭʿihā*), the prayer is invalid, because *niyya* is firm resolve (*al-niyya ʿazmu jāzimu*)" (2:133). On the term 'resolve' (*ʿazm*), see chapter 2, n. 2 above.

to the prescribed categories of *fiqh*. It may thus serve the psychological function of producing or confirming knowledge that a given act was performed and a duty fulfilled. But it is not, in any overt or explicit way, spiritual, even in the context of prayer, presumably the most spiritual of the *ʿibādāt*.

The casuistic detail recounted in the previous chapter may seem beside the point to a reader in search of the 'spirit of Islam'; that is precisely my point. I recount this material to show how *niyya* is actually discussed in the legal sources, because any analysis of *niyya* must deal with these facts. Like most legal systems, Islamic law generates a complex normative taxonomy of human activity, defining the types of actions one should or should not do to fit into the system. Muslim jurists are not strict behaviorists, and *fiqh al-ʿibādāt* conceptualizes action in a way that includes intention. One must get the outward form right, but one must get the inner form right as well. *Niyya* is a function of the mind, the rational faculty, and its link to the spirit/soul (itself a corporeal entity) is indirect; it is depicted as being spoiled not by 'sin' but by 'slipping the mind'. The call to formulate *niyya* is the call to focus the mind on the *ʿibādā* at hand. *Niyya* is definitive of actions, critical to making a given set of movements and utterances into one type of act and not another—such as performing ablutions, not cooling off or cleaning up; or the noon prayer not the evening prayer; or someone else's *ḥajj*, not my own. Thus *niyya* helps make a person's particular action into the named type of action identified and required by the law.

If *niyya* has elements of a spiritual quality in *fiqh al-ʿibādāt*, it does so indirectly, as an intention to perform an act of worship. An *ʿibāda* is an act of obedient service in accord with the will of God. *Niyya* is not simply the intention, for example, 'that I bow at the waist, then kneel, then touch my forehead to the floor'. Rather, *niyya* is specifically the intention 'that I pray', 'that these actions constitute *ṣalāt*', and, implicitly, 'that my action be an *ʿibāda*'. A valid *ʿibāda*, then, must be accompanied by *niyya* with the goal 'that this action be done to accord with the will of God'. Thus *niyya* can perhaps be described as a 'religious' or 'spiritual' component of the *ʿibādāt*, if by this we mean it is an intention to fulfill the will of God as expressed in the *sharīʿa*. This is how we ought to take al-Qarāfī's assertion that *niyya* is the intention "specifically that the act is for God" and "accomplishes the glorification of the Lord." The *sharīʿa* governs actions in this life, including what might seem to some to be quite mundane matters. This is one way of understanding what many Muslims mean when they insist that Islam is not a 'religion' as modern

Westerners often use the term, but rather a 'way of life'. Proper religion does not necessarily involve Denny's disembodied "descent into the self's core," for 'religion' in *fiqh al-ʿibādāt* is consistently presented in bodily, formalistic terms, as an embodied orientation toward God. *Niyya* is Goldziher's "supreme religious principle" only if one takes 'religion' in this embodied sense, and even then, there are plenty of other 'principles' at least as important as *niyya.* The jurists treat the *qalb* as part of the body, which must be properly aligned when performing the *ʿibādāt.* It would be better to recognize that all the *ʿibādāt,* in all their aspects, are properly religious and spiritual, than to designate *niyya* as the element that makes them such.

I wish to be emphatically clear: I am not making the absurd claim that there is nothing spiritual (in the more interioristic, disembodied sense) about anything in the many and varied Islamic religious traditions. Nor am I arguing that no Muslim ever uses the term *niyya* in a spiritual way.[46] *Fiqh al-ʿibādāt* is not the whole of Islam, and there are contexts and genres in which the term *niyya* is given a different, more spiritual cast than in *fiqh.*[47] For example, al-Ghazālī, who in Goldziher's account is the savior of Muslim interiority, addresses *niyya* at some length in his *Iḥyāʾ ʿulūm al-dīn*, devoting an entire chapter (*kitāb*) to "*niyya, ikhlāṣ,* and *ṣidq* (intention, sincerity, and truthfulness)."[48] This text does indeed treat *niyya* as a spiritual element, a kind of conduit between the believer and God, even as Wensinck's "religious and moral criterion superior to that of the law."[49] Goldziher, then, is partly correct: Ṣūfī

---

[46] Anecdotally, it should be noted that the many Muslims with whom I have discussed *niyya* attribute a wide range of connotations to the term. My initial interest in the topic was only sharpened by the apparent lack of worry about *niyya* reported by several fellow students of mine at the College of Islamic Law at the University of Jordan. My inquiries about *niyya*, especially my expectation that one might fret over the indeterminacy of one's own *niyya*, often inspired quizzical responses and calm assurances that one 'simply does the *niyya*'. Others, however, have told me that they very much see *niyya* as a crucial spiritual element in their religious practice, especially *ṣalāt*, describing *niyya* in terms of spiritual insight or comfort. My point is not that the latter Muslims are wrong, but that the former are also right.

[47] See, for example, Padwick, *Muslim Devotions*, 48–54.

[48] Abū Ḥāmid al-Ghazālī, *Iḥyāʾ ʿulūm al-dīn* (Cairo: Lajnat Nashr al-Thaqāfa al-Islāmiyya, 1938), 14:154–177.

[49] Al-Ghazālī maintains that God rewards good intentions even if not put into action, suggesting that for him *niyya* is the ethical core of an individual's actions, the aspect of one's behavior that matters most to God. Al-Ghazālī cites a *ḥadīth*, "the *niyya* of the believer is more important than his action" (*Iḥyāʾ ʿulūm al-dīn*, 14:162). However, no *fiqh* manual I have consulted cites al-Ghazālī's opinion, or this *ḥadīth*, which al-Ghazālī's editor notes is considered "weak" (*ḍaʿīf*) (14:162, n. 1).

writings often do tend to have a more interior-oriented notion of religion, including religious praxis, than do *fiqh* texts. No doubt we would do best to talk about a variety of views within Islam—some scholars have even suggested adopting the plural term 'Islams'. Certainly there is variety and debate within the sweep of Islamic history, and Denny, if perhaps not Goldziher, does well to represent some Muslim points of view on the relationship between *niyya* and spirituality, or between spirituality and the law. But *fiqh* is no minor part of the Islamic tradition, and no sweeping characterizations of 'Islam' that misrepresent significant elements of *fiqh* will do. Casting Ṣūfism—itself far more diverse than is often recognized—as 'superior' to other manifestations of Islam, as the cure to some legalistic disease, is inappropriately normative and historically simplistic.

Efforts to spiritualize *niyya* serve a broad agenda of correcting a 'defective' Islam. They seem wedded, moreover, to an ethical vision focused on the 'inner self' as a complex site of conflicting drives and, indeed, as the principal battleground of good and evil.[50] According to this view, proper objective action is not sufficient, but proper internal disposition is also required. Further—and this is crucial, for this is where Islamic ritual law really veers from this course—not only is the person divided into inner and outer, but the inner self is seen as itself divided and unruly, capable of the worst kinds of betrayals. 'Ethical profundity' here emerges as a hermeneutic of suspicion of one's own actions that refuses to be satisfied, and that consistently distrusts the interior self. However, the 'inner self' as presented in *fiqh al-ʿibādāt* is not so complex. If, as Brinkley Messick has observed, Islamicists are not yet at the point of offering a systematic theory or genealogy of the Islamic legal self on the order of Michel Foucault's or Charles Taylor's work on Western selfhood, a few preliminary observations are in order.[51] There is no Fall in the general Islamic view of history or human nature. As Denny himself points out, "*fiṭra*, humankind's God-given sound, original nature" is, as God's creation, inherently good.[52] Most Muslims

---

[50] For one account of the history of such views in Christianity, see Owen C. Thomas, "Interiority and Christian Spirituality," *Journal of Religion* 80, 1 (2000): 41–60.

[51] See Messick, "Indexing the Self," 151–152. See also Fazlur Rahman, "The Status of the Individual in Islam," in *The Status of the Individual East and West*, ed. Charles A. Moore and Aldyth V. Morris (Honolulu: University of Hawaii Press, 1968), 217–225.

[52] Denny, "Ethical Dimensions," 203; cf. MacDonald "Fiṭra." See also chapter 1, n. 22 above.

think themselves born as 'blank slates' rather than ones needing erasure of inherited mistakes. Islamic ritual law does not envision the inner self as unruly and rebellious, 'fallen' and prone to betrayal.[53] The jurists do not treat *niyya* as a slippery slope; one need not pile layer upon layer of *niyya*, so that one must not only 'mean it' when he acts, but 'mean to mean it', and so on indefinitely. And *niyya* is not depicted as conflicted, in some Augustinian turmoil of self-doubt, wanting to 'mean it' but not being able to. *Niyya*, the internal, subjective dimension of right action, is presented as generally stable and subject to the will. Subsequently, the ethic pervading ritual law texts is not one of an elusive, unattainable standard, such as the claim that one's *niyya* can never be deep or lasting enough. One can actually get the actions right, both inside and out. The jurists are scrupulous in assessing actions in both their subjective and objective aspects, but it is not the runaway, insatiable, interioristic scrupulousness that Goldziher, Denny, and others seem to harbor as a model of ethical profundity. Denny is not wrong in suggesting that Islamic ritual is profound, but the specific model of profundity he seeks inappropriately constrains the data.

The actions governed by Islamic ritual law are presented as valuable and moral in and of themselves, not as symbolic surfaces, signifiers, or metaphors. The texts of Islamic ritual law, when addressing the nature and role of *niyya*, do not say that *niyya* 'puts one in the presence of one's creator', or that '*niyya* gives these acts their ethical meaning and religious worth'; they do not say 'be spiritual' or 'be moral' when doing these acts. Rather, they say, 'formulate *niyya* when doing these acts', which is to say, 'do these acts and not others, *for one is being religious*

[53] Beyond treating *niyya* more spiritually, Ṣūfīs also tend to see the internal self as complex, multi-layered, and potentially divided, even dangerous. Abū ʿAbdallāh Ḥārith b. Asad al-Muḥāsibī (d. 243/857), for example, is representative of a strain of Ṣūfī thought regarding the complexity of the inner self: "The person who falls into vanity does not hesitate to become mired in self-delusion (*ghirra*) ... [and] even goes so far as to lie about God Most High while thinking that he is being true, to stray into error while thinking he is well guided" (*Kitāb al-riʿāya li-ḥuqūq Allāh*, ed. Margaret Smith [London: Luzac, E.J.W. Gibb Memorial, 1940], translation provided by Michael Sells, *Early Islamic Mysticism* [New York: Paulist Press, 1996], 172–173). Michael Sells notes that many Ṣūfīs more systematically divided the self (*nafs*) into three phases, "the phase of ego-domination (*an-nafsu l-ʿamāra*), the phase of self-blame (*an-nafsu al-lawāma*), and the phase of peace and security (*an-nafsu al-muṭma'inna*)," a distinction derived from Qur'ān 12:53, which refers to "the self that dominates with wrong" (*an-nafsu l-ʿamāratu bi s-suʿ* [*sic*]) (Sells, 178, n. 19; the translations and transliterations here are from Sells).

and moral by doing these acts'. Of course, many Muslims see morality and religion as involving much more than just these acts. But Western scholarship has often overlooked a crucial aspect of *niyya* in *fiqh al-ʿibādāt*: its technical aspect as a discrete step in embodied and mindful ritual duties. Western scholars have too often tried to wash away the sticky 'problem' of this formalism with the monotheistic universal solvent of 'spirit'. Such an approach to *niyya* is defensive and apologetic, meant to show the spiritual depth of Islamic practice, but ironically it only perpetuates the characterization of Islam as rigidly formalistic. Making *niyya* into the spiritual side of praxis pushes back against, and thus props up, a misunderstanding of Muslim ritual actions as somehow spiritually defective.

Part 2. *Explaining Ritual Intent*

A. *Intending Ritual Action*

If *niyya* is not the spiritual component of Islamic ritual law, we still face the question of why Muslim jurists insist on its inclusion in ritual acts. Rather than thinking of *niyya* as spiritual in the sense considered above, we ought to think of it as not simply intention, but as a specific kind of intention. As we have seen in the previous chapter, *niyya* is primarily a taxonomic matter. But to this we must add another aspect of meaning: conscious, sincere, focused attention on the act at hand. As a mental act defining a ritual action, *niyya* involves the focusing on the mind, consciousness, and attention on that action. The 'spiritualist' explanation discussed above takes this valid point and runs with it, turning it into a vague, ephemeral, disembodied phenomenon that supposedly gives otherwise meaningless acts a meaning. However, a more accurate understanding sees the kind of attention *niyya* entails as more modest, straightforward, and as concrete as mental states can be. The call to 'pay attention' while performing a ritual may seem self-explanatory—the *ʿibādāt* are manifestly very important, so one ought to pay attention to them. But perhaps this too is misleading. The attention and sincerity called for in the *ʿibādāt* is not the treacly stuff of romantic notions of spirituality, but simple deliberateness, the intentional authoring of the act at hand. Why this should necessitate a legal requirement presents a mystery: If an act is done by a person, is it not therefore that person who authors the act? The solution to the mystery lies in recognizing that ritual is a peculiar context in which intentions do not operate the same way they do in other kinds of actions.

As the first step to understanding *niyya* as sincere, focused attention, we must address the relation of *niyya* to *ikhlāṣ*. The Qur'ān passage most often cited in relation to *niyya* appears in *sūrat al-Bayyina*, 98:5: "And they have been commanded no more than this: To worship God, offering Him sincere devotion, being true (in faith), to establish regular prayer, and to practice regular charity, and that is the religion right and straight." This verse is part of a short, eight-verse *sūra* that considers the errors of "Those who reject (truth), among the People of the Book, and among the polytheists" (98:1 and 6). In its quranic context, verse 5 provides the positive content of what the People of the Book are called to do. Classical commentaries confirm this, explicitly identifying the referent of "they" in 98:5 as Jews and Christians.[54] However, the *fiqh* manuals cite only the portion "And they have been commanded no more than this: To worship God, offering Him sincere devotion, being true (in faith) (*li-ya'budū Allāha mukhliṣīn lahu al-dīn* [*mukhliṣīn* is a plural active participle of *ikhlāṣ*, meaning '(as) people who are sincere']),"
which they treat as a generic command to all Muslims, and not to the People of the Book, that is, Jews and Christians. Still, such a reading is not inaccurate; surely Muslims, "Those who have faith and do righteous deeds" (98:7), are called to do at least as much as wayward Peoples of the Book. This is an instance of the common legal method of isolating a verse from its quranic context in order to support a legal ruling.

Many *fiqh* manuals cite this verse somewhere amidst discussions of *niyya* in the *'ibādāt*. Ibn Rushd, for example, remarks (in a passage previously cited above):

> The *'ulama'* of the cities disagree as to whether *niyya* is a requirement for valid *wuḍū'* or not, despite their agreement on the stipulation of *niyya* in the *'ibādāt* according to what [God] Almighty said, "And they have been commanded no more than this: To worship Allāh, offering Him sincere devotion," and according to what [the Prophet Muḥammad] said, "Actions are defined by intentions," the famous *ḥadīth*.[55]

[54] See, for example, the commentary of Abū Ja'far Muḥammad b. Jarīr al-Ṭabarī, *Jāmi' al-bayān 'an ta'wīl āy al-Qur'ān* (Cairo, Maktabat Muṣṭafā al-Bābī al-Ḥalabī wa-Awlāduhu, 1954–1968), 29:263–264.

[55] Ibn Rushd, *Bidāyat al-mujtahid*, 1:8; *DJP*, 1:3.

Ibn Rushd gives no further explanation, simply taking the Qur'ān passage as an indicant that *niyya* is required by God in acts of worship. Ibn Qudāma similarly cites this verse as the basis for requiring *niyya* in prayer,[56] and returns to it again when discussing the relation of *niyya* to the *takbīr*:

> Shāfiʿī and Ibn al-Mundhir say it is required that the *niyya* be simultaneous with the *takbīr*, according to what [God] Almighty said, "And they have been commanded no more than this: To worship Allāh, offering Him sincere devotion" (*mukhliṣīn lahu al-dīn*). [God] said "*mukhliṣīn*" referring to their state (*ḥāl*) at the time of the *ʿibāda*,... and *al-ikhlāṣ* is *niyya*, and the Prophet said "Actions are defined by intentions," because *niyya* is a requirement, so it is not permitted for the *ʿibāda* to be void of *niyya*.[57]

Ibn Qudāma uses his interpretation of the Qur'ān verse to demonstrate not only the required status of *niyya*, but that *niyya* (taken to be synonymous with *ikhlāṣ*) must be present "at the time of the *ʿibāda*."[58] In short, *niyya* is asserted as the equivalent of *ikhlāṣ*, and thus the Qur'ān makes *niyya* a necessary aspect of all acts of worship.

These references to the Qur'ān clearly serve to establish a link between the terms *niyya* and *ikhlāṣ*, but just what kind of link is this? It is tempting to leap to the philological conclusion that '*niyya* = *ikhlāṣ*, *ikhlāṣ* = sincerity, therefore *niyya* = sincerity'. However, such an equation is overly simplistic, resting on the misguided notion of a one-to-one correspondence when moving between languages. Further, attempting a more sophisticated version of the same equation, by exploring the full range of meaning of *ikhlāṣ* to see how this informs our understanding of *niyya* would still mislead, for the question is not 'What could these terms mean in the full sweep of the language?', but 'What do these terms mean for these authors?' The answer is that the meaning—the range of referential possibilities—of the term *ikhlāṣ* is of minimal concern to these jurists. Their discussions of this issue evince no interest in the semantic nuances of either term or the relationship between them.

---

[56] Ibn Qudāma, *al-Mughnī*, 2:132; and see also 2:136.

[57] Ibid., 2:136.

[58] Qarāfī likewise employs Qur'ān 98:5 to assert the identity of *niyya* and *ikhlāṣ*: "[God] Almighty said 'And they have been commanded no more than this: To worship Allāh, offering Him sincere devotion'. *Ikhlāṣ* is the will (*irāda*) orienting an action toward God, purely, and the goal (*qaṣd*) of an action so oriented toward God is *niyya*. The strict sense of this verse is that what cannot be intended is not commanded, and what is not commanded is not an act of worship (*ʿibāda*)" (*al-Umniyya*, 19).

Instead, these discussions provide a quranic proof text for the requirement of *niyya* in the *ʿibādāt.* The structure of the argument in all the examples cited is simple: the terms *niyya* and *ikhlāṣ* are asserted to be synonymous, and the Qur'ān is cited to show that *ikhlāṣ* is a requisite element of the *ʿibādāt*; therefore, *niyya* is a requisite element of the *ʿibādāt.* This constitutes a straightforward argument from divine authority, and solves the jurists' problem of the lack of discussion of *niyya* in the Qur'ān. Significantly, the jurists do not use the occasion to argue that *niyya* means sincerity, or to assert a moralistic imperative to 'be sincere, mean what you say!' Rather, the jurists simply provide a quranic proof text for the requirement of *niyya* to complement the *ḥadīth* proof text, which is especially helpful since the latter does not specifically refer to ritual.

However, the fact that the equation of *niyya* with *ikhlāṣ* does not establish that *niyya* has an aspect of sincere, focused attention does not necessarily mean that it never has this meaning. We must simply look elsewhere for the proof. This aspect of *niyya* is somewhat more elusive than the others discussed above, as direct proof, such as an array of quotations and citations, that *niyya* is used in this way is harder to come by. However, this aspect of *niyya* is pervasive and indeed lies behind much of the discussion of *niyya* throughout the sources, including many passages cited throughout the previous chapter. *Niyya* in *fiqh al-ʿibādāt* is often a technical term, referring to a specific internal action, a discrete step in the performance of acts of worship. But underlying this technical usage is a simple impulse to insist that ritual performances be done in a state of sincere, focused attention. This is a more general, nontechnical aspect of the term, yet one still peculiar to ritual law settings.

Searle's view of intentional action suggests a way to understand this aspect of *niyya*, providing a philosophical analysis of what most people intuitively know: an action need not be cognitively conscious or 'thought about' to be intentional. Prior intentions may necessarily be conscious in some way.[59] But not all actions have prior intentions—some only have intentions in action, and intentions in action need not necessarily be present to one's awareness. 'Acting without thinking' may

[59] As explained in chapter 1, prior intentions are mental representations of their conditions of satisfaction (i.e., they are causally self-referential); Searle does not explicitly address whether they are conscious or not.

still be acting intentionally.[60] A 'thoughtless' action—such as catching an object accidentally dropped, or running into the street to pull a child from in front of an oncoming car—may not involve conscious awareness, but is still an intentional action. Similarly, a familiar and oft-repeated action, like walking, may be done without paying attention, yet is certainly intentional.[61] Calling these actions 'intentional' is, for Searle, the same as calling them 'actions'. But intention is not the same as 'conscious awareness', nor does the presence of the former guarantee the presence of the latter.

Islamic jurists seem to have recognized this possibility and viewed it as a potential problem, at least for acts of worship. The jurists offer prescriptions of how one ought to act, not descriptions of all possible parameters of action. Like most human actions, the *ʿibādāt could* be done without conscious cognitive awareness, but these acts, perhaps above all others, *should not be.* The prescriptions of *niyya* in the *ʿibādāt* function to legally require attentiveness on the one hand (the act is technically invalid without *niyya*), and to simply remind, even prod the actor to 'pay attention' and 'be sincere' on the other hand. In this non-technical sense, if one does not have the *niyya*—if one does not pay attention—it does not count. Perhaps the clearest demonstration of all this is the discussion of *niyya* 'slipping away' (*ʿazaba*) during an act of worship: this would not turn the act into a Searlean unintentional or accidental occurrence, but it does render it invalid. This must be because *niyya* has the connotation of paying conscious attention.

Similarly, al-Qarāfī's discussion of acts and states that do not require *niyya* is telling in this regard. *Niyya* is not needed for belief in, or pious

[60] For Searle it is technically incorrect to call an involuntary movement, such as a sneeze, an 'action', even if in common speech we might do so.

[61] Debates persist among philosophers about how to parse the intentionality of complex actions (and on closer analysis, isn't virtually every action complex?). It seems that the resolution to these issues is rooted in practical concerns rather than in pure logic. Those components of a complex action that matter in any analysis are exactly that: the components that *matter.* One could expand a true description of an action quite far, including such things as 'firing neurons in the brain', 'contracting muscles', 'displacing air molecules', and so forth (see Searle on the 'accordion effect', *Intentionality*, 98–100). But while these might be part of an action, they may not matter in a given context. Searle asserts that things not included in the Intentional propositional content of the intention are not actions at all, but "unintended occurrences that happen as a result of [an] action" (100). I am asserting that the line between what is considered a component of an action and what is an unintended occurrence seems to depend on the practical (or ideological, strategic, etc.) considerations of the situation in which the line is drawn.

fear of, God, for these in effect cannot occur without the object of the Intentional mental state being God. But *niyya* is needed for actions that could possibly be done without a mental focus on God or on duty to God, as a matter of 'mindless' repetition. It hardly seems impertinent to observe that *ṣalāt*, for example, might possibly be done inattentively; having repeated the act five times daily for years, one could certainly get the objective movements right as a matter of rote, just as one could walk a familiar route without focusing on each step. The juristic treatment of *niyya* both deems such inattentive prayer invalid, and it seems, rhetorically admonishes the believer to pay attention.

Paying attention ought perhaps to be distinguished from being sincere. Sincerity is a matter of the outward expression (i.e., the speech act or other communicative action) corresponding to the Intentional state it purports to express. This is a complicated way of saying that sincerity is a matter of 'meaning what one says'. It is, of course, possible to be insincere in communicating, as Searle puts it, "expressing an Intentional state, where one does not have the Intentional state that one expresses," or, in a word, to lie.[62] In *fiqh al-ʿibādāt* texts, however, the objective action is depicted as more or less an end in itself—there is no consideration of the symbolic expression of prayer, for example, such as suggesting that the prostrations of prayer express humility and self-abnegation, or that paying alms means one loves one's less fortunate Muslim brethren. Such meanings may well be attached to these actions by practitioners, but the law texts do not deal with such matters. So the issue is not one of being 'insincere' in one's symbolic communication. The legal definition of 'sincere prayer' is simply prayer done while consciously focused on prayer.

However, sincerity in this regard does not mean simply that the Intentional state corresponds to outward expression. Sincerity here must be defined in terms of the meaning of the *ʿibādāt*. As discussed earlier in this chapter, an *ʿibāda* is an act of obedient service in accord with the will of God manifest in the *sharīʿa*. *Niyya* is not simply the intention in action that constitutes the Intentional component of an action, such as the intention 'that I bow at the waist, then kneel, then touch

[62] Searle, *Intentionality*, 9–10. Searle's idea of 'sincerity conditions' is a logical relation between Intentional states and illocutionary acts: the former is the sincerity condition of the latter (9). If both the Intentional state and illocutionary act were put into words, the illogic becomes obvious; for example, if one were to say 'It's snowing but I don't believe it is snowing'. However, this is a lie only if one knows it to be mistaken and says it anyway; otherwise it is simply mistaken.

my forehead to the floor'.[63] Rather, *niyya* is specifically the intention 'that I pray', and, moreover, 'that my action be an *'ibāda*'. A sincere *'ibāda*, then, must be accompanied by *niyya* with the goal 'that this action be done to accord with the will of God'. The sincerity component of *niyya* that I am identifying here is the need for the outward expression to correspond to a particular Intentional state, so that one performs the *'ibādāt* as *'ibādāt*, as obedient service in accord with the will of God. As al-Qarāfī puts it, the reason *niyya* is required in some actions is that *niyya* "distinguishes that which is for God from that which is not."[64]

There is a potential problem in that Intentional states are not readily available for objective evaluation. While *fiqh al-'ibādāt* texts define and prescribe the proper ways to perform acts of worship, the subjective element of any action, *'ibādāt* included, is exactly that: subjective. There may be outward signs suggesting the nature of the subjective state; one might be looking around the room or laughing while ostensibly praying, for example. But having the correct objective form of an action is only a suggestion of the subjective state. Fully evaluating *niyya* is, in the end, irreducibly subjective. *Fiqh al-'ibādāt* can establish objective criteria for the objective aspect of acts of worship, and using these criteria, one could evaluate this aspect of another's performance. But whether one meets the criteria established for the subjective components of acts of worship is only available for subjective evaluation.

B. *Intending the Non-Intentional*

We have still not moved very far toward explaining the jurists' treatment of intentions. To push in this direction, we may ask whether there is anything special about ritual contexts and ritual actions that makes intentions especially problematic. This question is raised from two different angles. First, as already noted, *fiqh* texts raise the question by fretting so much over *niyya*, oddly admonishing Muslims to 'intend!'

---

[63] For Searle, merely recounting the most basic propositional content of an intention in action is not an 'explanation' of an action, or at least not a useful one, but rather is a tautology. For example, to say "I raised my arm because I intended to raise my arm" is true but explains nothing, "because by identifying the action ... we have already identified it in terms of the intention in action" (*Intentionality*, 105–106). An explanation, in this account, requires reference to a more complex Intentional component, for example, "I raised my arm to cast my vote." This seems to me, however, to be a different matter than 'paying attention' or 'being sincere', which could involve simply being cognitively conscious of one's intention.

[64] Qarāfī, *al-Umniyya*, 20.

while performing acts of worship. Why so much concern over intentions in ritual law? (In the other legal spheres, again, it is assumed that actors have intentions, not that they need to be told to have them.) Second, ritual studies scholars raise this question by arguing for the special nature of ritual actions and contexts. Is there something peculiar about ritual that might help explain the Islamic legal approach to intentions?

To address both aspects of the question, I will draw on the ritual theory of Caroline Humphrey and James Laidlaw, presented in their book *The Archetypal Actions of Ritual.* Humphrey and Laidlaw focus on the specific characteristics of human actions—especially their mental and psychological aspects—in ritual contexts, seeking to discern how what they call 'ritualized action' differs from 'normal action'. Taking a formalist approach, Humphrey and Laidlaw argue that, in ritual action, actors have a unique relationship to their own actions. Ritualized action has four peculiar characteristics: (1) ritualized action is non-intentional: "while people performing ritual acts do have intentions ..., the *identity* of a ritualized action does not depend, as is the case with normal action, on the agent's intention in acting." (2) Ritualized action is 'stipulated' in that "the constitution of separate acts out of the continuous flow of a person's action is not accomplished, as is the case with normal action, by processes of intentional understanding, but rather by constitutive rules which establish an ontology of ritual acts." (3) The "acts are perceived as discrete, named entities, with their own characters and histories," and thus can be called 'elemental' or 'archetypal', and (4) because the acts are felt to be external, they are also 'apprehensible', "available for a further reassimilation to the actors' intentions, attitudes, and beliefs," such as "by consciously intending to mean some proposition by the act, or by a spontaneous 'thoughtless' identification with the act itself as a physical activity"—such as perceiving one's own action as bodily practice without mental content.[65]

The first two characteristics are especially important for my argument. Humphrey and Laidlaw argue that ritual action differs fundamentally from non-ritual action in that "intentions no longer play the immediate role which they normally do in determining the identity

[65] Humphrey and Laidlaw, *Archetypal Actions*, 88–89, emphasis in original. A broadly similar approach to ritual is taken by Roy A. Rappaport, "The Obvious Aspects of Ritual," in *Readings in Ritual Studies*, ed. Ronald M. Grimes (Upper Saddle River, N.J.: Prentice Hall, 1996), 427–440.

of the acts performed."[66] Rather, in ritual the identity of an action is provided by 'prior ontological stipulation'. Ritual actors follow constitutive rules that determine the identity of the acts they perform, and defer (though they do not lose altogether) what Humphrey and Laidlaw call their 'intentional sovereignty'.[67] This is more than to say that ritual actors follow rules, it is to say that ritual actors have a unique relationship to the identity of their actions, standing one step removed from authoring their actions. What counts as a ritual is not that one does a certain act, but that one does a certain act stipulated as that named ritual act, like 'prayer' or 'puja'. To extend Clifford Geertz's example, if a 'twitch' is a physical movement free of intent, and a 'blink' or 'wink' is the same movement imbued with intent, a 'ritual blink' is done intending not simply to blink, but intending to do the action whose identity is defined by prior stipulation as 'ritual blinking'.[68]

Humphrey and Laidlaw clarify their view of ritual by comparing ritualized action with the use of language. When using language, "our words can have a meaning which is to some degree independent of our intention in using them—they can, so to speak, escape our intentions." By saying one thing intentionally, a person may convey other meanings not intended. For example, intending to warn someone not to go on the ice may also non-intentionally inform that person about the thickness of the ice. This is not a matter of misunderstanding, but of the limits to the control we have over the meaning of our words. In spite of this potential gap, Humphrey and Laidlaw assert that in language, "What you aim at ... is that your words will indeed match your intended meaning." If they do not, it makes perfect sense to correct yourself, saying "that is not what I meant."[69] While this overlooks the possibility of intending to be ambiguous, as a poet might do, it makes the important point that in using language, the author has a direct intentional connection to part—though only part—of the meaning of the words. A speaker normally speaks to enact an intention, even if that intention only partly governs the meaning of the act.

In ritualized action, the separation between the actor's intentions and the meaning of the action is more acute and, moreover, is defini-

---

66 Humphrey and Laidlaw, *Archetypal Actions*, 94.

67 Ibid., 98–99.

68 See Clifford Geertz, "Thick Description: Toward an Interpretive Theory of Culture," in *The Interpretation of Cultures: Essays in Interpretive Anthropology* (New York: Basic Books, 1973), 6–7; he borrows this distinction from Gilbert Ryle.

69 Humphrey and Laidlaw, *Archetypal Actions*, 98.

tive of ritual. In speaking, the gap between intention and meaning may often be accidental, the unintended meanings ancillary to the intention of the actor. According to Humphrey and Laidlaw, "In ritual, on the other hand, you do not choose your acts in order to enact your intention, so that so long as you follow the rules, there is never any call to correct what you have done because it was not what you meant."[70] They further assert that this is no accident, that it is "the point" of ritual that "the meaning of a ritual act diverges from the intention of the agent."[71] Of course one still does the action, yet it is "you, in intending to perform your act as ritual, who constitutes your action as ritualized and thus *make it the case* that you are no longer, for a while, author of your acts. You set at one remove, or defer, rather than give up, what one might call the 'intentional sovereignty' of the agent."[72] You are performing acts defined by prior stipulation, not by your intentions. This is the odd intention to do that which is not defined by your intention.

This does not make ritualized actions into non-actions or unintentional actions, like 'absent-mindedly scratching your chin', or 'clumsily knocking something over'. As Humphrey and Laidlaw put it, "The actor feels there to be some reason for the act, that the ritual has its own point, or, speaking metaphorically, that the act has its own ritual 'intention'."[73] Humphrey and Laidlaw suggest that the ritual actor's "particular intentions no longer fix the act she is performing," creating what they refer to as a potential "gap" between the actor's intentions and her actions. Thus, having made an intentional decision to perform a ritual, what they call the "ritual commitment," the actor may even have "some quixotically unrelated intention" and still perform the ritual.[74]

---

[70] Ibid.

[71] Ibid., 98–99.

[72] Ibid., 99, emphasis in original.

[73] Ibid., 101.

[74] Ibid., 99. Humphrey and Laidlaw at times problematically mix description with explanation in a way that undermines the power of their theory. For example: "when acting ritually, it is because your act is other than an ordinary intentional act that you perform it" (99), implying that rituals are driven by a desire to experience a different kind of intentionality. They similarly assert, as noted, that it is "the point" of ritual that "the meaning of a ritual act diverges from the intention of the agent" (98–99). They make an offhand and unconvincing aside that this "potential freedom from the everyday and inexorable suffusion of action with personal intentions ... may suggest a reason why people perform ritual" (99). Whether their description of ritualized action

This account is compelling and helpful in understanding the Muslim jurists' treatment of *niyya* in ritual law. In the light of Humphrey and Laidlaw's theory, one can see that, in the *ʿibādāt* of Islamic ritual law, the identity of acts is provided by the rules of ritual performance given in the texts. The actor performs one of these acts not by (re)inventing an act to be defined as prayer, for example, but by 'stepping into' the acts stipulated by ritual law. The rules establish that there is this named action required of Muslims, and what particular movements and utterances will count as valid performance. The actor then acts, making the movements and utterances required by the law, and these movements may be deemed valid enactments of the stipulated actions. Intending to perform an *ʿibāda* is intending to step into an act whose identity is authored, in effect, by ritual law, the jurists, and God. This illustrates the fact that ritual is an odd situation where the acts can look exactly correct, yet the actor is not 'authoring' them, not imbuing them with intention, not making them what they appear to be. In ritualized action, intention is a particularly precarious part of action.

However, I also find that analysis of intentions in Islamic ritual law illuminates some significant limitations to Humphrey and Laidlaw's theory. This theory seems, at first blush, to explain exactly what we find in Islamic ritual law: that the jurists think ritual actions are removed in some special way from the actor's intentions, and so the jurists command the actor to intend her ritual actions. That is, ritual actions are a special kind of action that can be done without intending, and still be that action, so the jurists insist on intention to fill this potential gap. However, looked at in the light of Islamic ritual law, there are two significant shortcomings in this view of ritualized action: first, the theory sells short its own insight into the social nature of ritual and displays a truncated notion of audience. Second, it belies an overly physical notion of ritual action.

Regarding the first point, while Humphrey and Laidlaw are correct in identifying the 'prior stipulation' aspect of ritual action, they fail to recognize a key implication of this insight: that ritual is inherently social. *Someone* must do this stipulating. Humphrey and Laidlaw pay insufficient attention to the crucial issue of audience, that is, to whom an act must 'count' as a particular ritual action. Their theory presupposes a social context—the ritual is defined and judged by a social

---

is accurate or not, this justification of the existence of ritual and the motivation of ritual actors seems misguided, or at least badly underdeveloped.

group—but does not pay attention to the full implications of this fact.[75] Thus, they are correct only on one level: a ritual action may be deemed to 'count', to *be* a ritual action, without the direct intention of the actor, only in terms of an onlooking audience without access to intentions. I agree that ritual is peculiar in that it can look like an action that it is not, that a ritual actor can go through the motions without the attendant intentions and still get the motions right. In contrast, I cannot, for example, raise my arm without intending to do so. If there were a machine hooked up to my brain that made my arm go up without my control, this would not count as 'I raised my arm (intentionally)'. However, to an observer it may count as 'he performed the arm-raising ritual'. I can appear to 'do ablutions' while intending to cool off, get clean, or just splash around in the water. But this only counts if 'doing ablutions' means appearing to make the motions of ablutions in the eyes of others.

The Islamic approach to ritual law provides a counter-example, a vision of ritual that only 'counts' if intentional. Islamic prayer has as one of its constitutive rules that the actor intend the action. Extending our example, Humphrey and Laidlaw imply that prayer would count if the actor were hooked up to a machine that made him or her go through the motions. But this is only true if counting occurs only in the eyes of other people. Islamic law adds one, and probably two, additional audiences: the self and God. On Humphrey and Laidlaw's view, no one in the audience can know if the intentions fit the movements, but in the *'ibādāt*, the audience includes the one person who can know this, namely, the actor himself. Certainly, one could still 'get away with' a disingenuous or vacuous performance, but the same texts that stipulate the movements (accessible by others) also stipulate the intention (known only by oneself), and in a very real sense, ritual action without intention *does not count*. Further, though the texts are not explicit in this regard, it seems fair to say that they assume that God is also watching. Their very definition of ritual is an act done in obedience to, and worship of, God, and God is the one other being who knows a person's intentions. A fully valid ritual is one that God recognizes and accepts, and while no one can know whether God will accept even an objec-

[75] The analogy they draw between language and ritual (above) highlights the social aspects of language—that the audience to a linguistic act is partly responsible for establishing the meaning of that act. However, Humphrey and Laidlaw do not explicitly make this point.

tively and subjectively proper ritual, the jurists assert that without both components, God will certainly not accept it.

Humphrey and Laidlaw's discussion of 'archetypal' and 'apprehensible' qualities of ritual action answers this charge to some extent, seeming to include the ritual actor as audience for his own actions, perceiving these acts as entities outside himself that he temporarily inhabits. While this may be an accurate description of ritualized action, here Humphrey and Laidlaw again understate the importance of audience. These 'archetypes' must exist in one's mind and memory, and in the collective minds, memories, and texts of a community.[76] What is at stake in a given ritual performance is whether it happened correctly or not, whether the specific enactment fits the archetype—in short, whether it 'counts'. And 'counting', again, is a social matter, a question of audience. When Humphrey and Laidlaw say that in ritual "there is never any call to correct what you have done because it was not what you meant" they fail to realize that the call could come from somewhere other than the audience of outside observers.

A second, and related, shortcoming in Humphrey and Laidlaw's theory revealed by the lights of Islamic law is its overly physical view of ritual action. For Humphrey and Laidlaw, what counts as a proper ritual action is a proper set of bodily movements done in accord with prior stipulation. Because they only pay attention to the audience of other people, they only consider that a ritual will count when this audience sees the right movements and hears the right words. If I happened to splash around in water in a certain way, this would count as ritual ablution. While they appear to focus on the mental or psychological state of ritual actors, Humphrey and Laidlaw actually treat ritual in a very physical manner. Again, it is a genuine insight of theirs that ritual is an unusual case of physical action that can count as a particular named action regardless of the actual intention of the actor. However, by defining a 'ritual that counts' in such a physical way, they fail to pursue the interior mental or psychological aspects of ritualized action.

Islamic law, by including an audience of both the self and God, includes a subjective element in the very constitution of the ritual. The jurists implicitly recognize that a gap potentially exists between ritual

[76] It should be noted that Humphrey and Laidlaw's idea of 'archetypes' is altogether distinct from that of Carl Jung: "we do not think our archetypes derive from particular collective experiences of humankind as a whole, nor, very emphatically, that they have universal symbolic meanings" (*Archetypal Actions*, 158).

actor and action. They fill this gap by insisting that what goes on in the heart or mind is as much a part of a 'ritual that counts' as is where to stand and walk when on pilgrimage. Again, this indicates the limits of one person to assess the ritual of another, and the provisionality of such an assessment. But it is not true of Islamic ritual law to say that all rituals count as long as the bodily movements and utterances are correct. Even if we assume that intentions are not available for objective assessment, we need not exclude them from the definition of a valid ritual. We must simply expand our definition of validity, and reduce our certainty about assessing it. This is exactly what Islamic ritual law does.

In short, what Humphrey and Laidlaw have identified is that absent-minded, accidental, or even duplicitous ritual still looks like ritual, and if looking like ritual is all that matters, then absent minded or insincere ritual is valid ritual. In the Islamic case, we see the jurists realizing this odd fact, and responding by making intention part of the ritual. *Niyya* in *fiqh al-ʿibādāt* is perhaps best understood as a specifically ritualistic form of intention—the intention to participate in a ritual and to assent to the ontological stipulation of the ritual action. The jurists may not be able to tell whether I really intend my performance or am only trying to fool them, but they have told me that the latter does not count, and that they are not the only, or most important, audience. If jurists did not stipulate *niyya*, then trying to look like one is praying in order to fool others, would still be prayer. But since the ritual law includes *niyya* along with the stipulated movements, only prayer intended as prayer is prayer. The acts of ritual worship are given by the law, but only *happen* if actors intend them to.

CHAPTER FOUR

INTENT IN ISLAMIC CONTRACT LAW

Introduction

Contracts and business transactions are subsets of the law of social transactions, *fiqh al-muʿāmalāt.* As noted above, *fiqh al-ʿibādāt* (ritual law) deals with divine-human relations, while *fiqh al-muʿāmalāt* deals with inter-human relations. Contract law constitutes a critical component of many legal systems, helping to determine how law contributes to social and economic order. Islamic contract law allows for a wide range of economic activity while establishing parameters reflecting religious and ethical concerns. In the law of social transactions, we find a significantly different set of actions and a different legal agenda than in ritual law. *Fiqh al-muʿāmalāt* is not meant to enjoin ritual behavior—behavior elevated above the norm—but to bring a religious evaluation system to bear on ordinary life. The legal sphere of social transactions is not governed by an overarching imperative, as is the ritual sphere; rather here jurists address actions marked by a wide range of choice, establishing parameters of how one must act if one chooses to act at all.[1] If the *ʿibādāt* are morally positive (hence the imperative to do them), civil acts are morally neutral—certain forms are pre- and proscribed if one chooses to act, but one need not act at all. Put differently, while *fiqh al-ʿibādāt* consists largely of constitutive rules, *fiqh al-muʿāmalāt* consists largely of regulative rules. In the *ʿibādāt* the jurists prescribe *niyya* along with the other elements of actions, while in the *muʿāmalāt*, intentions are largely assumed to exist and are regulated and assessed

[1] Recall Qarāfī's definition of the *muʿāmalāt* (from chapter 2 above): these are those acts the performance of which achieves the benefit for which God commanded them, as opposed to the *ʿibādāt*, for which the external performance alone does not achieve the benefit—the intention of the performance is necessary for the act to fulfill the duty/accrue the benefit. In the *muʿāmalāt*, compliance with the rules, regardless of intention, brings direct results and benefits (at least to someone other than the actor—e.g., payment of a debt) (see Qarāfī, *al-Umniyya*, 27–28, and Jackson, *Islamic Law and the State*, 201).

along with other elements of actions. Contracts in Islamic law hinge on speech acts, performative utterances that accomplish some end, such as the transfer of property, goods, money and the like, or commit the participants to some temporary or permanent terms and relations.[2] The treatment of intent here revolves around the intent behind a given speech act.

I will demonstrate that *fiqh* texts consistently treat speech acts in these legal matters as potentially being of three types. First, jurists distinguish between speech that is explicit and direct (*ṣarīḥ*) or allusive and indirect (*kināya*). The latter category is further divided (often implicitly rather than explicitly) into speech that is allusive yet clear in meaning, and that which is entirely ambiguous. Thus, we find three types of speech acts, which I will call type 1, explicit and unambiguous; type 2, allusive or indirect, yet sufficiently clear in meaning; and type 3, ambiguous to the point of not being clear in meaning. The jurists treat intentions—in terms of basic sincerity—as being a crucial factor only for type 2. Type 1 speech acts are legally binding regardless of intention (sincerity), while type 3 speech acts are too ambiguous to have legally binding effects. In other words, the sincerity of speech acts of types 1 and 3 does not matter—their objective formal qualities determine their legal effects. Speech acts of the second type, however, are defined by intentions; the words themselves have the potential to be legally valid performative utterances, but they also have the potential to be otherwise, and it is the intention of the speaker that determines into which category they fall. As we shall see, however, the jurists do not establish clear objective criteria for assessing intentions in these cases.

The issue of basic sincerity, however, does not exhaust all the implications of considering intentions in assessing performative speech acts. Another important matter is the potential complexity of the intention, or the possibility of intending a single act to have multiple meanings and effects. Searle describes this as the 'accordion effect' of intentional action: a single intentional action can stretch to encompass multiple intentional, not to mention unintentional, results. These results may be other actions or events, responses, symbolic meanings, and so forth. In short, an intention can be complex. Here we may recall Searle's dis-

[2] Whether such speech acts in Islamic law are truly performative utterances or, alternately, 'informational reports', is a matter of some debate, as will be seen later, especially in the conclusion of chapter 5.

tinction between intention-in-action and prior intention. All intentional actions have an intention-in-action, and some actions also satisfy a prior intention, formed at some temporal remove from the action. One way in which an action can be complex is by satisfying an intention-in-action while also contributing to the satisfaction of a prior intention. For example, one action could satisfy the intention-in-action 'that I get on the bus' while also contributing to the satisfaction of a prior intention 'that I go to work', an intention not finally fulfilled until several other components of the complex action come to pass. The intention to board the bus, then, would be a complex intention.

Muslim jurists recognize the potential complexity of intentions, and they seek to address this fact in contract law. For some jurists, the validity of the contract hinges not only on its formal qualities and direct effects, but also its wider consequences, if these are intended by the contracting parties. The classic example is the case of selling grapes to a winemaker: selling grapes is legal, making wine is not, and so in some cases the legality of the sale of grapes (satisfying a legal intention-in-action) is eclipsed by the additional intention to make wine (abetting an unlawful prior intention).

In sum, Muslim jurists address two broad categories of intent in contract law, basic sincerity and complexity. On the one hand, the jurists consider the exact words uttered and determine whether they are sufficiently explicit to be effective regardless of intention (type 1), or, if not fully explicit, whether they are close enough to potentially count (type 2) or not (type 3). If the words are deemed allusive but potentially effective (type 2), jurists then ask whether the speaker intended them to count. The issues here include the exact verbal form of the utterance and the speaker's basic sincerity—whether the speaker 'meant it' to be a certain kind of utterance. On the other hand, jurists sometimes also address the complexity of intentions, the wider intended consequences of an act. The issues here include whether those wider effects are legally relevant, and how or where the line is to be drawn between intentional effects that matter and those that do not. In other words, the jurists sometimes—but not always—question whether a person 'meant it' (basic sincerity) when speaking, and sometimes 'what (else) he meant' (complexity).

All of these issues—verbal form, basic sincerity, and complexity—play specific roles in the different subsets of *fiqh al-muʿāmalāt*. In this and the following chapter I will demonstrate that jurists treat intentions as crucial to the identity of some, but not all, actions. In certain cases, jurists systematically avoid assessing actions according to intentions and focus instead on the formal qualities of the (speech) act. Thus, not all actions depend on *niyya* or any other form of intention, as the famous *ḥadīth* insists they do; some actions are legally effective and binding regardless of intentions.

An additional aspect of the legal treatment of commercial transactions is a significant shift in the terminology of intent. The previous chapters have shown that in ritual law, jurists employ the term *niyya* almost exclusively and with specific technical implications. *Niyya* in *fiqh al-ʿibādāt* serves a principally taxonomic function, giving actions the identity of the named religious duties of the *sharīʿa*. Moreover, *niyya* is morally colored by this close association with acts of obedient worship, emerging as the good and proper intent to worship God in fulfillment of the law. In commercial law, and in *fiqh al-muʿāmalāt* in general, the term *niyya* looses many of the specific technical implications it had in *fiqh al-ʿibādāt*, and jurists also employ other terms when referring to intentions, foremost among them *qaṣd* and *irāda*. Intent remains essentially taxonomic, serving at times to define actions and locate them within the available legal lexicon. But intent itself becomes morally neutral, as it can be the intent to do good, bad, or neither. The terms employed slide toward the generic and interchangeable, reflecting a shift away from the specificity of usage in ritual law.

Explicitness and Sincerity of the Contract

Freedom to contract is generally supported in Islamic law, and the various rules governing contracts and commerce function to provide the parameters of this freedom.[3] Contracts in Islamic law are generally oral in nature, consisting of terms and conditions established and accepted through speech acts. The record of the contract is established by eyewitnesses, usually two *mukallaf* male Muslims, and the terms of the contract, such as the price and the exact merchandise involved, must be explicit.

[3] Oussama Arabi emphasizes the limits Islamic law places on this type of activity, asserting that "Islamic law does not permit freedom of contract." He notes three general types of restriction: prohibition of usury, constraints on licit objects of legal obligation, and the attaching of stipulations to contracts ("Contract Stipulations [*Shurūṭ*] in Islamic Law: The Ottoman *Majalla* and Ibn Taymiyya," *International Journal of Middle East Studies* 30 [1998]: 29).

Writing the contract is neither legally necessary nor, according to *fiqh* manuals, even legally efficacious. This is, however, a clear instance of an ideal not always reflected in actual practice.[4] Jeanette A. Wakin has shown that medieval Muslims employed documents in several significant areas, and some jurists wrote treatises on *shurūṭ* (or *wathā'iq*, in the Mālikī west), about regulating the usage of written documents, especially in contracts and testimony. However, jurists developed two parallel approaches to the law, one more religiously idealistic, the other more pragmatic. The *fiqh* manuals under scrutiny in my study belong to the former, while the subgenres of *shurūṭ/wathā'iq*, *ḥiyal* (legal devices or evasions, sg., *ḥīla*),[5] and *maḥāḍir* and *sijillāt* (collections of model documents for use by *qāḍīs* and their clerks) all belong to the latter.[6] In *fiqh* manuals, jurists consistently rejected the use of written documents for contracts of sale, and for the structurally similar practice of recording and notarizing witness testimony in *qāḍī* court procedure. The Qur'ān and *ḥadīth* both do provide potential support for the use of written documents, especially in contracts of sale.[7] Wakin notes that,

[4] Joseph Schacht makes the more general observation that "The actual practice of commerce in the Muslim Middle Ages was controlled not by these theoretical rules of Islamic law but by a customary commercial law which had been called into being by the normal needs of commercial life in the great cities of Islam, and was elaborated by the legal advisers of the merchants, who were competent specialists in Islamic law" ("Bay'," in *Encyclopaedia of Islam*, new ed.). On the use of written records in *qāḍī* courts generally, see Hallaq, *Origins*, 60–61, 91–96.

[5] Wakin observes that the *ḥiyal* are "legal devices or evasions. Often compiled by the great jurists themselves, *ḥiyal* works were handbooks showing interested persons, particularly the merchants, how they could follow the letter of the law and yet arrive at a different result than that intended by the law" (*The Function of Documents in Islamic Law* [Albany: State University of New York Press, 1972], 11, and see her n. 1). See also J. Schacht, "Ḥiyal," in *Encyclopaedia of Islam*, new ed.

[6] See Wakin, *Documents in Islamic Law*, 1–15. She also considers several other subgenres which are more explicitly woven into *fiqh* manuals to be representative of the pragmatic, as opposed to idealistic, impulse: *adab al-qāḍī* (the duties of a *qāḍī*), *waqf* (pious endowments), *waṣāyā* (legacies), *farā'iḍ* (the law of succession), and *nafaqāt* (maintenance of a wife). These works (along with the *ḥiyal*, *shurūṭ*, and so forth) "were all loosely tied together by the fact that they tended to appear in connection to the same authors and because a certain literary continuity was maintained over the centuries" (12). While the parallel field of practical literature was kept separate from the more idealistic fields of *fiqh*, much of the practical literature was written by the same authors who produced the idealistic works. Moreover, Wakin observes that, by recognizing the need to address pragmatic concerns and doing so themselves, "the aim was to keep practice under the control of doctrine, for otherwise their own system would have been undermined" (10).

[7] See Qur'ān 2:282; on the *ḥadīth*, see Wakin, *Documents in Islamic Law*, 5–6. The Qur'ān also supports the use of oral testimony (as did prevailing Near Eastern practice)

> Despite all this, the jurists never modified their attitude toward written documents and managed to avoid the quranic injunction by interpreting it as a simple recommendation … Thus oral testimony provided the only form of proof in the Sharīʿa … The personal word of an upright Muslim was deemed worthier than an abstract piece of paper or [in regard to circumstantial evidence] a piece of information subject to doubt and falsification.[8]

While in practice written documents played a significant role in the practical manifestations of contracts and testimony, and while legal subgenres emerged to regulate the use of documents, the *fiqh* manuals themselves generally insisted on the spoken word as the ideal contractual medium.

The work of Baber Johansen offers a useful starting point for analysis of contract law in Islam. Johansen, who works mainly on Ḥanafī sources, distinguishes between 'commercial exchange' and 'social exchange'. In commercial exchange, such as sales of property, "commodities are exchanged for commodities," including any non-*ḥarām* objects or animals, as well as human slaves, while in social exchange (he also calls this "symbolic exchange"), such as marriage (the only example Johansen names), "goods or monetary values are considerations for non-commodities, or non-commodities are reciprocally given and taken."[9] Johansen argues that commercial transactions involve a relatively high degree of concern for intent, while social transactions involve a relatively low degree. He asserts that this is because the latter involve a risk of social disruption that necessitates a firm finality and stability to the contractual exchange, while the former do not. Com-

---

and, as Wakin observes, the Qur'ān's "emphasis on witnesses to prove crimes punishable by *ḥadd* may have influenced the attitude toward oral testimony in civil transactions" (6).

[8] Wakin, *Documents in Islamic Law*, 6; she further asserts that "if the paradox in the official rejection and widespread use of written contracts epitomizes the conflict between theory and practice, the very existence of these *shurūṭ* works shows us how the scholars tried to make that conflict less sharply felt" (10–11). She emphasizes that Ḥanafīs tend to be the most 'practical' or 'pragmatic' in their approach to the law, and the most likely to employ quasi-legal stratagems (10–13). However, she also notes that, even though less inclined in this direction, Ḥanbalīs employed them as well (13, n. 5).

[9] Johansen, "The Valorization of the Human Body in Muslim Sunni Law," in *Law and Society in Islam*, Devin J. Stewart, Baber Johansen, and Amy Singer (Princeton: Markus Wiener, 1996), 71. Similarly Oussama Arabi notes that "In the domain of civil transactions (*muʿāmalāt*), Muslim jurists distinguish an exchange in which both terms have monetary value—*muʿāwaḍa mālīya*—whose model is the sale contract (*al-bayʿ*), from those in which only one term of the transaction has monetary value, i.e., marriage (*nikāḥ*), donation (*hiba*), and testation (*waṣīya*)" ("Intention and Method," 209, n. 24).

mercial exchange, he claims, "presupposes the complete and voluntary consent (*riḍā tāmm*) of the partners to a contract"; duress invalidates a contract unless retroactively authorized by any participant who acted under duress.[10] Thus, "The contracts have to be interpreted in light of the parties' intentions (*nīya*) and purposes (*maqṣūd*). They cannot be interpreted in a formalistic way." In contrast, contracts of social exchange, because they indicate social ranking by classifying "people into those whom one can marry and those whom one cannot," imply "a high social risk of rupture and conflict, because the refusal of a demand in marriage ... indicates negative ranking and classification."[11] While marriage conventionally includes much negotiation before the contract is finalized, once it is finalized "the subject matter is much too explosive ... to leave the parties the same range of maneuvering that they enjoy in commercial exchange." Therefore, "These contracts follow the principle of a strict formalism which leaves very little place for intent, purpose, and knowledge of the parties concerned."[12] In other words, in commercial exchange the risks of social disruption are relatively low, so intentions can come into play in spite of their potentially disruptive effects, while too much is at stake in social exchange to allow the parties to make claims about objectively non-verifiable matters such as intentions.

This argument suggests a sociological explanation for why intentions matter in some *muʿāmalāt* issues and not in others: intentions matter in commercial exchange because such transactions must be undertaken freely (people must be sincere, presumably impossible under duress), while intentions do not matter in social exchange because this could cause social disruption. This implies that jurists will consider inten-

---

[10] Johansen, "Valorization," 73, citing Y. Linant de Bellefonds, *Traité de Droit Musulman Comparé* (Paris: Mounton, 1965), 1:69–71.

[11] Johansen, "Valorization," 73. Earlier he explains that "admission to social exchange is selective. It depends on the family's standing in the five major social hierarchies, which are determined by religion, gender, kinship, generation and the relation of free persons to slaves" (72). See also Susan A. Spectorsky, *Chapters on Marriage and Divorce: Responses of Ibn Ḥanbal and Ibn Rāhwayh* (Austin: University of Texas Press, 1993), 14–16, where she discusses the idea of *kafāʾa*, or equality in terms of "religion, lineage, means, and freedom" as a condition of marriage; and Mona Siddiqui, "Law and the Desire for Social Control: An Insight into the Hanafi Concept of *Kafāʾa* with Reference to the Fatawa ʿAlamgiri (1664–1672)," in *Feminism and Islam: Legal and Literary Perspectives*, ed. Mai Yamani and Andrew Allen (New York: New York University Press, 1996), 49–68.

[12] Johansen, "Valorization," 73–74.

tions whenever they can, to make sure people act freely and sincerely, unless considering intentions threatens social stability. In this understanding, consideration of intentions is inherently risky, presumably because intentions are not objectively verifiable and allow the parties to 'maneuver', to make up or change their minds after the fact. This makes transactions less stable, which is tolerable in commercial exchange, but not in social exchange. This meshes with Schacht's view, which, as will be seen below, assumes that reference to intentions creates potential loopholes for escape from a contract.

Johansen's view has several shortcomings which limit its explanatory power. First, he draws only on Ḥanafī sources, and it remains to be seen if his findings apply to jurists of other *madhhab*s. Second, he omits any consideration of divorce, where (as we will see in the next chapter) intentions matter a great deal. Of course, divorce is technically not a contract but the dissolution of one, yet it is certainly a contract-related matter that implicates the same social ranking issues as marriage. Third, the implication that commercial exchange does not affect the social fabric is not convincing: since commercial exchange is socially open in ways marriage is not, a failed contract of sale may not carry the symbolic weight of marriage, but it could certainly rend important social connections. Finally, and perhaps most importantly, Johansen discusses intentions only in terms of the basic sincerity of the speech act that forms a contract—whether one meant what he or she said, and was not lying (whether voluntarily or under duress). However, I will show that for many jurists, it is the potential complexity of intentions that matters in contracts, the possibility that a person may enter an apparently legal contract intending to achieve illegal ends.

Brinkley Messick's views on intention in *mu'āmalāt* settings move beyond those of Johansen in some helpful ways. Messick surveys sources from a wider range of *madhhab* affiliation, highlighting the variety of positions held by various jurists—some take a formalistic approach to contracts, treating verbal expressions as key, while others consider basic intentional sincerity more important than words. Further, where Johansen looks only at bilateral contracts, Messick distinguishes between these and unilateral declarations, specifically, repudiatory divorce [*ṭalāq*]. More importantly, Messick notes a general tension in Islamic law, revolving around intention's "role as a foundation of legal authority and ... associated problems concerning the aims and means of legal interpretation"—that is, intent is crucial element constituting legal subjects and their actions, yet is essentially subjective and elusive.[13] A central component of Messick's interpretive approach is the idea of a "foundationalism … that locates the site of authoritative meaning-generation internally, within the self, and thus beyond direct observation."[14] As he puts it, the consideration of intentions in a contract indicates a particular view of the self and of authoritative speech:

> In and of itself, then, the specific wording employed in sale and related contracts is not to be considered constitutive or binding, but, at the same time, this same wording serves as a principal type of contextual indicator concerning that which is constitutive and binding, namely, consent. In such analyses, a kind of culturally specific foundationalism assumes that a bedrock of human authority and truth exists, located at a remove from ordinary discourse, inwardly (in the "heart" or in the "self") in the elemental 'language,' if that is the appropriate term, of human intention (*qaṣd, niyya*).[15]

In this view, consideration of intentions in contractual exchange is more than an insistence on consent, it is also an indication that verbal forms and other outward signs are indices of a deeper level of expression, an internal formulation of intention that authorizes the words. In short, verbal expressions are indirect evidence of 'what is really going on', which takes place in the subjective states of the contracting parties. This foundationalism is manifest in varying degrees over time and place, and among jurists and *madhhab*s. Facing this problem of "attempting to know that which is defined as essential and yet, by its understood nature, inward and inaccessible," has led jurists to "contested solutions … [that] involve the study of manifest signs and forms of legal expression, including, but not limited to, individuals' spoken words and writings."[16] Messick focuses his energies on the manifestations of these issues in the context of modernizing Zaydī Yemen, but his more general doctrinal observations will be of use as we pursue an analytical framework in this and the following chapters.

In *fiqh* works, as noted above, contracts of sales are essentially speech acts, even if sometimes accompanied by written deeds, and subjective states come into play primarily in terms of the intent of the speakers while pronouncing the contract. Johansen indicates that jurists tend

---

[13] Brinkley Messick, "Indexing the Self," 152–153.

[14] Ibid., 153.

[15] Ibid., 161–162. Cf., Brinkley Messick, "Written Identities: Legal Subjects in an Islamic State," *History of Religions* 38, 1 (August 1998), 45.

[16] Messick, "Indexing the Self," 153.

to weigh intentions heavily when assessing the validity of commercial contracts, in order to affirm that a contract is undertaken freely. I will first show that while Johansen is correct that some jurists weigh basic sincerity in contracts of sale, others do not. In terms of the basic sincerity of the speech act forming a contract of sale, jurists display a range of views. Many jurists tend to insist on type 1 speech and only deem a contract valid if it is explicit and fits all the formal requirements of a contract. In these cases they make no mention of intentions and simply insist on the explicitness of all aspects of the contract, which is then binding. Other jurists, however, make a distinction between explicit (*ṣarīḥ*) speech, which is binding regardless of intention, and allusive (*kināya*) expressions that can only effect a contract if intended to do so. Still others, in accord with Johansen, explicitly insist that a contract be formed with the proper intention, that is, the intention that a given utterance be a contract. In this context, jurists tend to use the term *niyya* with the meaning of intention-in-action that a given speech act have a particular meaning and legal effect.

Jurists agree that the key element of a sale is a verbal offer of sale and a verbal acceptance of the offer.[17] Ibrāhīm al-Bayjūrī's view is exemplary: "A sale must include an offer and an acceptance. The former is something such as the seller or his agent saying 'I sell it to you and it is your property' or the like, followed by the buyer or his agent saying 'I buy it and it is my property', and the like."[18] The order of offer and acceptance can be reversed, or take different grammatical forms such as the perfect tense.[19] The exact terms of the sale, such as cost, and the specific items involved, must be explicit. Bayjūrī simply insists on explicitness while saying nothing about intention, and in this he is representative of many jurists.[20]

[17] See, for example, Ibn Qudāma, *al-Mughnī*, 6:7–9; and Bayjūrī, *Ḥāshiya*, 1:654–655.

[18] Bayjūrī, *Ḥāshiya*, 1:654–655.

[19] See, for example, Ibn Naqīb, *'Umdat al-sālik*, 378, where he notes that the buyer's acceptance may precede the seller's offer; Ibn Qudāma, however, notes a disagreement over this matter, and over the use of the imperative and other grammatical issues (*al-Mughnī*, 6:7–9). Mūṣilī notes that a sale by a mute or blind man is valid if it is made clear that he understands the terms (*al-Ikhtiyār*, 2:3–4, 10), an issue on which most jurists agree.

[20] See, for example, the Ḥanafī 'Alī b. Abī Bakr al-Marghīnānī (d. 1197), *al-Hidāya, sharḥ bidāyat al-mubtadī* (Cairo: Maktabat Muṣṭafā al-Bābī al-Ḥalabī wa-Awlāduhu, 1975), 3:21–24; this text is partially translated into English by Charles Hamilton as *The Hedaya, or Guide: A Commentary on the Mussulman Laws* (Lahore: Premier, 1870), see 241–243. Ibn Rushd says nothing about intentions in contracts of sale.

Other jurists discuss whether the utterance is considered explicit, and thus binding regardless of intentions, or insufficiently explicit, in which case intentions may matter. This is an issue of the sincerity of the speech act and whether a given speech act was 'meant to be' a contract. If an utterance is deemed too ambiguous to be automatically binding, but clear enough to be potentially valid (type 2, *kināya*), then intentions are decisive. The Shāfiʿī jurist Aḥmad Ibn Naqīb al-Miṣrī (d. 769/1368) offers a representative statement on such matters. After defining contracts of sales in much the same terms as Bayjūrī above,[21] Ibn Naqīb adds that

> [In addition to] unequivocal expressions (*ṣarā'iḥ*) ... sales can likewise be effected by indirect expression with intention (*bil-kināya maʿ al-niyya*), such as "take it for such-and-such an amount," or "I consider it yours for such-and-such an amount," intending thereby a sale which is accepted. If [the speaker] does not intend thereby a sale, it comes to nothing.[22]

Implicit in this statement is the threefold schema discussed above—explicit and binding, allusive and made valid and binding by *niyya*, and unacceptably ambiguous. Ibn Naqīb provides examples of statements that are close to explicit, implying that some statements would be too ambiguous to count even with *niyya*.[23] However, Ibn Naqīb gives no indication of how others' intentions are to be ascertained.

---

[21] "A sale is not valid unless there is a spoken offer and spoken acceptance. 'Offer' means the statement of the seller or his agent 'I sell it to you' or 'I make it yours'. 'Acceptance' means the statement of the buyer or his agent 'I buy it' or 'I take possession of it' or 'I accept'" (Ibn Naqīb, *'Umdat al-sālik*, 377). Note that I have modified the given English translation.

[22] Ibid., 378.

[23] In a section dealing not with sales but with guaranteeing payment of another's debt (*ḍamān dayn al-ghayr*) Ibn Naqīb and his 19th-century commentator, 'Umar Barakāt (d. after 1890), further discuss the issue of explicitness and the role of *niyya* in commercial transactions; the heart of the matter here is the specificity of the terms of the guarantee (the words in parentheses are those of the commentator): "It is necessary that the guarantor make the guarantee in words (or the written equivalent with *niyya*) that imply he is effecting it, such as 'I guarantee your debt (that So-and-so owes you)', or 'I will cover it' or the like. (These are explicit [*ṣarīḥa*] expressions in that they mention the guaranteed financial obligation. When it is not mentioned, the expression is allusive [*kināya*], which is valid provided the speaker intends [*nawā*] the financial obligation and that he knows the amount, for otherwise [*kināya*] is not valid)" (ibid., 414–415, my translation). Here Ibn Naqīb's commentator inserts two references to *niyya*: first, a written guarantee, regardless of its degree of explicitness, is equivalent to an ambiguous spoken guarantee in that it depends on *niyya*. Second, for a spoken, ambiguous/allusive guarantee, the *niyya* specifies the terms of the agreement that are not sufficiently specified in the explicit expression. In either case, however, the text gives no indication of how intentions are to be ascertained.

Note that Ibn Naqīb's statement above only gives intentions a role in making an ambiguous statement into an act of sale: *niyya* makes 'take it' or 'I consider it yours' equivalent to 'I sell it'. Even in these cases, the terms of the sale are presented as being explicit: 'take it *for such-and-such an amount*'. Thus, Ibn Naqīb holds that the terms of any commercial transaction must be made explicit for the transaction to be valid.[24] Intentions cannot take the place of an explicit statement of terms, such as intending a certain price without stating it explicitly; intentions can only make type 2 utterances count. This view largely retains its formalism, in that a type 1 utterance is treated formalistically, binding based on its explicit form, and *niyya* has no role. *Niyya* only matters for a type 2 utterance, in which case the indirect expression must be accompanied by the intention that it count.

This emphasis on formalism can have surprising consequences. For example, like most jurists, Ibn Naqīb insists that a seller is obliged to disclose any defects he knows of in the article he is selling.[25] However, according to Ibn Naqīb, even when the seller knows of a defect and does not disclose this information, such a seller has "cheated" (*ghashsha*), but the sale is nonetheless valid.[26] Here even intentional deceptiveness is not sufficient to invalidate a formally valid sale. Schacht comments on such treatment of explicit (*ṣarīḥ*) speech as binding regardless of intentions or outcomes, asserting that

> this tendency originates in the idea of the magical effect of the right word, and leads to formalism; the evidence of witnesses, for instance, is valid only if preceded by a derivative of the root *sh-h-d* 'to give testimony'. But this formalism has a rational basis; in order to create a *mufāwaḍa* (unlimited mercantile partnership), for instance, either this term must be used or every single legal effect mentioned.[27]

Schacht does not pursue this suggestion of echoes of archaic magic. However, this affinity between legal formalism and magic is intriguing, and whether or not the two are related through historical development as Schacht implies, legal formalism does resemble giving speech 'magical' power. Schacht's similarly terse assertion of the rational basis of this formalism suggests an important legal function of this approach to

---

[24] See ibid., 377–379, where, like all jurists with whom I am familiar, Ibn Naqīb insists that a sale must include explicit agreement upon price and exactly what article is being sold.

[25] Ibid., 392.

[26] Ibid.

[27] Schacht, *Introduction*, 116.

intentions and speech acts: it facilitates precisely locating a given speech act in the legal taxonomy, and thus clarifies the exact form and legal implications of the transaction being enacted. Using the term *mufāwaḍa*, for example, establishes exactly what kind of transaction is taking place and what rules apply. In the absence of the term, the details of the transaction must be spelled out to achieve this clarity.

Some jurists take a different approach, treating intentions in terms of basic sincerity as elemental to the formation of a contract. For example, the Ḥanafī Kāsānī (one of Johansen's sources) contends that the validity of a contract rests in part on the sincerity of the contracting parties:

> The present-tense form [of a contract of sale] is that the seller says to the buyer "I sell this thing to you for such and such [an amount]" and intends [by this] an offer of contract (*nawā al-ījāb*) and the buyer says … "I buy this thing from you for such and such [an amount]" and intends [by this] an offer of contract (*nawā al-ījāb*) … this satisfies the requirements [of a valid contract] (*yatimmu al-rukn wa yanʿaqidu*), however we consider the intention (*al-niyya*) here … Whether [the form of the contract] is explicit or metaphorical (*ḥaqīqatan aw majāzan*), I insist on the specification [of the contract] by *niyya* (*fa-waqaʿtu al-ḥāja ilā al-taʿyīn bil-niyya*).[28]

Here Kāsānī insists on basic sincerity (using the term *niyya*)—one must intend that his or her statement be a contract of sale, or it is not a valid contract. For Kāsānī, the form of the contract is less important than the intention *that it be a contract*. He allows either explicit or metaphorical terms—licensing type 2 speech, with *niyya*, to produce a valid contract—but even explicit speech requires basic sincerity, *niyya*.

According to Johansen, such an approach results from a primary concern that a contract be entered voluntarily. However, Schacht notes another important effect of this emphasis on intentions, namely the creation of loopholes in the law. Having observed, as noted above, the possibility of formalistic approaches to verbal utterances, Schacht continues:

> On the other hand, even a very imperfect declaration accompanied by *niyya* is regarded as legally valid whenever possible … By means of a complicated network of casuistry all possible forms of declaration are tested as to whether they are valid on their own, or only if accompanied

[28] Kāsānī, *Kitāb badāʾiʿ al-ṣanāʾiʿ*, 5:133.

> by *niyya*, or not at all ... This tendency often affords the possibility of evading the resulting obligation.[29]

Making contracts contingent on intentions gives contracting parties and judges leeway in assessing a transaction. In short, reference to intentions, which are understood to be at some remove from direct assessments, introduces a loophole whereby a person can escape from a contract by denying having had the requisite intent. Whether such loopholes were, in fact, taken advantage of is beyond the scope of the present inquiry, but the implications of this possibility are significant and suggest one explanation of why intentions were incorporated so fully into *fiqh al-bayʿ*. Moreover, as Messick notes, this approach treats the real contract as taking place in subjective states, not objective wordings, treating the latter as mere simulacrum of the former.

The issue of consent that many secondary scholarly works emphasize in contracts ought to be distinguished from the related, but separable, idea of sincerity. Jurists agree that consent is a necessary condition for all contracts, and one may not be coerced into entering into commercial (or social) exchange. However, for some jurists, in the absence of coercion, a tendency toward formalism becomes dominant even in contracts of sale. That is, some hold that non-coerced but insincere or unintended explicit statements are valid and binding. Kāsānī represents an alternative view, which holds that sincerity or intent is necessary regardless of how explicit a statement might be.

Complex Intentions in Contracts of Sale

The other major issue regarding intent in contracts of sale is that of the complexity of intentions—the possibility that, while intending a particular phrase to count as a contract, a person might also intend that the contract further some other ends. If such ends are illegal, a question arises about the legality of the contract even if its immediate terms are legal and the contracting parties are sincere and uncoerced. This is a question of whether the 'accordion effect' of a commercial transaction involves illegal actions, and whether the contracting parties' intentions and knowledge of these effects compromise the legality of the contract. The simplest answer is that it is not lawful to contract a sale that leads

[29] Schacht, *Introduction*, 116–117.

immediately to illegal results. Thus, trade is unlawful for certain *ḥarām* materials like wine, carrion, swine, and idols, or in certain situations, such as selling property one does not have rights over.[30] However, the issue is more complex for a contract the immediate terms and effects of which are legal, but which leads to illegal ends. Returning to the example of selling grapes to a winemaker: selling grapes is perfectly legal, whereas making wine is prohibited. So what of selling grapes when the buyer intends to make wine? Likewise, the selling of a sword is permitted, but what if the buyer intends to kill with it? These matters hinge mainly on intentions, and evince a recognition by the jurists of the potential complexity of intentions. Jurists disagree over the legal relevance of complex intentions or, more precisely, where to draw the line between intentional effects that matter and those that do not.

Ibn Naqīb demonstrates the potential diffculty of these matters by saying, "[It is unlawful] to sell grapes to someone who will make wine from them. If anyone makes such an unlawful (*muḥarrama*) transaction, the agreement is valid."[31] This seeming contradiction—an unlawful transaction that is nonetheless valid—is explained by one of Ibn Naqīb's commentators, ʿAbd al-Wahhāb Khallāf, as resolved by distinguishing between intrinsic unlawfulness (*al-muḥarram aṣālatan*) and extrinsic unlawfulness (*al-muḥarram li-ʿāriḍ*).[32] Acts of the former type are wholly forbidden and void (*bāṭil*) and cannot be a legal *sabab* (the legal grounds of rights and obligations[33]) or form the basis for further legal consequences—for example the sale of an unslaughtered animal carcass. Such acts have no legal standing and cannot give rise to subsequent actions with legal standing—for example, giving away the invalidly purchased unslaughtered animal carcass as alms. Acts of the latter type, however, are unlawful for extrinsic reasons and can be legal *sabab*s and form the basis of subsequent legal consequences. The sale

---

[30] See, for example, Ibn Rushd, *Bidāyat al-mujtahid*, 2:126–128; *DJP*, 2:155–157; the materials listed are considered 'filth' (*najāsa*). There are also a number of substances over which jurists disagree, such as bristles of swine hair, oil from prohibited animals, elephant tusks, dogs, cats, and human milk. Bayjūrī similarly observes that one cannot sell something impure, like wine, and extends this to something that is of no beneficial use, like a scorpion or an ant (*Ḥāshiya*, 1:657–658).

[31] Ibn Naqīb, *ʿUmdat al-sālik*, 390–391.

[32] Ibid., 36–37.

[33] *Sabab* in classical sources means what Oussama Arabi calls "the objective cause of legal obligation"; Arabi gives an example from Qarāfī: "The marriage contract is the legal cause (*sabab*) of procreation" (*al-Furūq* [Cairo: 1344–1346 H], 3:171; in Arabi, "Intention and Method," 203, n. 8).

of grapes to a winemaker is, for Ibn Naqīb, unlawful in this extrinsic sense, while the act of selling grapes is intrinsically lawful, so the sale is valid. Here 'extrinsic unlawfulness' appears to take on a moral quality, akin to assessing something as 'reprehensible' (*makrūh*), rather than a strictly legal one.

Not all jurists endorse this intrinsic/extrinsic distinction; Ibn Naqīb's solution is one among several offered by various jurists to the problem of illegal ends being furthered by a legal transaction. Further illumination of these issues, in both the classical period and the modern, is provided by the work of the twentieth-century Egyptian jurist ʿAbd al-Razzāq al-Sanhūrī, who oversaw the preparation of the New Egyptian Civil Code of 1949.[34] Oussama Arabi's study of Sanhūrī provides a convenient synopsis of the range of approaches and opinions in classical *fiqh* manuals to the question of complex intentions in contracts of sale, as well as a glimpse into how modern jurists have approached these issues.[35] For present purposes, however, it is Sanhūrī's survey of classical sources that is most useful.

Unlike the analytical approaches considered so far, Arabi, in presenting Sanhūrī's views, distinguishes between basic intentional sincerity (or consent) on the one hand, and the wider, complex intentions of contracting parties on the other. Arabi observes that the subjective conditions of contract validity potentially include both consent (*riḍā*) on the one hand and ulterior motive (*qaṣd*) or intention (*niyya*) on the other.[36] Arabi asserts that consent is recognized by all schools of law as a factor in contracts. In my view, this is an overstatement, for while all jurists may agree that a contract is invalid if coerced, not all agree that, in a context free of coercion, a person must be sincere in agreeing to a contract—some treat this situation formalistically, as seen above.

---

[34] Arabi focuses on Sanhūrī's *Maṣādir al-ḥaqq fī al-fiqh al-islāmī: dirāsa muqārina bil-fiqh al-gharbī* (Cairo: n.p., 1954–1959).

[35] Sanhūrī surveys the four major Sunnī *madhhab*s, thus moving beyond Chafik Chehata's study of Ḥanafī approaches to contract law (*Théorie Générale de l'Obligation en Droit Musulman Hanéfite* [Paris: Editions Sirey, 1969]). Chehata concluded, based on Ḥanafī sources, that "Motive is so little taken into consideration that the sale of an object is clearly considered to be valid even if the ends it serves are illegal" (70, cited by Arabi, "Intention and Method," 201). For his own version of reformulated 'modernized' Islamic law, Sanhūrī insists that the validity of contracts must hinge on this subjective cause. The reader will note that I rely heavily on Arabi's important article, with gratitude to the author and with permission from the publisher.

[36] Arabi, "Intention and Method," 209.

Regarding the issue of multiple, complex intentions (i.e., the prior intentions to act illegally that may accompany the intention-in-action to form a contract), Arabi notes that jurists disagree over the implications of these for the validity of the contract. He employs a variety of terms—particularly *qaṣd*, *niyya*, and *sabab*, treated largely as synonymous—to refer to this aspect of intentions in contracts. Sanhūrī focuses on "the subjective determining motive or cause for contract" (*al-sabab*), the further goal or end intended by the contracting parties.[37] This encompasses both the immediate goal and what we are calling the accordion effect, insofar as the latter effects are intended. Selling grapes which inadvertently spoil and ferment, for example, involves no intent to produce alcohol and does not affect a sale prior to spoilage. As noted, jurists agree that the immediate effects of a contract must be legal, but Sanhūrī finds that some jurists largely disregard any wider motives,

[37] Ibid., 201. Sanhūrī employs the term *al-sabab*, but gives it a novel meaning as subjective rather than objective cause; Arabi notes the classical scholars did not use the term *sabab* this way (202–203; on the classical meaning, see n. 33 above). On a separate but related matter, Arabi asserts that "Sanhūrī unearthed a more complex reality of interrelation between ritual law and the law of contract" (202). Arabi expands on this point by observing that "In Islamic law the centrality of the inner world of the Muslim subject shows foremost in the law of worship (*ʿibādāt*). In Islam, piety in prayer is a legal matter, and legal structures are erected to see to its respect by individual Muslims … The subject's *intention* (*nīya*) to pray is not left to the vagaries of his psyche, but explicitly posited as a *legal category in its own right*. Still, when it comes to mundane transactions (*muʿāmalāt*), the specific modes of the implication of the subject in the act are viewed differently by the different schools" (211, emphasis in original). And, further, "the insistence on sincerity of intention (*nīya*) in worship (*ʿibādāt*)—a fundamental dimension of Muslim religious experience embodied in law—was not to remain without effect on the implication of subjective intent in the other legal domain, that of mundane transactions (*muʿāmalāt*). For despite the marginalization of the ulterior motive in Ḥanafī and Shāfiʿī contract law, Sanhūrī demonstrates that the Mālikīs and more markedly, the Ḥanbalīs … took the licitness of motive as a necessary feature of the validity of contracts" (222). Arabi here seems to conflate the fact that all jurists weigh intentions in acts of worship with the fact that Mālikīs and Ḥanbalīs weigh intentions in contract law. Sanhūrī's work serves to show that a modernized Islamic law can weigh intentions in contract law without breaking from its own legal traditions. He does this by drawing not only on Ḥanafī materials, as many of his predecessors in legal reform had done, but by drawing on all four major Sunnī *madhhab*s. Arabi does not indicate that Sanhūrī based his incorporations of intentions into contract law on the role of intentions in ritual law. As I endeavor to show in this study, there is some overlap of treatment of intentions between ritual and civil law, but the specific notions of intention shift markedly between the two spheres. The jurists' understanding of *niyya* in *fiqh al-ʿibādāt* does not seem to me to be the cause, as Arabi implies it is, of some jurists' consideration of intentions in contracts; the simple fact that Ḥanafīs include *niyya* as a crucial part of many acts of worship but not of contracts challenges this explanation.

while others give them substantial weight.[38] Sanhūrī finds in classical Islamic law a *madhhab* split on this issue, with Ḥanafīs and Shāfiʿīs de-emphasizing subjectivism in favor of strict formalism, and Mālikīs and Ḥanbalīs tending to treat subjective motives as determinative of the validity of the contract even if not explicitly mentioned in the contract.[39]

In describing the formalistic approach, Arabi asserts that "the marginalization of subjective intent in commercial transactions when that intent is not made manifest in the terms of the contract is representative of a strong trend in Islamic legal thought."[40] To demonstrate this tendency toward formalism Arabi quotes from Shāfiʿī's *Kitāb al-umm*:

> No contract is nullified except due to its own terms ... Sale contracts are not nullified on grounds of pretext or evil intention (*nīyat sūʾ*) .... Thus if a man buys a sword intending to kill with it, the sale is permissible; though the intention is not admissible, it does not invalidate the sale .... The Book, followed by the Sunna and the general judgment of Islam, all indicate that contracts have legal effect according to their manifest content and are not invalidated by the intention of the parties.[41]

Shāfiʿī provides further explanation, which Arabi calls "the strongest statement in this sense":

> The principle I follow is that any contract which is valid in appearance, I do not nullify (*anna kull ʿaqd kana ṣaḥīḥan fīʾl-ẓāhir lam ubṭilhu*) on grounds of suspecting the parties: I validate it by the validity of its appearance; I take their intention to be reprehensible (*akrah lahumā al-nīya*) if—*were it made explicit*—that intention would invalidate the sale. Thus I reprehend the purchase of the sword by the man if he plans to kill with it. Yet its sale by the vendor to the man who kills unjustly with it is not prohibited, for he might not kill with it; consequently, I do not invalidate the sale. Similarly I reprehend the sale of grapes by the vendor to a person whom he sees is making wine from it; but I do not void the sale of the grapes, because they were sold legally (*ḥalālan*). Just as the buyer of the sword might not kill anybody with it, so the buyer of the grapes might not make wine.[42]

---

[38] According to Arabi, within contract law, "Sanhūrī discerns an inverse proportion between the centrality of subjective cause and formalism in legal systems" (ibid., 206); that is, as jurists pay more attention to intentions, they reduce their emphasis on formal aspects of the contract, such as the precise wording of it.

[39] This insight is built on the work of Linant de Bellefonds; see Arabi, "Intention and Method," 220, including n. 58.

[40] Arabi, "Intention and Method," 209.

[41] Shāfiʿī, *Kitāb al-umm* (Cairo: n.p., 1325 H), 7:270; in Arabi, "Intention and Method," 209–210.

[42] Shāfiʿī, *Kitāb al-umm*, 3:65; in Sanhūrī, *Maṣādir*, 4:57–58; in Arabi, "Intention and Method," 212, italics added by Arabi.

Only if explicitly mentioned in the contract does an illicit intent invalidate the contract. Otherwise, while such intentions are 'reprehensible' (*makrūh*), they do not invalidate the sale.[43] Knowledge of the possibility, or even probability, that the buyer has illicit plans does not invalidate the contract; context and norms, such conducting the sale in front of a distillery, do not come into play. In short, for Shāfiʿī subjective states have no effect unless made overt.[44]

This formalistic view emphasizes immediate intentions-in-action over more distant complex prior intentions—Shāfiʿī is quick to assert that the buyer may not act on these complex intentions. Legal and moral responsibility for subsequent actions is placed on the buyer alone, and the seller is released from responsibility to inquire into motives or to consider the possible outcomes—even the likely normal outcomes—of a given transaction. Further, this view treats the sale as a series of discrete steps, each having only limited connection to the others, and treats temporal sequence as crucial: in other words, a given step in the process is insulated from later steps, so that an illegal result does not reach back to affect earlier actions. The legally relevant intentions are the immediate intentions-in-action that constitute the discrete, explicit, and objectively legal actions of the sale. Shāfiʿī compresses the accordion of complex intentional effects of an act, considering only a narrow set of such effects.

While Sanhūrī groups Ḥanafī law with that of the Shāfiʿīs in this regard, within Ḥanafī law he sees two divergent "modes of legal efficacy of the subjective cause," which hinge on the degree of explicitness: either the subjective intent is explicit, and thus affects the validity of the contract, or it is implicit, in which case there is a difference of opinion among Ḥanafīs.[45] Regarding the first issue, Sanhūrī cites an example from the Ḥanafī Kasani and asserts that a transaction is invalid if it has a declared purpose which is illicit: "The hiring (*ijārah*) of concubines for fornication (*zinā*) is not permissible as it is a hiring for disobedience

[43] Note the similarity to the Shāfiʿī Ibn Naqīb's notion of 'extrinsic unlawfulness' (at least as interpreted by his commentator), discussed above.

[44] Sanhūrī's point is that Ḥanafīs and Shāfiʿīs both generally favor formalism, ignoring the ulterior motive if it is not explicit, even if it is quite obvious (Arabi, "Intention and Method," 215). As further evidence of this characterization, Sanhūrī observes that Ḥanafīs and Shāfiʿīs tend to allow both *ʿīna* sale, a loophole allowing the collection of interest, and the marriage contract of *taḥlīl*, a loophole allowing remarriage after triple divorce (see 219–220). Both are cases where the formal requirements of the law are met, and even though the parties' intentions are illicit, the transactions are valid.

[45] Ibid., 212.

(*maʿṣīya*) of the law."[46] Sanhūrī presents this as a case where "the contracting party expressly indicates his motive for concluding the transaction." Kāsānī indicates that such a sale is altogether "null and void." This coheres with the Shāfiʿī position that *explicit* expression of intent can invalidate a transaction.

However, in the case of a non-explicit illicit motive, Sanhūrī sees a split among Ḥanafīs, a split hinging on conflicting views of the relevance of indirect evidence such as context and norms. The case Sanhūrī considers is that of the sale of items generally deemed to have no licit purpose. Some such items, like pork, are explicitly prohibited by the Qurʾān and *sunna*, while others are not—for example, monkeys and musical instruments, problematic because their main function is entertainment—leading to questions regarding their status as objects of licit exchange (*māl*). Abū Ḥanīfa, like Shāfiʿī, is reported to have allowed the sale of such items "as long as the contracting party is silent about the use to which he intends to put them," while the influential Ḥanafīs Abū Yūsuf and Muḥammad al-Shaybānī held that, as Arabi puts it, "as the dominant intent behind such transactions is unlawful in the majority of cases," such a contract is invalid.[47] This latter position weighs context and norms when assessing a contract, at least to the point of invalidating the sale of objects normally used for illicit ends. Thus, this line of Ḥanafī thought shades into the 'Mālikī/Ḥanbalī' position of 'subjectivism'. However, even Abū Yūsuf and Muḥammad al-Shaybānī favor formalism when the objects of sale are normally subject to a range of uses that readily includes legal ones, as is the case with grapes.

In contrast, Sanhūrī asserts that the Ḥanbalī and Mālikī schools typically approach intentions differently from the Ḥanafī and Shāfiʿī schools. The former pair place emphasis on recognition of 'dominant intent' and tend to hold a contractor responsible for the other party's illegal motive.[48] This position has much stronger tones of moralism, holding both contracting parties responsible for the wider effects of a transaction and holding each party at least partly responsible for the actions of the other. As Arabi observes, paraphrasing Sanhūrī,

---

[46] Kāsānī, *Kitāb badāʾiʿ al-ṣanāʾiʿ*, 4:190 and 5:169; in Sanhūrī, *Maṣādir*, 4:59; in Arabi, "Intention and Method," 213.

[47] Arabi, "Intention and Method," 213–214.

[48] Ibid., 217; Ḥanbalīs, for example, do not allow *ʿīna* or marriage contracts of *taḥlīl* (219).

> Ḥanbalī jurisprudence erects subjectivist constraints which parallel the scruples of the medieval Church-jurists who were the precursors of modern French law: their shared concern is for the spiritual purity of the individual as measured by the extent of his submission to the edicts of Divine Law.[49]

Ibn Qayyim al-Jawziyya (a Ḥanbalī, d. 1350) holds that a commercial transaction hinges on the participants' intentions:

> Should the law take into account only the manifest meaning of expressions and contracts even when the purposes and intents (*al-maqāṣid wa'l-nīyāt*) appear to be otherwise? Or do aims and intentions (*al-quṣūd wa'l-nīyāt*) have an effect which requires paying attention to them and taking them into consideration? The evidence of the Law (*adillat al-sharʿ*) and its rules concur that intentions in contracts do count and that they affect the validity and invalidity of the contract (*annahā tu'aththir fī ṣiḥḥat al-ʿaqd wa-fasādih*), determining whether the contract is legal or illegal.[50]

Arabi observes that according to this view, "two transactions with the same formal terms but with opposite intents cannot enjoy equal juridical status."[51] As Ibn Qayyim asserts:

> Thus if a man buys a slave-girl intending that she be for his employer, then she is legally forbidden for the buyer; whereas if he buys her for himself, then she is permissible for him. Though the form of the act and the contract (*ṣūrat al-fiʿl wa'l-ʿaqd*) is the same in both cases, the intent and aim (*al-nīya wa'l-qaṣd*) are distinct .... Also if one sells a weapon to someone whom he knows will use it to kill a Muslim; then the sale is forbidden and invalid as it promotes crime and aggression; however the sale is valid if he sells the weapon to someone engaged in holy war in God's way.[52]

Here the knowledge of the seller and the norms of the circumstances under which the sale takes place are both taken into account as factors in the validity of the sale: if either indicates that the buyer intends illicit ends, the transaction is invalid.[53] The transaction effectively hinges on the seller's knowledge, perceptions, and expectations regarding the

---

49 Ibid., 217.

50 Ibn Qayyim al-Jawziyya, *Iʿlām al-muwaqqiʿīn ʿan rabb al-ʿālamīn* (Cairo, al-Munīriyya, n.d.), 3:96–98; in Arabi, "Intention and Method," 218.

51 Arabi, "Intention and Method," 218.

52 Ibn Qayyim al-Jawziyya, 3:96–98, in Arabi, "Intention and Method," 218.

53 However, Ibn Qayyim apparently does not make the seller retroactively responsible for the buyer's actions. Presumably, when selling a sword to someone engaged in holy war, if the buyer proceeded to kill a Muslim, the seller would not be responsible and the sale would remain valid because the seller acted in good faith, even if in fact the buyer used the context to shield his true illicit motives.

buyer's intentions. Note, however, that those intentions do not have a 'magical' effect on the seller, for he is obliged only to pay attention to objective indications of relevant norms and context.

The Ḥanbalī Ibn Qudāma provides further evidence of this tendency away from formalism toward subjectivism:

> The sale of grape juice to someone whom the vendor is aware is making wine from it is null and void (*bāṭil*) ... The sale is prohibited and nullified if the vendor knows the intention of the buyer ... to make wine, whether from the buyer's declaration or from specific signs indicating this.[54]

Here again a sale transacted with illicit intentions is invalid. Again, the decisive issue is the seller's knowledge of the buyer's illicit intention, garnered either through explicit declaration or "specific signs indicating this," presumably the objective, if circumstantial, evidence of norms and circumstances. Thus, while this Mālikī/Ḥanbalī position gives greater weight to intentions, the legal status of the transactions still effectively rests on objective criteria rather than some 'magical' effect of purely subjective intention. Arabi points toward the wider significance of this description:

> The Ḥanbalīs [and Mālikīs] ... represent the close association between pietist ethical and properly legal considerations in Islamic law. Ḥanbalī jurists ... are not satisfied with mere moral responsibility upon knowledge of unlawful ends to be achieved by seemingly legal means. Ḥanbalī law readily transforms moral condemnation into a legal interdiction which implicates the driving motive of both parties within the law [and] ... deduces legal consequences from the intentional stand of the parties irrespective of whether this stand finds expression in the terms of the contract or not.[55]

The tendency to emphasize intentions in contract law corresponds, in other words, to a tendency to view of Islamic law not in narrowly legal terms, but in broadly moral ones. While Arabi does not pursue the implications of this observation, one of them seems obvious: the position attributed to the Ḥanafī/Shāfiʿī group, in contrast, views Islamic law less as a broad moral discourse and more as a specific set of rules whose scope is largely limited to assessing the immediate form and impact of Muslims' acts. This latter position also corresponds, as seen

[54] Ibn Qudāma, *al-Mughnī* (Cairo: n.p., 1341–1348 H), 4:283–284; in Sanhūrī, *Maṣādir*, 4:78–79; in Arabi, "Intention and Method," 219.

[55] Arabi, "Intention and Method," 221.

above, to a tendency to break actions into their constituent elements, isolating the intentions behind each element from the others and from any wider potential consequences. In contrast, the Ḥanbalī/Mālikī position tends to treat actions not only as cohesive units in themselves, but also as immediately connected to their wider impact.

If, as it appears, Sanhūrī is correct in finding a *madhhab* split, or at least in identifying two general positions on intentions is sales—whether or not these fully correspond to his *madhhab* characterizations—this suggests a divergence in understanding the very nature and role of the law. The putative formalist Shāfiʿī/Ḥanafī position presents the transaction in terms of immediate intentions-in-action, preserving the contract in spite of wider implications and prior intentions. The responsibility for any illicit ends is left to rest on the buyer.[56] In contrast, the subjectivist Mālikī/Ḥanbalī position emphasizes the moral aspects of the transaction, its potential to enmesh the parties in illegal and immoral acts. This position pushes the seller to ascertain the motives and intent of the buyer, and perhaps vice versa, holding her or him responsible for the wider ends furthered through the transaction, and to pay attention to context and norms. In the former case, the law appears as a dispassionate set of regulations, while in the latter case the law appears as a sweeping moral vision, a rhetorical discourse admonishing the adherent to seek moral perfection.

For his part, Sanhūrī's ultimate goal was not just a study of premodern Muslim approaches to intent in contracts. He was seeking "to elaborate a 'theory of cause in Islamic law' that will be in harmony with the concepts of modern French jurisprudence, the backbone of much of his and Egypt's modern judicial experience." To this end, he sought to displace Ḥanafī law, with its minimization of motive as a factor in contracts, with the approaches taken by Ḥanbalīs and Mālikīs, where he perceived "a more complex reality of interrelation between ritual law and the law of contract," which I take to mean a more consistent emphasis on the importance of intent in the constitution of actions.[57] Whatever Sanhūrī's goal here, it seems to me that such a substitution

---

[56] Presumably, the roles of buyer and seller could be reversed if the seller were transacting a legal sale and using the proceeds for illicit ends, for example. Jurists do not explicitly consider this possibility, however. As with some aspects of the treatment of *niyya* in *fiqh al-ʿibādāt*, some jurists seem to employ a rhetorical strategy by which concerns for the legal effects of intentions also express concerns for the moral qualities of actions.

[57] Arabi, "Intention and Method," 202.

would have the general effect of restricting freedom of contract, not enhancing it. That is, the Ḥanafī position can be read as offering maximum leeway to contracting parties by insisting on merely formal propriety, while the contrasting approach would force the evaluation of contracts based on a much wider range of factors.

Conclusion

In Islamic contract law, intentions come into play primarily in terms of performative utterances. When they consider the intent of a speech act, the jurists assess the intent of the speaker on two levels, that of basic sincerity and that of complexity or the wider ends he or she intends to achieve with a given speech act. In terms of basic sincerity, a central argument developed in this chapter is that, in civil law, Islamic legal texts tend to treat speech acts as being of three types: (1) clear, explicit, and unambiguous; (2) allusive or metaphorical, yet generally clear in meaning; or, (3) ambiguous to the point of not being clear in meaning. The jurists consistently treat intentions as a crucial factor only in category (2); speech acts of the first type are legally binding regardless of intention, so that one might say that 'what you say is what you get', while speech acts of the third type are too ambiguous to have legally binding effects. Speech acts of the second type, however, are presented as defined by intentions—the words themselves have the potential to be legally valid performative utterances, but they also have the potential not to be such, and it is the intention of the speaker that determines into which category they fall.

Comparing ritual to contract law, it is clear that the language of intent and subjective states is significantly less technical in the latter than in the former. In ritual law, the term *niyya* is nearly the exclusive term used for intentions, and further, the term has numerous technical connotations. *Niyya* is a necessary part of the ritual itself—what one does with the mind while one moves the body in the requisite ways. In civil law, *niyya* is still a common referent for intentions, but here it is intermixed rather freely with other terms, especially *irāda* and *qaṣd*. Throughout the *mu'āmalāt*, the jurists are concerned with intention as that which determines the meaning and legal status of speech, especially ambiguous speech.

As for the treatment of intentions in contracts, Johansen's approach to intentions in contracts of sale, combined with Schacht's complementary view of the potential for reference to intentions to create legal loopholes, offers a partial explanation in sociological terms. On this view, jurists strategically emphasize or deemphasize intentions (basic sincerity) in the service of both individual autonomy on the one hand, and social stability on the other. Allowing parties to disclaim a contract based on subjective states provides a measure of room to maneuver within the legal system, to 'evade the resulting obligation' of an ill-considered or regretted speech act. Sanhūrī's and Arabi's *madhhab* typology offers an additional or alternative theory, that specific rulings on issues of complex intent in Islamic contract law reflects wider views of the very nature of Islamic law. We have also seen evidence of Messick's "foundationalism" in the tendency of some jurists to treat intent as decisive in contracts, as well as evidence of the tension he highlights in the jurists' approaches to interpreting intentions through outward indicants. Full assessment of these arguments will have to wait until the next chapter, where we will explore their value in illuminating the role of intent in the 'social transactions' and 'symbolic exchange' of Islamic personal status or family law.

CHAPTER FIVE

INTENT IN ISLAMIC PERSONAL STATUS LAW

Introduction

In addition to sales contracts, *fiqh al-muʿāmalāt* includes rules of marriage, divorce, and inheritance, which together have come to be known as family law or the law of personal status (*al-aḥwāl al-shakhṣiyya*). In many present Muslim states, this is one of the few areas in which classical Islamic law is routinely applied. In Jordan, for example, most legal matters are governed by a secular legal code derived from that of the European colonizers, but personal status is governed by Islamic religious law. Students studying law at the University of Jordan take most of their courses from the faculty of secular law (*kulliyyat al-qānūn*), but study personal status law with the faculty of Islamic law (*kulliyyat al-sharīʿa*). Personal status law has remained in force despite the pressures of colonialism and modernization, in part because of the relative explicitness of the Qurʾān on matters of marriage, divorce, and inheritance, and because the intensely personal and communal nature of these issues makes them too ingrained to be easily put aside. Enforcing these rules may also aid governments who wish to appear properly pious.

Marriage and divorce, like sales, hinge on performative utterances, and may be analyzed according to the three-fold distinction developed in the previous chapter—speech types 1, 2, and 3. In marriage law jurists systematically discount the role of intentions, insisting on certain verbal formulas which are valid and binding regardless of intent. Only explicit (*ṣarīḥ*, type 1—valid and binding regardless of intent) speech is allowed, and allusive (*kināya*) speech, regardless of intention, cannot form the basis of a valid marriage. Johansen's sociological view of contracts helps clarify this situation by suggesting that marriage relations implicate a wide range of social ties and thus must be treated formalistically for maximum stability. As in contracts of sale, Johansen's approach meshes with that of Schacht, who observes that reference to intentions in a transaction creates loopholes that allow a party to renege based on claims about subjective states. Such loopholes are not allowed in marriage.

The role of intentions in divorce law is decidedly more complex than in marriage. In the case of unilateral repudiatory divorce (*ṭalāq*), jurists consider a wide range of potential verbal expressions, and generally allow not only fully explicit (*ṣarīḥ*), type 1 speech, but also allusive (*kināya*) type 2 speech if the intention of the speaker is to effect a divorce. Jurists casuistically distinguish among phrases that fit either of these categories, or fall into the third category of phrases too ambiguous to count regardless of intentions. Further, *ṭalāq* may be pronounced multiple times with varying effects, and intentions may affect the number of *ṭalāq*s enacted by a given pronouncement. Thus, divorce law at times ignores intent and at other times treats it as determinative either of validity or number, or both. Schacht, Johansen, and Messick all overlook this double aspect of intent in divorce, that is, that intention can determine both whether a *kināya* pronouncement is sincerely meant to enact *ṭalāq*, on the one hand, and the number of *ṭalāq*s a valid pronouncement enacts, on the other.

Inheritance law is less amenable to the kind of analysis useful for marriage and divorce because speech acts play a less determinative role here. In defining bequests and inheritance, jurists modify the normally liberal rules of sales and gifts, insisting that a dying person follow the quranically prescribed rules for devolving property after death. However, while the law may appear to hinge on the intentions of the dying person—an intention, say, to give all of one's property to a single child or business partner rather than parcel it out in accord with the legal rules—the jurists actually treat this situation formalistically. That is, they ignore intent while measuring actions by such criteria as prevailing norms and expectations regarding a given illness and the amount of time spent ill. Any illness normally expected to cause death has the legal effect of invalidating transactions for a period of time (usually one year) prior to death. The intent of a person to follow or flout the law is, theoretically, completely subordinated to the objective facts of the case, such as the type of illness or the timing of any transactions.

Part 1. *Marriage*

Marriage (*nikāḥ*) is generally considered a *sunna* act, at the least permitted, often preferred, and sometimes even called a duty.[1] In legal terms, marriage is a contractual commitment that binds parties to certain rights and obligations, including mutual sexual access and fidelity. For women, marriage precludes marriage to other men, while for men it precludes marriage to more than three other women.[2] *Fiqh* manuals discuss a great number of additional details, such as degrees of blood and legal relation that preclude marriage, details of the *mahr* (bridal price), and rules of comportment within a marriage.[3] The marriage contract hinges on the verbal recital of the contract—a performative speech act that brings the marriage contract into effect or, as Mūṣilī puts it, "the basis [of marriage] is offer of contract and acceptance of it."[4] The contract involves no necessary written document. A *mukallaf* man contracts on his own behalf, while jurists debate the necessity of a *mukallaf* male Muslim to serve as a guardian or agent (*walī*) for a woman.[5] All major jurists agree that the verbal exchange constituting

[1] Ibn Rushd reports that "A group [of jurists] says that marriage is recommended (*mandūb*), and these are the majority. The Ẓāhirīs say that it is obligatory. The later Mālikīs hold that for some it is obligatory, for others recommended, and for the rest it is permitted (*mubāḥ*). This depends on the extent to which an individual fears falling into evil" (*Bidāyat al-mujtahid*, 2:2; *DJP*, 2:1). That is, if one fears that he or she might be tempted to act illegally (e.g., to fornicate) outside of marriage, some say marriage becomes an obligation. Mūṣilī offers the following definition: "*nikāḥ* is a state of temperance (*i'tidāl*), a confirmed and desired *sunna*, and it should be [undertaken] in a state of desire, for [marriage undertaken] in fear of harm is detestable (*makrūh*)" (*al-Ikhtiyār*, 3:82).

[2] See J. Schacht, "Nikāḥ," in *Encyclopaedia of Islam*, new ed.

[3] The wife is entitled to material support (e.g., food, shelter, and clothing) commensurate with women of comparable social and economic status (See, e.g., Ibn Rushd, *Bidāyat al-mujtahid*, 2:51–52; *DJP*, 2:60–61). A marriage payment, usually called a *mahr*, is paid by the husband to the wife. The *mahr* is accepted by the woman as part of the marriage contract, and becomes her property. It is generally held that a divorce prior to consummation of the marriage leads to a return of half the *mahr*; in divorce after consummation nothing is returned. His property does not become jointly owned; with the exception of the *mahr*, the husband is the legal owner of the property, but is obligated to support his wife "in a style befitting her position" (Schacht, "Nikāḥ"). The *mahr* is a gift, not a purchase price, for, as Johansen notes, "according to the Hanafite jurists, a free person can never become the object of commercial exchange" ("Valorization," 74).

[4] Mūṣilī, *al-Ikhtiyār*, 3:82.

[5] On these debates, see Ibn Rushd, *Bidāyat al-mujtahid*, 2:8–17; *DJP*, 2:9–19. See also Schacht, "Nikāḥ."

the marriage contract must be witnessed by at least two *mukallaf* male witnesses.[6]

Fiqh texts display a marked tendency toward formalism regarding marriage, as intentions play virtually no role in determining the validity or meaning of a marriage contract. Muslim jurists do not discuss the potential complexity of intentions in the context of marriage. Marriage is a binary matter—either a speech act produces a marriage, or it does not. The details of the marriage, such as the *mahr* or the living arrangements, are all worked out explicitly but are not mentioned during the verbal exchange that enacts the marriage. Thus the 'accordion effect' of complex intentional action does not come into play.

Matters are slightly more complicated in terms of the intention issues of explicitness and basic sincerity. Jurists envision marriage as enacted by type 1, explicit and inherently binding, speech acts. They unanimously agree that a marriage contract is valid if it employs some form of the terms *nikāḥ* (marriage, also used as a term for conjugal intercourse) or *tazwīj* (lit., joining two things together), the two most common and direct terms for marriage. If the offer and acceptance explicitly employ these terms, without adding other elements that create ambiguity, the contract is unquestionably valid and binding. This form of marriage contract is deemed *ẓāhir* (manifest) or, more commonly, *ṣarīḥ* (explicit). In such cases, jurists largely disregard issues of intent, taking into consideration only the explicit wording, so that 'what you say is what you get'.

In arriving at this strict formalism—and at times slightly mitigating it—jurists consider four possible general circumstances in which intentions might matter for *ṣarīḥ* marriage contracts: (1) coercion; (2) indirect, silent, or non-verbal expression of consent; (3) jest; and (4) intoxication. Regarding coercion, many jurists agree that both parties must consent to the marriage and cannot be coerced,[7] although many Ḥanafīs as well as the Ḥanbalī Ibn Qudāma hold that even coercion

[6] As Ibn Rushd observes, "[Jurists] agree that a secret marriage is not valid" (*Bidāyat al-mujtahid*, 2:17; *DJP*, 2:19). Ibn Qudāma quotes a *ḥadīth* which holds that "every betrothal (*khuṭba*) without a witness is like the hand of a leper" (*al-Mughnī*, 9:464–465).

[7] An underage girl may be given in marriage by her father, not necessarily having obtained her consent. See, for example, Spectorsky, *Marriage and Divorce*, 92–93, citing Aḥmad Ibn Ḥanbal's (d. 241/855) opinion that a girl under seven can be married off by her father (but not any other agent) without her permission, but after age nine she must be consulted, even by her father. Note that this leaves unclear what to do with an eight-year-old.

does not mitigate a formally valid marriage contract.[8] Jurists also disagree as to which objective actions signal consent. Regarding indirect, silent, or non-verbal expression of consent, a non-virgin (widowed or divorced) woman must give explicit consent, but a virgin is deemed by some to consent by silence.[9] Laughter or crying (or, presumably, nodding or signaling with the hands) may also be deemed consent, especially if these are seen as typical ways a given women indicates her assent.[10] A non-virgin is generally allowed to contract her own marriage, and Ibn Qudāma remarks that he knows of no disagreement regarding the position that she must consent explicitly through words, "for the tongue is the bridge to what is in the heart."[11] In this regard, at least, basic sincerity theoretically matters to most—save many Ḥanafīs and Ibn Qudāma—but this is effectively the only situation in which intentions matter in marriage contracts.

The ruling on jest in a marriage contract is apparently universal: an explicit expression of marriage, even in jest, is valid and binding. The proof text is an oft-cited *ḥadīth*: "There are three things in which joking is treated as earnestness, and earnestness is taken as earnestness: divorce (*ṭalāq*), marriage (*nikāḥ*), and revocation of divorce (*raj'a*)."[12] In short, the speech act of a marriage contract is unaffected by an intent to jest, and a joke is simply assessed terms of explicitness, like any other statement of marriage. Of course, one can imagine both parties deciding not to pursue a marriage under such circumstances, but the legal texts envision adherence to the *ḥadīth*. This is consistent with wider views of a marriage contract—if formally sound, it is valid and binding, regardless of intent, and jest is simply a subset of intent.

Jurists disagree about a marriage contracted while intoxicated. As with jest, intoxication generally is treated as irrelevant. However, some

---

[8] On the Ḥanafī position, see Johansen, "Valorization," 74. Ibn Qudāma says "a marriage contracted in jest or under coercion (*talji'a*) is valid" (*al-Mughnī*, 9:463).

[9] Ibn Rushd, *Bidāyat al-mujtahid*, 2:4; *DJP*, 2:3; and Schacht, "Nikāḥ."

[10] Spectorsky notes that this approach to the consent of a virgin is taken because "she is presumed to be shy" (*Marriage and Divorce*, 9).

[11] Ibn Qudāma, *al-Mughnī*, 9:407–408. Note that this principle is not consistently applied outside of marriage. Here Ibn Qudāma implies that objective acts are direct indicants of intentions, but this is often not assumed to be the case, as in divorce law, as will be seen below.

[12] Ibid., 9:463. There are several variants of this *ḥadīth*, including another cited by Ibn Qudāma: "A marriage, divorce, or emancipation done playfully is binding." Ibn Qudāma, as previously noted, here also says "a marriage contracted in jest or under coercion (*talji'a*) is valid."

analogize intoxication to insanity, and thus treat it as a loss of *compos mentis* and the accompanying ability to enter a valid contract. Mālik considers marriage and sales contracted while intoxicated to be invalid, but holds the intoxicated person liable for divorce, manumission, and injuries or homicide; Abū Ḥanīfa holds the intoxicated person liable for all acts, though some of his followers disagree.[13] Others deem the speech of an intoxicated person void, but hold him liable for physical actions.[14] Similar disagreements arise over a divorce pronounced under the influence, as we will see below.

Jurists debate the use of terms other than *nikāḥ* and *tazwīj*. The Ḥanafī Mūṣilī, for example, considers the contract valid if it employs not only the terms *nikāḥ* or *tazwīj*, but also *hiba* (gift), *ṣadaqa* (giving, donating), *tamlīk* (ownership, control), *bay'* (sale), or *shirā'* (purchase).[15] Mūṣilī makes no mention of *niyya* or any other terms for subjective states, but simply expands the sphere of type 1 pronunciations of marriage. In general, Mālikīs and Ḥanafīs allow the terms *hiba*, *bay'*, and *ṣadaqa*, while Shāfi'īs insist on using *nikāḥ* or *tazwīj*.[16]

---

[13] Ibn Rushd, *Bidāyat al-mujtahid*, 2:82; *DJP*, 2:98.

[14] Ibid. According to Ibn Rushd, "The reason for their disagreement is whether the *ḥukm* (assessment) is the *ḥukm* of the insane, or there is a difference between [the intoxicated and the insane]. Those who hold that [the intoxicated] and the insane are similar, for both have lost their senses, and the condition of liability is sanity (*'aql*), say that [the pronouncement of divorce of the intoxicated one] does not come into effect. Those who hold that there is a difference between them because the intoxicated person had muddled his senses by his own volition, in contrast to the insane person, say that [the divorce] is effective." Note that the *DJP* translation mistakenly inserts the word "not" into the second case, wrongly implying that the divorce of the intoxicated person who "has muddled his senses by his own volition" is also not effective.

[15] Mūṣilī, *al-Ikhtiyār*, 3:83; he does not allow terms of 'rent' (*ijāra*).

[16] Ibn Rushd, *Bidāyat al-mujtahid*, 2:4; *DJP*, 2:3. Ibn Rushd observes rather obscurely that "The reason for their disagreement lies in whether [marriage] is a contract in which, along with intention (*niyya*), a particular word is required, or whether the employment of such a word is not necessary for its validity. Those who attach it to the category of contracts that require the consideration of both factors [i.e., word and intent] say that a marriage cannot be contracted except by [explicit] use of the terms *nikāḥ* or *tazwīj*. Those who say [particular] words are not a condition of [a marriage contract], in keeping with contracts in which [particular] words are not a condition, permit marriage by means of any word that renders the legal meaning (*ma'nā*); that is, if the word and the legal meaning are consonant." Here Ibn Rushd seems to attach *niyya* to all marriage contracts, whether they use the two explicit terms or a narrow range of terms deemed by some to have the same effect, the 'legal meaning' of a marriage contract. This seems to treat *niyya* as the basic sincerity of the speech act. However, the texts I have consulted do not employ *niyya* in this manner, that is, as a requisite of all marriage contracts.

Ibn Qudāma asserts that "if the *khāṭib* (male person seeking betrothal) says to the *walī* (the agent of the woman) 'do you marry?' (*a-zawwajta*) and he replies 'yes' and he says to the husband 'do you accept' and he replies 'yes', then the marriage is contracted if there are two witnesses present." However, Shāfiʿī insists on more explicit wording than just 'yes'—the *walī* must say "I marry you to my daughter (*zawwajtuka ibnatī*)" and the man must reply "I accept this marriage (*qabiltu hadhā al-tazwīj*) because these two [statements] are the two fundamental features (*arkān*) of the contract and there is no contract without them."[17] According to Ibn Qudāma, Shāfiʿī insists on explicit use of the terms *nikāḥ* or *tazwīj* in both the offer and the acceptance "because this would [otherwise] be *kināya* in marriage involving *niyya* and hidden ideas (*al-iḍmār*), and the contract cannot be based on these, just as [it cannot be based on] expressions of 'gifts' or 'sales'." In short, Shāfiʿī defines simply saying 'yes' as type 2 speech, and insists that the marriage contract must be type 1. Ibn Qudāma says that when someone simply answers 'yes' to a direct and explicit question it is binding. This is not a disagreement about the necessity of type 1 speech, but about what qualifies as such.

In support of this kind of formalism, Ibn Qudāma cites a Qurʾān passage, 33:50: "O Prophet, We have made lawful to thee … any believing woman who offers herself to the Prophet if he wishes to wed her—this is limited to thee, and not for the believers."[18] Ibn Qudāma takes this as proof that a marriage contract without the words *nikāḥ* or *tazwīj* is only allowed for the Prophet.[19] Ibn Qudāma gives the following noteworthy explanation: "This is because witnessing is required for a marriage, and indirect expressions (*al-kināya*) are made known [or 'made effective'[20]] by *niyya* and *it is not possible to witness the niyya, for [the witnesses] lack access to it* (*liʿadam iṭṭilāʿihim ʿalayhā*), so this is necessarily not a [valid] contract—and in this it is different than all other contracts and from divorce."[21] That is, *kināya* expressions cannot enact a marriage

[17] Ibn Qudāma, *al-Mughnī*, 9:459–460.

[18] Ibid., 9:460.

[19] Thus one cannot contract a marriage this way, with such terms as 'hire' (*al-ijāra*), 'permission' (*al-ibāḥa*), or 'lawfulness' (*al-iḥlāl*), because these are not explicit (*bi-ṣarīḥ*) [references to] marriage, so it is not possible to contract by them. Ibid., 9:460–461.

[20] The edition used reads *tuʿlamu*, but the editor notes that two manuscripts here read *taʿmalu*, which in my opinion is probably correct (9:461, n. 15).

[21] Ibid., 9:461, emphasis added.

because they depend on *niyya*, and *niyya* cannot be known by the witnesses who validate the marriage. On this view, the requirement of witnesses to the contract necessitates the formalism characteristic of marriage law.

In sum, jurists consistently exhibit a relatively strict formalism regarding marriage contracts. Only explicit, direct (type 1) expressions are allowed, though the jurists disagree over the exact boundaries of this category. The basic sincerity of the pronouncement does not matter, nor does any element of complexity. Ibn Qudāma gives one possible explanation for this formalism, namely that, because it cannot be confirmed by witnesses, intent (*niyya*) cannot be a part of a marriage contract. Alternatively, Johansen, as noted above, suggests that this formalism emerges because contracts of social exchange implicate social ranking by classifying "people into those whom one can marry and those whom one cannot" and thus imply "a high social risk of rupture and conflict, because the refusal of a demand in marriage … indicates negative ranking and classification."[22] In short, "the subject matter is much too explosive and the risk of frustration and strife too important to leave the parties the same range of maneuvering that they enjoy in commercial exchange."[23] In social exchange, then, too much is at stake to include objectively non-verifiable matters such as intentions, because such loopholes could threaten the marriage and the social order. Whether this sociological theory fully explains the jurists' motives is beyond the scope of our inquiry, but it seems to be at least plausible. It accurately predicts a deemphasizing of intent in marriage law, and nothing in the legal texts proves the theory false. We will have more to say on this particular theory below.

Part 2. *Divorce*

A. *Unilateral or Repudiatory Divorce:* Ṭalāq

Many jurists cite a *ḥadīth* to the effect that "the most loathsome of things permitted by God is divorce (*ṭalāq*)."[24] However loathsome, it

---

[22] Johansen, "Valorization," 73.
[23] Ibid.
[24] See, for example, Ibn Qudāma, *al-Mughnī*, 10:324, for two variants of this *ḥadīth*.

is generally agreed that divorce is permitted.[25] Most forms of Islamic divorce hinge on a performative utterance. In contrast to its role in marriage, intent plays a major role in divorce, and as with their general approach to contracts, the jurists assess a divorce pronouncement in terms of both basic sincerity and according to the potential complexity of intentions behind the pronouncement. Jurists treat certain explicit terms as binding regardless of intention, and also allow a relatively wide range of metaphorical or indirect terms if intended as divorce. Further, an expression of divorce may count for more than a single pronouncement if so intended.

Divorce can take a variety of forms, but the most basic and prominent in the texts is called *ṭalāq* (lit. 'release [from marriage]', sometimes translated as 'repudiation'), which itself can take several forms.[26] The husband makes a verbal pronouncement of *ṭalāq* after the wife has finished a menstrual period and before he resumes sexual relations with her. She then begins her *ʿidda*, a waiting period of three menstrual cycles, or three months if she does not menstruate, to establish whether she is pregnant—if she is pregnant, the *ʿidda* ends at delivery. The *ʿidda* also allows opportunity for reconciliation. The husband may revoke most formulations of *ṭalāq* during the *ʿidda*, but if he does not, the couple may reconcile only with a new marriage contract. Certain verbal formulations are considered irrevocable (*bāʾin*), and even if pronounced only once they necessitate a new marriage contract for reconciliation. A couple may divorce and remarry twice, but after a third divorce they can only reconcile after the wife has married and divorced another husband.[27] Similarly, three pronouncements of *ṭalāq* during one *ʿidda* make the divorce irrevocable, and the couple may then reconcile only after her marriage to, and subsequent divorce from, another man. While they often frown on such 'triple *ṭalaq*s', calling them *makrūh* (detestable)

---

[25] See ibid., 10:323; as Ibn Qudāma observes, "*ṭalāq* dissolves the marriage contract, and this is legal (*mashrūʿ*), and the basis (*al-aṣl*) of this legality is the Book [i.e., the Qurʾān], the *sunna*, and consensus."

[26] For a general discussion, see Schacht, *Introduction*, 163–166; and Spectorsky, *Marriage and Divorce*, 27–28.

[27] See Ibn Rushd, *Bidāyat al-mujtahid*, 2:63–64; *DJP*, 2:75–76; and Spectorsky, *Marriage and Divorce*, 27–28. For some reason, one common understanding of Islamic divorce closely resembles that of Denny, who asserts that "The formula 'I divorce you' is uttered three times, the first and second being followed by a prescribed waiting period" (*Introduction*, 279). As noted below, such repetition is allowed, but is not required.

or *ṭalāq al-bid'a* (divorce through innovation), most jurists consider these valid and binding.[28]

Intent matters in *ṭalāq* in two general ways: first, in terms of 'basic sincerity', as certain phrases are binding regardless of intent or sincerity (type 1), while some must have been intended as *ṭalāq* in order to actually be *ṭalāq* (type 2), and all others simply cannot count (type 3). Second, intent matters in terms of 'complexity', or the wider effects of intentional action. The key issue here is the number of *ṭalāq*s effected by a given pronouncement. Although an explicit statement of number is usually binding, the husband's intent can potentially increase the number of *ṭalāq*s effected by a single pronouncement, but can never reduce the 'number effect' of an explicit statement. In short, intent potentially enters into *ṭalāq* by affecting the validity of a type 2 pronouncement, and/or by increasing the 'number effect'. The jurists employ the term *niyya* extensively in discussing divorce, but they also use other terms (e.g., *irāda* and *qaṣd*) more or less synonymously.

Because the exact wording of a pronouncement of *ṭalāq* determines its precise legal effects, *fiqh* discussions of the topic are decidedly casuistic.[29] Susan Spectorsky usefully delineates ten categories of *ṭalāq*, and while not exhaustive or necessarily reflective of the explicit taxonomy used in *fiqh* texts, this helps to clarify the matter. Since I will use it as a framework for my own analysis, I will quote it at length:

> In the first category are those statements that clearly result in divorce, such as statements that include the use of a word with the root letters *ṭ l q*, as well as those that do not include such a word but are treated as unambiguous circumlocutions. In the second category are ambiguous circumlocutions that result in divorce only if the speaker intended them to. Discussion of both of these categories includes the question of whether these statements effect single, double, or triple divorce, and whether the speaker's intention is to be taken into account. The third, fourth, and fifth categories all consist of statements that are treated as oaths, that is, as commitments to future action. A man can be released from an oath either by fulfilling it or by expiating it with a compen-

[28] Ibn Rushd says Abū Ḥanīfa held that *sunna* calls for the husband to make a single pronouncement of repudiation during three successive periods of purity, while refraining from sexual intercourse; Mālik held that *sunna* only calls for a single pronouncement, and additional pronouncements deviate from *sunna* (*Bidāyat al-mujtahid*, 2:63–64; *DJP*, 2:75–76).

[29] Schacht also attributes this casuistry to the fact that "repudiation is a disposition with immediate effect" (*Introduction*, 164). That is, the stakes are high at the moment of the pronouncement, so precision and clarity in establishing the legal taxonomy of various possible forms of expression is needed.

> satory action. In the third category are, for example, conditional statements by means of which divorce is made dependent upon the occurrence of a future event or upon ascertaining whether a certain fact is true. The fourth category consists of general statements such as "Any woman I marry is divorced." In the fifth category are statements including the words "God willing" (i.e., making an exception: *istithnā'* or *thunyā*). Then, sixth, there is silent divorce, when a husband does not utter a divorce aloud but thinks it; and seventh, a divorce statement made under coercion. Category eight contains questions not about the nature of the divorce statement per se but about the status or condition of the husband who makes the statement. Category nine concerns the divorce of the husband who is terminally ill. Category ten addresses the question of whether the sale of a female slave automatically results in her divorce.[30]

Before taking these in order, I will begin with Spectorsky's seventh, eighth, and ninth categories, all of which deal in some way with the "status or condition of the husband who makes the [divorce] statement," his mental capacity and free will. In the first place, the husband must be *mukallaf*, although a minor may be allowed to divorce if deemed sufficiently mature, and a slave has the ability to divorce, but cannot be forced to do so.[31] A divorce pronounced while sleeping has no effect, nor does the divorce of the insane (*majnūn*) or delirious; a deaf or mute person may divorce through indications other than words, provided he is understood.[32] Regarding *ṭalāq* pronounced under intoxication, most jurists hold it binding, as they do with a pronouncement of marriage. For example, Ibn Ḥanbal follows Shāfiʿī in validating the divorce of the intoxicated man.[33] According to Ibn Rushd, most jurists say the intoxicated person's mind is muddled by choice, so his acts are binding; if one is foolish enough to act while drunk, he must face the consequences. Ḥanafīs, however, disagree among themselves, with Abū Ḥanīfa holding the intoxicated liable for all acts, while his disciples liken the intoxicated to the insane and disregard his *ṭalāq*.[34]

As for coercion (Spectorsky's seventh category), most jurists hold *ṭalāq* pronounced under duress invalid, with two exceptions. First, some

[30] Spectorsky, *Marriage and Divorce*, 28–29.

[31] See ibid., 36, 130, 131, 165.

[32] See ibid., 36, 105, 110.

[33] See ibid., 36–37. As seen above in the case of marriage, the disagreement here reflects a disagreement over the legal agency of an intoxicated person. In the case of divorce, Ibn Rāhwayh (d. 238/853) assesses liability according to degree of intoxication (See ibid., 37 [and 37, n. 131], 73–74, 120, 127, 164–165). See also Linant de Bellefonds, *Traité de Droit Musulman Comparé*, 2:344–345.

[34] Ibn Rushd, *Bidāyat al-mujtahid*, 2:82; *DJP*, 2:98.

Shāfiʿīs hold that if the husband is under duress, yet still intends the divorce to be effective, it is.[35] In this view, while words may be coerced, intentions cannot be; the coercion is seen as coincidental to the intended pronouncement, which is held binding. Second, as they do with marriage, some Ḥanafīs profess a strict formalism: coercion has no effect on the pronouncement, which they liken to one made in jest.[36]

Spectorsky's ninth category, divorce by a terminally ill husband, reflects the same situation as a deathbed commercial transaction and its effect on inheritance, as discussed below. As in the case of inheritance law, a terminally ill person faces certain restrictions, especially as his behavior might affect the division of his estate: if deemed terminally ill, his transactions are invalidated. Thus, a dying man is generally not allowed to divorce his wife. Such a divorce is invalid, and if the man dies having done this, his wife still retains her status.[37]

We may now turn to Spectorsky's first category, "statements that clearly result in divorce, such as statements that include the use of a word with the root letters *ṭ l q*, as well as those that do not include such a word but are treated as unambiguous circumlocutions." This category encompasses *ṣarīḥ* speech and, for some jurists, some forms of *kināya* speech.[38] Two intention issues arise here: the basic sincerity of the pronouncement, on the one hand, and the complexity of the

---

[35] Ibid., 2:81; *DJP*, 2:97. See also Spectorsky, *Marriage and Divorce*, 36, n. 129 on coercion. Ibn Rushd observes that "The reason for the disagreement is whether a person under coercion has any choice, for there is no coercion in the pronouncement if the words have been uttered of his own volition. The person coerced does not in fact possess a will for the performance of anything." That is, if he wills it, it is not coerced, by definition, even in a situation that looks like coercion. Ibn Rushd says both sides of the debate rely on the same *ḥadīth*: "Liability is removed from my community for mistake, forgetfulness, and for what they are coerced to do"; he also cites a Qurʾān passage: "... except him who is coerced and whose heart is still content with faith" (16:106). Ibn Rushd's interpretation is that a coerced person should not be held accountable, and that intentions do not matter—his point seems to be that intentions formed under duress are no more reliable than overt actions under duress (2:81–82; *DJP*, 2:97).

[36] Ibn Rushd, *Bidāyat al-mujtahid*, 2:81–82; *DJP*, 2:97; Ibn Rushd adds, "Abū Ḥanīfa differentiates between sales [where coercion invalidates the transaction] and *ṭalāq*, for *ṭalāq* is a solemn matter (*mughallaẓ*), and so jest is equated with seriousness." See also Linant de Bellefonds, *Traité de Droit Musulman Comparé*, 2:342–343.

[37] See Spectorsky, *Marriage and Divorce*, 37 (and 37, n. 132), 220.

[38] Ibn Rushd, *Bidāyat al-mujtahid*, 2:74; *DJP*, 2:88; he makes this distinction for 'unrestricted divorce' (*al-ṭalāq al-muṭlaqa*) and observes that jurists "disagree over the details [of the distinction] between direct and indirect expression, and the legal implications of each."

intention and the wider effect of the intentional action, on the other. In terms of basic sincerity, all pronouncements in Spectorsky's first category are effective regardless of intentions, and they are what I am calling type 1 speech.[39] The key question for this category of *ṭalāq* is simply what words fall into it. Most texts agree that the clearest and least problematic pronouncement is 'I release you' or 'you are released', using forms of the word *ṭalāq*.[40] Again, such a statement is binding regardless of intent.[41] As we will see below, jurists disagree over the role of intent in determining 'number' here, but all agree that, in terms of basic sincerity, intent does not matter for *ṣarīḥ* speech. Most jurists recognize the possibility of using the term *ṭalāq* metaphorically, if the context so indicates. For example, it is not a necessarily *ṭalāq* if a husband releases a wife from physical shackles and says to her 'you are released (*ṭāliq*)'.[42]

Some jurists, especially Mālikīs and Ḥanafīs, "hold that the only *ṣarīḥ* term is *ṭalāq*, and any other expression is *kināya*."[43] However, many jurists add other terms and phrases to this category. Shāfiʿī and some Ẓāhiris count three terms as *ṣarīḥ*: *ṭalāq*, *firāq* (separation), and *sarāḥ* (release), because they are mentioned in the Qurʾān.[44] Shīrāzī says that "if one addresses [his wife] with one of these terms, then says 'I meant (*aradtu*) something other [than *ṭalāq*], but my tongue slipped', this claim

39 Note that Spectorsky's first category does correspond exactly with my type 1, but it does not correspond exactly to *ṣarīḥ*; all *ṣarīḥ* speech fits Spectorsky's first category and my type 1, but so does some *kināya* speech, at least according to some definitions.

40 '*Ṭāliq*', an adjectival form, can only apply to females and thus does not take the usual grammatical feminine marker of *tāʾ marbūṭa* (Spektorsky, *Marriage and Divorce*, 28, n. 99). She cites W. Wright, *A Grammar of the Arabic Language*, 3rd ed. (Cambridge: Cambridge University Press, 1967), 1:187.

41 See, for example, Ibn Rushd, *Bidāyat al-mujtahid*, 2:74–75; *DJP*, 2:88–89; Mūṣilī, *al-Ikhtiyār*, 3:125.

42 Ibn Rushd, *Bidāyat al-mujtahid*, 2:75; *DJP*, 2:89.

43 Ibid., 2:74; *DJP*, 2:88.

44 Ibid. The Ẓāhirīs do not allow any other terms for divorce, only these three mentioned in the Qurʾān. The text continues interestingly: "Those who hold that divorce is not effective except by these three words do so because the *sharʿ* employs only these words, so using them [to enact a *ṭalāq*] is an act of obedience (*ʿibāda*), and the [exact] expression is legally determined [rather than rationally determined]. Thus it is obligatory that such use be confined to the words laid down by the *sharʿ*" (2:74). The *DJP* translation (2:89) is an example of the difficulties caused by translating *ʿibāda* as 'ritual': the translation renders this "their [i.e., the three terms'] use is a kind of predetermined ritual," which garbles the meaning. The translator does, however, helpfully indicate that Ibn Rushd here is distinguishing between revealed and reasoned proofs. That is, the reason these three terms can be used is because the revealed sources so indicate, not because human reason or logic establishes them as legally binding.

is not accepted, for it runs counter to what is manifest." Likewise, if he claims to have meant one of these explicit terms metaphorically, his claim is not accepted, as it runs counter to established usage.[45] Various other phrases are sometimes added to the list of terms considered valid and binding regardless of intent—for example, '*Anti khaliyya*', '*Anti bariyya*' (both meaning 'you [feminine singular] are free'), and '*Anti bā'in*' ('you are separated/cut off')—though it is not always clear why a given phrase has the effect it does.[46] A related issue is the possibility of 'jest' or 'play' in pronouncing *ṭalāq*. Many texts cite a variant of the *ḥadīth* quoted above regarding jest in marriage (i.e., "There are three things in which joking is treated as earnestness ...").[47] Thus, as with jest in marriage, if the pronouncement is formally a *ṣarīḥ* pronouncement of *ṭalāq*, then the fact (or the claim) that it was made in jest or play is of no consequence.[48] When discussing this set of issues, Shīrāzī recognizes a crucial general difficulty, that of reliably assessing intentions based on outward expressions, and he also seems to express some discomfort with the call to disregard intentions for explicit statements of *ṭalāq*. He asserts that, although the court holds a man accountable for the manifest meaning of his expression, God will recognize his true intention (*yudayyanu fīmā baynahu wa-bayna Allāh ta'ālā li-annahu yaḥtamilu mā yud'īhi*).[49] This suggests that Shīrāzī recognizes the assessment of the court to be provisional (a matter I will return to below, in regard to penal law).

[45] Shīrāzī, *al-Muhadhdhab*, 4:292.

[46] The three phrases mentioned are generally seen as effecting a triple divorce with a single pronouncement (see Spectorsky, *Marriage and Divorce*, 30 [and 30, nn. 104–105], 70; Spectorsky notes that Ibn Ḥanbal does not approve of these phrases). Regarding the term *batta* ("cut off"), Ibn Ḥanbal effectively equates this with *khaliyya, bariyya*, and *bā'in* divorces (i.e., triple/final), while Ibn Rāhwayh prefers to ask the husband about his intention regarding the revocability of the pronouncement (ibid., 30 [and see 30–31, n. 107]; "*batta*" figures in several important *ḥadīths* concerning the Companion Rakāna b. 'Abd Yazīd, who reportedly divorced his wife using this term, then was allowed by the Prophet to return to her). Ibn Ḥanbal says the phrase "you have free reign" effects triple divorce regardless of intention. A single *ṭalāq*, regardless of intention, results from "I have no wife," "I make a gift of you to your family" (but if the woman's family does not accept her, the words have no legal effect), and "begin an *'idda*" (which can be repeated three times in a row, and if intended to be a triple divorce, it is) (ibid., 31).

[47] See, for example, Shīrāzī, *al-Muhadhdhab*, 4:293: "There are three things in which earnestness is treated as earnestness, and joking is treated as earnestness: marriage (*nikāḥ*), divorce (*ṭalāq*), and revocation of divorce (*raj'a*)."

[48] See Linant de Bellefonds, *Traité de Droit Musulman Comparé*, 2:341–343.

[49] Shīrāzī, *al-Muhadhdhab*, 4:292. See also Nawawī, 18:239–241.

Interestingly, the prospect of writing—as opposed to speaking—one's pronouncement of *ṭalāq* also raises similar questions. Shīrāzī says of this situation that, "If one writes a *ṭalāq* to his wife using an explicit (*ṣarīḥ*) expression, but does not intend [it to be *ṭalāq*], it is not *ṭalāq*, for writing may be deemed capable of enacting a *ṭalāq* if the handwriting passes examination, but it cannot enact a *ṭalāq* on its own [without *niyya*]." That is, the same terms that when spoken can be effective regardless of intent are only effective when written if accompanied by *niyya*. However, Shīrāzī observes that jurists disagree over a written *ṭalāq* accompanied by *niyya*. Some say writing simply cannot enact a *ṭalāq*, which must be spoken, while for others such a written *ṭalāq* is valid, "because the letters convey the meaning of *ṭalāq*, and so they can enact a *ṭalāq* just like speech."[50] But if one does allow written *ṭalāq*, it must be both *ṣarīḥ* and accompanied by *niyya*. Put differently, written, *ṣarīḥ ṭalāq* is type 2 discourse, not type 1, in an odd instance of explicit discourse being dependent on intent.

Spectorsky's second category encompasses "ambiguous circumlocutions that result in divorce only if the speaker intended them to." This corresponds directly to what I am calling type 2 speech, and largely, though not completely, to what the jurists call *kināyat al-ṭalāq* (allusive expression of *ṭalāq*) The categories diverge in that *kināyat al-ṭalāq* bleeds into type 3 speech, that which is too ambiguous to count regardless of intent. Whereas intent (in terms of basic sincerity) plays no role in type 1 speech, it plays a crucial role here, determining the identity and validity of a given speech act as *ṭalāq* or otherwise. Again, I will address the issue of basic sincerity first, returning below to the issue of complex intentions.

Shīrāzī exemplifies the typical approach to *kināyat al-ṭalāq*. He asserts that a great many words can be used as *kināya* expressions of divorce—in fact, he gives some twenty examples (e.g., *bā'in, khaliyya, bariyya, ḥurra, wāḥida, ab'adī, aghrabī*), and notes that his list is not exhaustive. He observes that each term can "imply *ṭalāq* or not," and explains:

> If the speaker [i.e., the divorcing husband] intends (*nawā*) by [one of these terms] *ṭalāq*, then it is *ṭalāq*, and if one does not intend by it *ṭalāq*, then

[50] Ibid., 4:301. Ibn Naqīb and his commentators make a similar point, 414–415, and see chapter 4, n. 23 above. See also Brinkley Messick, "Indexing the Self," 172–174; Messick's sources confirm Shīrāzī's view that written *ṭalāq* is valid only if so intended, regardless of explicitness. What Messick calls "traceless 'writing'," such as in the air or on water, however, cannot be effective even if supported by intent.

> it is not *ṭalāq*. This is like refraining from food and drink, and whether one has thus undertaken a fast or not; if one intends by this [refraining] a fast, then it is a fast, and if one does not intend a fast, then it is not a fast.[51]

In *kināyat al-ṭalāq*, outwardly identical speech acts are differentiated by intent, and certain phrases enact a *ṭalāq* only if so intended. However, intent cannot make just any phrase into a *kināya* form of divorce, for norms of usage also partly determine the parameters of *kināya* expressions. Shīrāzī asserts that if "the use of [a given] phrase in the context of marriage is not customary (*muta'ārif*), it enacts a *ṭalāq* if there is *niyya* [and if *ṭalāq* is] among the [possible] meanings, and it does not enact *ṭalāq* without *niyya*, as is generally true of *kināya*."[52] There are limits, then, to type 2 speech, and if a word or phrase does not carry sufficient connotations of divorce, intention cannot make it effective as *ṭalāq*. (As we will see below, intent alone, with no verbal expression, cannot enact a *ṭalāq*.[53]) The exact boundaries of type 2 speech remain vague, as custom and context determine the parameters of what can be made, by intention, into a valid pronouncement.

Before continuing with Spectorsky's categories, we must address the issue of complex intentions in the first two categories. For Spectorsky's first category, intent in terms of basic sincerity has no effect on the legal standing of the pronouncement. For Spectorsky's second category the intention for a pronouncement to count as divorce is decisive. In both of these categories, intentions are also potentially complex, especially in terms of number, meaning the number of *ṭalāq*s enacted by a given pronouncement toward the total of three allowed before a marriage is irrevocably terminated. In other words, intent has a dual role in *ṭalāq*, affecting both basic sincerity, and complexity/number, and these roles

---

[51] Shīrāzī, *al-Muhadhdhab*, 4:294–295.

[52] Ibid., 4:295, emphasis added. Additionally, Shīrāzī discusses the timing of *niyya* in *kināyat al-ṭalāq*, noting that jurists disagree over whether the *niyya* must accompany the entire pronouncement, or if instead the *niyya* can be present merely at the start or finish of the pronouncement. Shīrāzī analogizes the situation to that of prayer, and holds that in *kināyat al-ṭalāq*, as in *ṣalāt*, the *niyya* must be present throughout (4:295–296). Here we see a partial return to the technical considerations characteristic of discussions of *niyya* in *fiqh al-'ibādāt*; this is an unusual usage in this sphere, where *niyya* is generally treated in a non-technical manner, interchangeable with other intention terms.

[53] Shīrāzī notes that certain phrases and words do not enact *ṭalāq* regardless of intention, "because these expressions do not convey *ṭalāq*, and if we were to [allow that] these enact *ṭalāq*, we would [allow] enactment of *ṭalāq* by sheer intention [with no verbal expression], and we have already established that *ṭalāq* cannot be enacted by sheer intention" (ibid., 4:296).

are independent of one another. Number can be determined either by the explicit content of the pronouncement, or, in some cases, by the speaker's intention.[54] Shīrāzī states that "if a man addresses his wife with [an explicit] expression of [singular] *ṭalāq* ... while intending (*nawā*) two or three *ṭalāq*s, it is so enacted." He analogizes this to *kināyat al-ṭalāq*, where the *niyya* is what makes the expression effective.[55] However, jurists disagree about a husband explicitly saying 'You [are divorced] once', while intending two or three *ṭalāq*s—some jurists say the additional *ṭalāq*s are valid, others do not.[56] In general, however, any explicit statement of number outweighs a divergent intent, but an implicit singular *ṭalāq* (that is, an explicit statement of *ṭalāq* but no explicit statement of number) may be increased in number by intent. Non-verbal indications of number, such as holding up three fingers while pronouncing an implicitly singular *ṭalāq*, are binding if the verbal expression is of type 1, or of type 2 and intended as *ṭalāq*.[57] Intent can

[54] Shīrāzī holds that a single *ṭalāq* is enacted if the husband says 'you are divorced part of a divorce', or 'half a divorce'; if he says 'three halves', or one and a half, some jurists consider this a single *ṭalāq*, others consider it two *ṭalāq*s; if he says 'half of two divorces', some consider this one *ṭalāq* (i.e., half of two), others two (since saying 'half a divorce' enacts one, doubling this would enact two) (ibid., 4:307–308).

[55] Ibid., 4:302–303. Shīrāzī cites as a proof text a *ḥadīth* using the term *irāda*. He says "the expression implies the number," indicating that *niyya* does not override explicit expression. Ibn Rushd similarly notes that "There is disagreement over the case of a man saying to his wife 'you are divorced' and then claiming that he meant (*arāda*) thereby more than one *ṭalāq*, either two or three. Mālik says that it is as the man intends (*nawā*), and this is binding on him. This is al-Shāfiʿī's opinion [also], unless the man [explicitly] restricts what he says, such as saying '*ṭalqa wāḥida*' (a single divorce) ... Abū Ḥanīfa said that the word *ṭalāq* does not effect [multiple *ṭalāq*s] because singular words do not imply multiple numbers, neither indirectly nor directly" (*Bidāyat al-mujtahid*, 2:75; *DJP*, 2:89).

[56] Shīrāzī endorses the latter opinion, noting that otherwise this would amount to "enacting *ṭalāq* on the basis of *niyya* [alone], and this is not permitted" (*al-Muhadhdhab*, 4:303).

[57] Shīrāzī says of non-verbal indications of number that, "If one says 'you' and holds up three fingers, intending by this triple *ṭalāq*, it comes to nothing, because simply saying 'you' is not an expression of *ṭalāq*, and *ṭalāq* cannot be enacted by *niyya* without verbal expression. But if one says 'you are divorced' while [intending triple *ṭalāq* and] holding up three fingers, a triple [*ṭalāq*] is enacted, for gesturing this way with the fingers indicates the number [of *ṭalāq*s] intended" (ibid., 4:303). In the first case here, the gesture is really not an issue, for the expression is simply not explicit enough to count (it is type 3 speech), and so regardless of *niyya*, there is no effect. In the second case the expression is explicit enough to enact *ṭalāq*; if a jurist holds that the *niyya* can then determine number, the gesture, it seems, would be redundant. However, for a jurist who does not see *niyya* as determinative of number, the gesture can take the place of words in explicitly expressing the *niyya* regarding number. Shīrāzī does not consider all the

also be determinative when grammar is ambiguous, such as saying 'You are divorced once in (*fī*) two', where 'in (*fī*)' might mean 'plus', for which the term *maʿ* is usually used.[58]

While a pronouncement explicit in basic form and number is binding regardless of intent, there seems to be some resistance to recognizing a single pronouncement as triple *ṭalāq*, leading to some rather convoluted rules. Saying 'you are divorced thrice' is binding as a triple divorce. However, if the husband instead repeats the phrase 'you are divorced' three distinct times, intentions come into play. If he does not intend multiple *ṭalāq*s, the first pronouncement alone is binding.[59] Shīrāzī says that the assumption is to treat the repetition as mere emphasis (*taʾkīd*) of a single pronouncement. However, if the man intends the repeated phrases to be a 're-commencement' (*al-istiʾnāf*) of the pronouncement of *ṭalāq*, then each repetition counts as an additional *ṭalāq*. The husband may mix and match, so to speak: the first pronouncement may be meant as *ṭalāq*, the second as emphasis, and the third as re-commencement, effecting a second *ṭalāq*.[60] Shīrāzī adds that if the husband uses different explicit (*ṣarīḥ*) terms for divorce (*firāq* or *sarāḥ*) each time, rather than repeating the exact same phrase three times, then each pronouncement is binding, regardless of intent.[61] Ju-

hypothetical possibilities, such as holding up three fingers while intending two *ṭalāq*s; presumably he considers an explicit indication of number by gesture to be binding. As we saw, however, some jurists allow saying 'one' and intending and enacting two or three; presumably these would allow the same in gesture, although the texts do not explicitly say this.

[58] Shīrāzī gives the example of saying "'You are divorced once in (*fī*) two'; [in this case] you look [into the matter]: if he intended (*nawā*) one *ṭalāq* plus (*maʿ*) two [more], then he has enacted three, since '*fī*' can mean the same as '*maʿ*'" (ibid., 4:304). Here the speaker's intentions determine the effect of indeterminate grammar. Shīrāzī adds that if the speaker has no *niyya* at all (*lam yakun lahu niyya*), again one must investigate, and if the speaker does not know arithmetic, and thus did not intend the results of the arithmetic (i.e., adding the *ṭalāq*s he pronounced), then it is a single *ṭalāq*; the speaker's intentions are here measured objectively, but are still deemed determinate. This is "like a foreigner pronouncing a *ṭalāq* in Arabic and not knowing the meaning of his words" (ibid.). If the man does know arithmetic, some consider this one *ṭalāq*, others consider it two.

[59] Ibid., 4:305–306; Shīrāzī notes that one opinion attributed to al-Shāfiʿī is that all three pronouncements are binding; one opinion attributed to Mālik held that only one is binding regardless of *niyya*.

[60] Ibid., 4:306. Here Shīrāzī treats '*niyya*' and '*irāda*' as effectively interchangeable, each referring to the subjective intentions of the speaker.

[61] Ibid., 4:306–307. Here again Shīrāzī observes that, although the court holds the man accountable for the manifest meaning of his expression, God will recognize his true intention (*yudayyanu fīmā baynahu wa-bayna Allāh taʿālā li-annahu yaḥtamilu mā yudʿīhi*).

rists are more apt to treat any expression of multiple *ṭalāq*s as binding in a non-consummated marriage, allowing such a union to dissolve more easily than a consummated marriage.

Spectorsky's third and fifth categories may be taken together. Category three consists of conditional pronouncements of *ṭalāq*, while category five concerns a specific form of condition, the *istithnāʾ* (saying 'God willing'). In a conditional (*muqayyida*) pronouncement, the husband establishes some sort of contingency that brings a *ṭalāq* into effect. A common example is the husband telling his wife, 'If you enter the house of so-and-so, you are divorced'. Such conditions are considered bad form, but are generally held valid and binding.

Ibn Rushd raises the interesting possibility of one man's *ṭalāq* being made contingent on another person's volition (*mashīʾa*).[62] If that other is a *mukallaf* (legally authoritative) person and his or her will can be ascertained, then this determines the effect of the pronouncement. Jurists disagree over the case of a non-*mukallaf* person—some liken it to a *ṭalāq* pronounced in jest, and rule accordingly, while others say the conditional *ṭalāq* does not come into effect because the condition is not met. If the *ṭalāq* is made contingent on the will of God, Mālik holds that the *ṭalāq* simply comes into effect, while Abū Ḥanīfa and Shāfiʿī hold the opposite.[63] Shīrāzī generally allows for the attaching of conditions of exception (*istithnāʾ*) to a pronouncement of *ṭalāq* when such conditions are stated explicitly. He notes that the exception must be consciously intended (*yaqṣud*), for if a man simply has the habit of always saying 'God willing' when he speaks, this does not count as a condition restricting a *ṭalāq*.[64] The tendency to disregard intent in cases of explicit speech breaks down here, for the exception must be both explicit and intended or it has no effect.

An exception attached only silently, 'in the heart' (*al-istithna' bil-qalb*) has no effect. This elicits an interesting comment from Shīrāzī:

---

[62] Ibn Rushd, *Bidāyat al-mujtahid*, 2:78–79; *DJP*, 2:93–94.

[63] Ibid., 2:79; *DJP*, 2:94. Ibn Rushd asserts that the key issue regarding exemptions is whether one holds that a future situation can affect a present act. That is, the pronouncement constitutes an act in the present, while the exemption refers to a future occurrence; those who hold that the future has no effect on the present hold that exemptions have no influence on the validity of the pronouncement.

[64] Shīrāzī, *al-Muhadhdhab*, 4:317; note that here 'habit' (*ʿāda*) implies that an act is non-intentional. He also observes that jurists disagree over the *niyya* of such conditionality (*niyyat al-istithnāʾ*). Some hold that the *niyya* for the condition must be present throughout the entire statement of divorce with its accompanying conditions, others that the *niyya* must simply be formed before finishing the statement (4:318).

> If one pronounces *ṭalāq* on his tongue, but makes an exception in his heart, [what is] manifest [is binding]; if he says "you are divorced" and intends (*nawā*) in his heart "God willing," the exception is not valid and is not considered in the legal assessment, and it is not recorded [as a legal decision], because *the explicit expression is stronger than the niyya (al-lafẓ aqwā min al-niyya), for the expression enacts a ṭalāq even without niyya, while niyya does not enact ṭalāq without expression.*[65]

The *ṣarīḥ* expression discussed here is binding regardless of intention, and an intention of exception without verbal expression has no standing. Intending an exception is a matter of basic sincerity—that is, it is akin to explicitly pronouncing a straightforward *ṭalāq* while intending something else. Disregarding such an exception is consistent with the general approach to *ṣarīḥ* speech: intention simply does not matter, and formalism predominates. The one major exception to this rule is that of number, which emerges as the only intention that can be effective without verbal expression.

As for attaching positive conditions (*shurūṭ*, sg. *sharṭ*), Shīrāzī focuses on explicit statements of conditionality and explicit explanations of meaning or interpretations of explicit statements, as when the husband says 'I meant (*aradtu*) by this (such and such a condition)'. However, Shīrāzī mentions *niyya*, saying "If one says 'you are divorced from this month' (*anti ṭāliq ilā shahr*), but does not have *niyya*, the divorce is enacted after that month," because the explicit phrase used (i.e., *ilā shahr*) is ambiguous, and could mean either the beginning or the end of the month, but it must mean no later than the end of the month, and thus only the end of the month can be established with certainty ("for a *ṭalāq* cannot be enacted in this situation despite the likelihood [that he means the beginning of the month], just as a *kināya* statement of *ṭalāq* is not effective without *niyya*").[66] This implies that if the husband does have *niyya*, it is decisive regarding the timing of such a *ṭalāq*.

Spectorsky's sixth category, silent divorce, involves some of the same issues as does contingent *ṭalāq*. As with unspoken exceptions intended to accompany a *ṭalāq*, many jurists give no legal weight to silent *ṭalāq*, that is, *ṭalāq* pronounced only in thought. Ibn Ḥanbal holds this opinion, for example, and includes in this assessment a divorce pronounced

[65] Ibid., 4:318, emphasis added. Shīrāzī continues, "and even if [he] informed us about the *niyya*, we would thereby elevate the weak over the strong, and this is not allowed, as [is shown by the fact that] the *sunna* [cannot] abrogate the Qur'ān, and a textual indicant (*al-naṣṣ*) [cannot be] disregarded [in favor of] analogy."

[66] Shīrāzī, 4:341.

under one's breath and inaudible—even if intended, such a divorce is invalid.[67] Ibn Rāhwayh, however, provides a rare example of a dissenting opinion, preferring to ascertain the man's intentions and treating those as determinate—though even here it seems some verbal confirmation of the silent thought is required.[68] Ibn Rushd argues that

> Those who hold *niyya* [without words] to be determinate (*fa-man iktafā bil-niyya*) argue on the basis of the words of the Prophet … "Actions are defined by intentions." Those who do not consider *niyya* [determinate] without the words argue on the basis of [the following *ḥadīth*]: "Liability of my community has been removed for a mistake, forgetfulness, and for what goes on in their souls" (*mā ḥaddathat bihi anfusahā*), for *niyya* is less [determinate] than what goes on in the soul. They hold that the stipulation of *niyya* in action by the former *ḥadīth* does not make *niyya* alone determinate.[69]

While I have not found other jurists explicitly employing these proof texts, Ibn Rushd's assertions are compelling, and point to two different basic approaches to intentions. Either intentions are themselves legally effective, or only as an element added to verbal pronouncements. However, it seems that even those who would prefer to take the former position face the difficulty of knowing another's intentions, and thus would likely be forced to refer to either context or an explicit inquiry, asking the man what his intentions are, thereby making the divorce hinge not on intentions per se, but on objective indications of them.

A final issue in *ṭalāq*, one not part of Spectorsky's categorization, is retraction of repudiation. Shāfiʿī says retraction is a matter of words alone.[70] Others say it may be effected through sexual intercourse, and this camp is divided in two: some say retraction through intercourse occurs only if the *niyya* of the husband during intercourse is that it effect a retraction, "because an act can only be equivalent to words when accompanied by *niyya*" (according to Mālik). The other opinion here is that, according to Ibn Rushd, "Abū Ḥanīfa permits retraction by sexual intercourse both with and without *niyya*."[71] Significantly, it seems

---

[67] Spectorsky, *Marriage and Divorce*, 36, 74, 131.

[68] Ibid., 36, and see 196. See also Nawawī, who notes that one of several opinions credited to Mālik allows silent divorce with *niyya* alone (*al-Majmūʿ*, 18:241).

[69] Ibn Rushd, *Bidāyat al-mujtahid*, 2:75; *DJP*, 2:90. The *DJP* translation inverts the term *dūna* (without) by rendering it "along with," garbling the issue at hand. Here we see reference to a *ḥadīth* not commonly cited in the *ʿibadāt* materials, one taken by some to trump the main *niyya ḥadīth*, '*innamā al-aʿmāl bil-niyyāt*'.

[70] Ibid., 2:85; *DJP*, 2:101–102.

[71] Ibid.; the *DJP* translation renders this "Abū Ḥanīfa permitted recourse through

that the jurists conceive of retraction of *ṭalāq* as an essentially verbal action, a performative utterance, and allow bodily action to stand in for the performative utterance under certain circumstances, specifically when it is so intended. If Austin shows how words can be equivalent to actions, here we see an effort to allow actions to be equivalent to words.

Though *ṭalāq* at first appears relatively simple, it clearly raises a host of intention-related issues. The general pattern, however, is clear. In terms of basic sincerity and effectiveness, explicit statements are valid and binding regardless of intent, allusive statements are valid and binding if so intended, and some statements are too ambiguous to count regardless of intent. Any valid pronouncement can potentially effect one, two, or three *ṭalāq*s, and while explicit indications are usually determinative, intent can potentially establish this aspect of *ṭalāq* even in the absence of verbalization. Because the juristic default position assumes the lowest number of *ṭalāq*s that a given pronouncement could effect, intent generally only increases number. While *fiqh* manuals do not usually discuss the issue of how intent is to be known, sporadic evidence suggests that a judge would be encouraged to investigate a divorcing husband's intent. Thus, theoretically, intent without objective indication might be deemed determinative, but in practice it seems likely that some outward expression would be needed in a disputed case. Since such expression might follow the initial pronouncement by some significant interval, it seems a divorcing husband would have some leeway to interpret his own actions as he sees fit at the later time. In this way, reference to intent in cases of *ṭalāq* appears to potentially enhance the husband's power, allowing him, for example, to turn a single pronouncement into an irrevocable divorce, or to back down from an ill-considered outburst, provided he did not use a *ṣarīḥ* expression.

B. *Divorce by Other Means*

Moving beyond *ṭalāq*, there are several other means of dissolving a marriage. Three of these, *ẓihār*, *īlā'*, and *li'ān*, may be grouped together in that each involves an oath of sorts. Each revolves around a specific speech act, and intent matters for each in terms of the basic sincer-

intercourse when he (the husband) meant it to be so, without manifest intention." I think this misses the point that intention does not matter here to Abū Ḥanīfa. Mālik requires *niyya* for retraction, and the *niyya* is presumed to precede the intercourse, and so it seems that the *niyya* effects the retraction and makes the sexual intercourse licit.

ity of the pronouncement and its identity or place in the legal taxonomy. Complexity and number are generally not at issue because each of these means of divorce is irrevocable and necessitates a new marriage contract should the couple regret the separation. *Ẓihār* and *īlā'* fit the basic pattern found in *ṭalāq*: certain explicit phrases are valid and binding regardless of intent, while other less-explicit phrases are binding if intended, and still other ambiguous phrases cannot count, regardless of intent. The primary issue, then, is determining in which category a given phrase belongs.

Ẓihār is the repudiation of a wife by means of a particular phrase, in which the husband says to his wife words to the effect of 'you are to me as my mother's back' (*anti 'alayya ka-ẓahri ummī*). This form of divorce is generally considered non-*sunna*, and is often deemed reprehensible (*makrūh*), yet according to most it still has binding effects.[72] A pronouncement of *ẓihār* does not immediately terminate a marriage. The pronouncement assimilates the wife into the category of women sexually forbidden (e.g., 'like my mother'); the husband must then either terminate the marriage by pronouncing a *ṭalāq*, which is in this case irrevocable, or restore the wife's licit status by performing an expiation (*kaffāra*—freeing a slave is stipulated by the Qur'ān). However, there is no clear limit on the amount of time the husband may delay resolution, leaving the wife in a state of limbo. Jurists discuss the various types and effects of *ẓihār* statements, and the expiation of *ẓihār* pronouncements.

The most prominent intention issue here is that of sincerity, along with the attendant issue of explicitness. As with *ṭalāq*, an explicit (type 1) expression of *ẓihār* is deemed binding and has certain unavoidable consequences. Intentions have no role, and insincerity, jest, or intending a mere admonishment do not mitigate the effect. Jurists disagree over exactly which phrases count as explicit, but tend to be rather strict in limiting the range of such expressions. For example, Shīrāzī includes only statements exhibiting minor variations, such as using prepositions

[72] This pre-Islamic practice is mentioned in the Qur'ān: "Those who pronounce *ẓihār* to their wives, [the wives] cannot be their mothers, for none can be their mothers save those who gave birth to them, and using such words is iniquitous and false … And those who pronounce *ẓihār* and then wish to retract the words they have uttered, they should free a slave [as expiation] before they touch each other" (58:2–4). The Qur'ān thus denounces the practice while indicating that it still has effects, rather than forbidding it outright. See Gerald Hawting, "An Ascetic Vow and Unseemly Oath?: *Īlā'* and *Ẓihār* in Muslim Law," *Bulletin of the School of Oriental and African Studies* 57 (1994): 117; and see 115 (esp. n. 9), on the various meanings of 'back'. See also Spectorsky, *Marriage and Divorce*, 39–42.

other than *'alayya* (to me) that are roughly equivalent in meaning, and also reference to some body parts other than 'back' and to sexually forbidden women other than one's mother.[73]

As for allusive expressions of *ẓihār* (*kināyat al-ẓiḥār*), we again see the pattern of jurists distinguishing between those clear enough that the effect depends on intention (type 2), and those so ambiguous as to have no effect (type 3). Shīrāzī includes in the category of allusive expression of *ẓihār* ambiguous phrases such as simply saying 'you are to me like my mother'; these are *ẓihār* only if the speaker intends them to be (he uses the term *niyya*).[74] Still other phrases are simply too far from the mark for *niyya* to make them into *ẓihār*: "If one says 'you are divorced' (*anti ṭāliq*) and intends this to be *ẓihār*, it is not *ẓihār*, and if one says 'you are to me as my mother's back' and intends by this a *ṭalāq*, it is not *ṭalāq*, for such statements are explicit (*ṣarīḥ*) in the context of a marriage, and *one cannot alter them from this meaning through niyya*."[75] Here again we see the limits of the power of *niyya* to determine the effects of a performative utterance. Shīrāzī asserts that a type 1 pronouncement simply cannot be anything else, regardless of intent. Put differently, a type 1 pronouncement in one category (e.g., *ṭalāq*) is binding in that category and cannot be shifted by intent alone into another category (e.g., *ẓihār*).

Jurists also consider certain other phrases in the context of discussions of *ẓihār*, determining whether these count as *ṭalāq*, *ẓihār*, or neither. The statements in question are typically some form of 'You are forbidden (*ḥarām*) to me' or 'What God has made lawful to me is forbidden to me'. For most jurists, *niyya* determines whether such statements are *ẓihār* or *ṭalāq*, and thus which rules apply. If the husband has no *niyya* at all when making the statement, then some hold that it is neither *ṭalāq*

---

[73] Shīrāzī, *al-Muhadhdhab*, 4:410–412. See also Ibn Qudāma, *al-Mughnī*, 11:57–67. Shīrāzī gives a representative account of the variety of specific expressions considered *ẓihār*, such as using different prepositions to express 'to me', or referring to a grandmother rather than a mother. He discusses certain phrases which cross the line into having no legal effect, such as referring to the back of one's father or of an animal.

[74] Shīrāzī, *al-Muhadhdhab*, 4:412. Ibn Rushd similarly observes that "If one says 'she is to me like my mother', but he does not use the word 'back', Abū Ḥanīfa and al-Shāfi'ī say that what he intends (*yanwī*) is determinative, because he may have meant (*qad yurīdu*) to indicate his respect for [his wife] and to elevate her standing. Mālik said this is *ẓihār* [regardless of intention]" (*Bidāyat al-mujtahid*, 2:105; *DJP*, 2:128). Note that virtually any discussion of metaphorical language raises issues of intention—an allusive utterance relies on intention and norms for its meaning. Note also that here we see Ibn Rushd employing *niyya* and *irāda* interchangeably.

[75] Shīrāzī, *al-Muhadhdhab*, 4:412, emphasis added.

nor *ẓihār*, because the phrase alone does not clearly belong to one category or the other, and it cannot simply mean that the wife is 'forbidden' (rather than 'divorced'), for a person cannot make forbidden what God has permitted.[76] Shīrāzī asserts that "if [the husband] did not intend anything," this counts as *ẓihār*.[77] Isḥāq Ibn Rāhwayh similarly holds that "If his intention cannot be ascertained, then what he said most resembles an oath [of *ẓihār*]."[78] If the man does have *niyya* it determines whether the phrase 'you are forbidden to me' is *ṭalāq* or *ẓihār*, for the phrase can imply either form of divorce. The effect of saying to one's wife 'you are to me like a corpse' or 'like blood' is similarly determined by *niyya*. If the husband intends *ṭalāq*, it is *ṭalāq*, if he intends *ẓihār*, it is *ẓihār*, but if he intends to make her 'forbidden', it comes to nothing and he owes an expiation for making a vacant oath. If he has no *niyya* at all, some say this is like saying '*ḥarām*' without *niyya*, and he owes an expiation, others that this is simply a form of *kināyat al-ṭalāq*—invalid in this case because not intended.[79]

Number, as mentioned above, does not matter in *ẓihār* as it does in *ṭalāq*, for a valid *ẓihār* either sets up an irrevocable *ṭalāq* or necessitates the husband's expiation. The question emerges, however, of what to do if a husband makes multiple statements of *ẓihār* but then seeks reconciliation rather than divorce, and here intent is potentially determinative. For Abū Ḥanīfa, the issue is whether the man intended the subsequent pronouncements as mere emphases of the first—in which case there is no (extra) expiation—or if he intended them as renewal (*arāda isti'nāf*) of the *ẓihār*, in which case he is liable for multiple expiations. For the other schools, intent has no role: Mālik says there is only a single expiation unless there is an explicit retraction of the first *ẓihār*

---

76 Ibid., 4:299–300. Note that here *niyya* means something other than simple intent to act, for the man in question surely intended to utter these particular words, but lacked the *niyya* which would give them a specific legally recognized meaning. See also Spectorsky, *Marriage and Divorce*, 41; and Ibn Rushd, *Bidāyat al-mujtahid*, 2:77; *DJP*, 2:92.

77 Shīrāzī, *al-Muhadhdhab*, 4:413. Note again that a lack of *niyya* does not make this statement 'unintentional', but rather mean that the speaker has not given the statement any specific identity within the legal taxonomy.

78 Cited in Spectorsky, *Marriage and Divorce*, 41, 164. Spectorsky notes that for Ibn Ḥanbal 'you are forbidden to me' is *ẓihār*, unless added to it are the words 'and I mean by this divorce' in which case it is triple (31 [and 31, n. 109], 71–72). Ibn Rushd recounts no fewer than seven other opinions on using the term 'prohibited' (see *Bidāyat al-mujtahid*, 2:77–78; *DJP*, 2:92–93). Clearly, this is a case on which no consensus exists. On the general nature of these kinds of pronouncements, especially as related to oaths and vows, see Hawting, "Ascetic Vow and Unseemly Oath?" *passim*.

79 Shīrāzī, *al-Muhadhdhab*, 4:300.

and then another pronouncement, in which case there is expiation for both pronouncements; Shāfiʿī holds that there is expiation for each pronouncement.[80]

The next type of divorce, *īlāʾ*, shares some structural characteristics with *ẓihār*. This is an oath taken by a husband that he will not have sexual relations with his wife for a specified period of time, typically four months, and at the end of the specified period he must either divorce her or take her back.[81] Jurists debate many details of *īlāʾ*, such as revocability, variations in the specified time period, intervention of a *qāḍī*, and so forth. There is no clearly defined verbal formula for *īlāʾ*, although, as Hawting observes, "it is generally stated that one must swear by one of the names of God or in a manner which involves an act of atonement (*kaffāra*) if the vow is broken."[82] Like *ẓihār*, an oath of *īlāʾ* can be revoked but, as with *ẓihār*, this necessitates *kaffāra*.

The central intention issue related to *īlāʾ* again revolves around the matter of explicitness and basic sincerity. Jurists discuss what phrases count as *ṣarīḥ* (type 1), and which as *kināyat al-īlāʾ* (type 2), in which case *niyya* determines their legal effects. Most jurists agree that valid *īlāʾ* must take the form of an explicit oath sworn in the name of God or a recognized term of reference to God, such as one of God's names or attributes.[83] But other parts of the oath may take more ambiguous forms. Shīrāzī, for example, considers the possibility of using a range of phrases to refer to sexual intercourse (*waṭʾ* or *waṭʾ fī al-farj*), and he considers *niyya* determinative in cases where the phrase is indirect

---

[80] Ibn Rushd, *Bidāyat al-mujtahid*, 2:113–114; *DJP*, 2:138. It should be noted that Abū Ḥanīfa here is credited with an opinion giving intentions a major role. Sanhūrī's analysis relating *madhhab* affiliation to emphasis placed on intentions suggested that the Ḥanafī *madhhab* downplays intentions in contracts of sale. But even if Sanhūrī is correct in his characterization, we can now see that the Ḥanafīs cannot be characterized simply as the *madhhab* which downplays intention. Rather, in both sales and here, the Ḥanafī treatment of intentions appears to serve an agenda of restricting the invasiveness of the law. That is, by downplaying intentions in sales, the Ḥanafīs give greater latitude to form contracts with less concern for wider effects; by emphasizing intentions in repetition of *ẓihār*, the Ḥanafīs give greater leeway to treat the pronouncements as mere emphasis, and in either case the result is diminished impact of the law.

[81] Hawting notes that Qurʾān 2:226–227 is taken to establish the four month waiting period after an *īlāʾ* before the divorce is final, and during this period the oath may be forsworn and an expiation made ("Ascetic Vow and Unseemly Oath?" 116).

[82] Hawting, "Ascetic Vow and Unseemly Oath?" 114.

[83] See, for example, Ibn Qudāma, *al-Mughnī*, 11:29. Ibn Rushd notes that Mālik held *īlāʾ* binding in the case of any kind of oath, not just those in the name of God or God's attributes (*Bidāyat al-mujtahid*, 2:101; *DJP*, 2:123).

(*kināya*) yet clear enough in meaning (e.g., 'I will not enter into you').[84] Shīrāzī also notes that some phrases are simply too ambiguous to be made into *īlā'* by *niyya*.[85] Discussing a closely related issue, Ibn Qudāma asserts that if a man with multiple wives swears an oath of *īlā'* without making explicit which wife he is addressing, his *niyya* determines this, and *niyya* can determine an ambiguous or unspecified time period.[86] *Fiqh* manuals do not indicate how the intentions are to be ascertained, but again we can infer that some objective indication is necessary.

A second intention issue, this one more specific to *īlā'*, arises in the case of a man who ceases marital relations with his wife but does not swear an oath of *īlā'*. Most jurists do not deem this *īlā'*, but Ibn Rushd observes that Mālik considers this *īlā'* if the husband intends to do his wife harm (*idhā qaṣada al-iḍrār*) by so refraining, in which case the rules of *īlā'* come to bear.[87] Ibn Rushd notes that "the majority consider [only] the apparent meaning (*al-ẓāhir*), while Mālik considers the meaning (*al-ma'nā*)" of the rules of *īlā'*. Here the jurists discuss the intention, not of a speech act, but of a bodily action, the refraining from sexual relations, and whether the intention makes the action equivalent to the speech act of pronouncing *īlā'*.

The third marriage-dissolving oath is the *li'ān*, which is a mutual swearing of husband and wife regarding her infidelity. This seems primarily to function as a means for the husband to deny paternity of a child the wife is carrying. Jurists typically present this as a case where the husband accuses the wife of infidelity and swears an oath four times to that effect, and the wife then swears an oath four times asserting her innocence. Each adds a fifth oath calling down 'the curse of God' if he or she is lying. This exchange dissolves the marriage but produces no liability for *zinā* (fornication) or for *qadhf* (unsubstantiated accusation of fornication). Significantly, jurists typically do not discuss intentions in relation to oaths of *li'ān*. Some debate the possibility of variant forms of the oath, such as substituting 'the wrath of God' for

---

84 Shīrāzī, *al-Muhadhdhab*, 4:388–390.

85 Ibid.; Shīrāzī notes that jurists disagree over which phrases fit this category.

86 Ibn Qudāma, *al-Mughnī*, 11:17–20.

87 Ibn Rushd, *Bidāyat al-mujtahid*, 2:101; *DJP*, 2:123. Ibn Rushd notes that Mālik held a similar position on *ẓihār*, ruling that a man who refuses to retract an oath of *ẓihār* even "when he is capable of doing so" becomes liable for the rules of *īlā'*, namely that he can be forced to chose either divorce or retraction, if the husband's intention in leaving his wife in the limbo of *ẓihār* is an injurious one (2:110; *DJP*, 2:134).

'the curse of God', but the majority simply allow no such variations.[88] In other words, formal explicitness is mandatory, as the texts do not allow the possibility of *kināya* forms of pronouncement, and intention is not considered. It seems that the weight of the oath itself is considered sufficient guarantee of sincerity.

While *ṭalāq*, *ẓihār*, and *īlā'* are the unilateral prerogative of the husband, and while *li'ān* involves participation by both husband and wife, there is a form of divorce that is the prerogative of the wife. Called *khul'*, there are debates about its precise form, but it generally involves payment by the wife to the husband in exchange for release from marriage. According to Ibn Qudāma, "if a woman hates her husband, finds his form detestable, or his character, his [lack of] piety, his old age, his feebleness, or the like, or she fears that she will not be provided for in obedience to God, she may obtain release from him (*tukhāli'ahu*) for compensation and ransom herself from him."[89] The payment may be return of the *mahr* (bride-price) or some other agreed-upon amount. In cases of *khul'*, two general intention issues emerge: first, discussions of *khul'* address the recurring question of explicitness and basic sincerity. Second, a specific question arises as to whether a *khul'* results in a *ṭalāq* or annulment (*faskh*), and whether intention can affect this. *Faskh* does not count in the calculation of the number of *ṭalāq*s, with its attendant implications for revocability of *ṭalāq* and for remarriage.[90]

As for the first issue, the general pattern holds that certain expressions deemed *ṣarīḥ* are valid and binding, while others are deemed *kināya* and are only effective if intended to be. For example, Ibn Qudāma asserts that "the expressions of *khul'* are divided into explicit and implicit, the explicit being three statements [using the terms *khul'*, *mufādāh* (ransom), and *faskh* (annulment)] ... and if one employs one of these expressions, it goes into effect without *niyya*." He then lists several expressions that count as *kināya* and are only effective with *niyya*.[91] The jurists only discuss the matter of the husband's *niyya*. There are two parts to the verbal exchange that effects *khul'*, and if the wife uses a *ṣarīḥ* expression when initiating the *khul'*, then even if he answers with

---

[88] Ibid., 2:119; *DJP*, 2:145.

[89] Ibn Qudāma, *al-Mughnī*, 10:267. See also Ibn Rushd, *Bidāyat al-mujtahid*, 2:66–70; *DJP*, 2:79–84.

[90] See Tahānawī, *Kashshāf*, 3:411.

[91] Ibn Qudāma, *al-Mughnī*, 10:275–276. For more on which terms are *ṣarīḥ* and which are *kināya*, see Jazīrī, *Kitāb al-fiqh 'alā al-madhāhib al-arba'a*, 4:387ff.

a *kināya* expression his *niyya* does not matter (in terms of sincerity—though it may affect the kind of separation).

The second issue is potentially a matter of complex intentions. Jurists debate exactly what kind of separation *khulʿ* is—specifically if it counts as *ṭalāq* or stands as a separate category—and for some jurists this depends on the *niyya* of the husband. Ibn Ḥanbal and Ibn Rāhwayh treat *khulʿ* as annulment (*faskh*), paying no attention to intention.[92] Abū Thawr says that if the *khulʿ* is transacted without the term *ṭalāq*, it is annulment, not *ṭalāq*.[93] According to Ibn Rushd, the majority of jurists agree that *khulʿ* is equivalent to *ṭalāq*. However, according to one opinion attributed to Shāfiʿī, he considered it to be annulment, because he deemed it a *kināya* expression, holding that if the husband "meant it to be (*arāda bihi*) *ṭalāq*, it is *ṭalāq*, and otherwise it is annulment."[94] Note that in this opinion, it is the husband's intention that matters, not the wife's, even though the *khulʿ* is putatively her prerogative.

There are several forms of divorce that involve the husband bestowing on the wife some degree of ability to effect a divorce.[95] These are typically called *takhyīr* (granting a choice), *tamlīk* (granting possession [of the right to divorce]), and *tawkīl* (granting of agency [to execute a divorce]). Though the details of each case—and what constitutes each case—vary among jurists,[96] the general principle is that these state-

---

[92] However, Aḥmad b. Ḥanbal treats remarriage after *khulʿ* as having two *ṭalāq*s in place (Spectorsky, *Marriage and Divorce*, 51, n. 182). Ibn Qudāma credits Ahmad b. Ḥanbal with two opinions on *khulʿ*, one that it is *faskh* (annulment), the other that it is *ṭalāq* (*al-Mughnī*, 10:274).

[93] Ibn Rushd, *Bidāyat al-mujtahid*, 2:69; *DJP*, 2:82.

[94] Ibid. Note that here Ibn Rushd uses a form of *irāda* where one might expect *niyya*, demonstrating that while the latter is typically used for such taxonomic intent, this usage is not without exception.

[95] See ibid., 2:71; *DJP*, 2:84.

[96] Jurists agree that in *takhyīr*, the husband offers the wife choice (usually presented as saying 'Choose!' [*ikhtārī*] or some phrase using this term, often employing 'yourself') and the wife must act on the choice immediately; she does not retain the right to choose after the conversation ends. *Tamlīk*, in contrast, remains her option until the couple have sexual intercourse or his retraction, whichever comes first (sexual intercourse also ends the period of *takhyīr*) (Spectorsky, *Marriage and Divorce*, 48–49). According to Ibn Rushd, Mālik sees *takhyīr* and *tamlīk* as different in that, in *tamlīk*, the husband gives the woman the right to make a pronouncement of *ṭalāq*, and she may pronounce one, two, or three; the husband, however, can limit her to one or two *ṭalāq*s, and may chose to add to this his own additional pronouncements that would lead up to irrevocable divorce. For its part, *takhyīr* may be restricted or unrestricted; for both Mālik and Shāfiʿī, in the latter case the wife has the right to terminate the marriage contract, but may not

ments, if made explicitly, are binding on the husband and allow the wife to enact a divorce. Most conditions, such as number and the duration of her license to choose, if explicitly imposed by his statement (or her reply, if he accepts it), are also binding. If no conditions are made explicit, then the husband's intention determines the specific terms of the situation, especially the number of *ṭalāq*s effected.

Jurists consider the intention of the husband rather than the wife when verbally enacting one of these procedures—the husband's intention determines the parameters of the wife's power. As Ibn Rushd observes about *tamlīk*:

> Shāfiʿī says [that saying] "choose [for] yourself" and "your affairs are in your own hands" are equivalent, but [these do not grant her the right to] divorce unless he intends (*yanwī*) this to be so, and whatever he intends takes effect; if he intends a single [repudiation, then it is] single, and if [he intends it to be] triple, it is triple.[97]

Thus, the husband largely controls the terms of the divorce, including whether his explicit statement actually grants her the power to effect divorce. The wife has only the option to enact what he specifies, and he can specify either explicitly or by silent intention alone. Conversely, Mālik holds that if the husband makes an explicit statement of *tamlīk*, this is binding on him, even "if he did not intend (*lam yurid*)" to grant her the right to divorce.[98] In short, as Ibn Rushd observes, "the basis of the disagreement is whether the dominant matter is the apparent meaning of the words or the *niyya*," and jurists disagree on this.[99]

---

choose a single or double repudiation—it is an all-or-nothing situation. Still, in effect, *takhyīr* and *tamlīk* are nearly identical—they each involve the husband devolving to his wife the right to execute divorce (*ṭalāq*, not *khulʿ*—she need not pay for release), and each may be restricted if the husband so desires. Mālik further differentiates *tawkīl* from *tamlīk* in that with the latter, this right cannot be taken from the wife once granted, while *tawkīl* can (*Bidāyat al-mujtahid*, 2:71; *DJP*, 2:85). According to Spectorsky, jurists debate whether the husband's offer enacts a *ṭalāq* that remains in place if the wife chooses to remain married (48–49).

[97] Ibn Rushd, *Bidāyat al-mujtahid*, 2:71; *DJP*, 2:85. According to the Shāfiʿī Shīrāzī, saying to one's wife 'choose [for] yourself' or 'your affairs are in your own hands' only enacts *ṭalāq* if the man intended this (*al-Muhadhdhab*, 4:298). Ibn Ḥanbal and Shāfiʿī both hold that if the wife chooses divorce, this establishes a single revocable *ṭalāq*, while Mālik and Ibn Rāhwayh both deem this a triple divorce unless the husband explicitly specifies otherwise (Spectorsky, *Marriage and Divorce*, 49; and see Jazīrī, *Kitāb al-fiqh ʿalā al-madhāhib al-arbaʿa*, 4:385).

[98] Ibn Rushd, *Bidāyat al-mujtahid*, 2:72; *DJP*, 2:86.

[99] Ibid., 2:72; *DJP*, 2:86–87.

The various forms of divorce provided for in Islamic law all adhere to the general pattern established for *ṭalāq*. If a given pronouncement explicitly fits the ideal form recognized by *fiqh*, then it is valid and binding regardless of intent. If not, the intent of the speaker may determine what, if any, legal effects it has. Number is usually not an issue for these forms of divorce, and so this aspect of complex intent does not arise. However, complex intentions may determine other aspects of the situation, such as whether *khulʿ* effects a *ṭalāq* or *faskh*. In general, however, complexity of intention is less of an issue outside of *ṭalāq* proper. The husband's intent remains the dominant concern of the jurists, even in forms of divorce where the wife has a significant role to play. And reference to intentions, inaccessible to others, continues to give the husband some leeway in shaping the specific effects of divorce proceedings.

Part 3. *Inheritance and Bequests*

Islamic law governs the passing on of wealth upon death, and intentions are largely disregarded in these matters, in spite of some appearances to the contrary. The law prescribes the basic parameters of inheritance, establishing what proportion of an estate is inherited by various categories of relatives.[100] Inheritance law (*ʿilm al-farāʾiḍ*, 'the science of the shares') determines, with little flexibility, the devolution of at least two-thirds of the estate, while a person may bequeath up to one third of his or her estate according to a testamentary will.[101] However, under the generally liberal rules regarding sales and gifts, a person may sell or give

[100] As noted above, testation is not a monetary exchange, according to Arabi, "Intention and Method," 209, n. 24. For a basic overview in English, see Schacht, *Introduction*, 169–174; Schacht, "Mīrāth," in *Encyclopaedia of Islam*, new ed.; and N.J. Coulson, *Succession in the Muslim Family* (Cambridge: Cambridge University Press, 1971). See also David S. Powers, *Studies in Qur'an and* Ḥadīth: *The Formation of the Islamic Law of Inheritance* (Berkeley: University of California Press, 1986); and Richard Kimber, "The Qur'ānic Law of Inheritance," *Islamic Law and Society* 5, 3 (1998): 291–325.

[101] On the authenticity of the *ḥadīth* that is the basis of this rule, see David S. Powers, "On Bequests in Early Islam," *Journal of Near Eastern Studies* 48, 3 (1989): 185–200. Powers argues, against Patricia Crone, that "although it is impossible to prove that the one-third restriction is authentic, the combined weight of the evidence suggests that it may in fact have originated in pre-conquest Arabian law," and since no compelling counterargument has yet been advanced, it is reasonable to assume that "this particular dictum reflects an actual ruling of the Prophet" (199; Powers quotes the *ḥadīth* on 185, citing Aḥmad Ibn Ḥanbal, *Musnad* [Cairo, 1895], 1:172–173).

away property under a wide variety of circumstances. Thus the possibility arises that a person could circumvent legally prescribed inheritance proportions by gifting or selling his property. While this appears to be a case where intent (i.e., the intent to circumvent the law) might be weighed in assessing an action, in fact jurists systematically discount the role of subjective states and determine the validity of such transactions based on objective factors.

The key issue in determining the validity of sales and gifts that might affect inheritance is death-sickness (*maraḍ al-mawt*, or simply *al-marīḍ*; also *al-maraḍ al-mukhawwif*, 'sickness causing fear [of death]', especially in early sources).[102] An illness leading to death produces certain legal effects, invalidating transactions that would harm the interests of heirs—unless, in most cases, those heirs approve of the transaction. The rationale of the rule would appear to be disallowing decisions made on the deathbed, perhaps because such decisions might be made in fear of death and thus reflect an unclear mind, or perhaps because such acts might be done to circumvent quranic inheritance law and devolve property in ways harmful to potential heirs, being done at the last minute to avoid difficult personal turmoil or legal challenge. In the latter case especially, intentions would seem central to the matter.

However, in most cases, jurists define the parameters of death-sickness in such a way that intentions play no role whatsoever. For the sake of activation of the rules governing devolution of property, death-sickness is defined in purely objective terms. The texts themselves can be misleading, mentioning 'fear of death' as an element in defining death-sickness, implying that, in such a state, a person would act irrationally or with the intention to circumvent the letter of the law.[103] However, in fact, the ill person's fear does not determine whether the relevant rules come into effect. Rather, the definition of death-sickness is sickness that is deemed normally to cause death and that does in fact cause death in a given case. A person is not prevented from acting while

[102] For a study of the early development of these matters, see Hiroyuki Yanagihashi, "The Doctrinal Development of '*Maraḍ al-Mawt*' in the Formative Period of Islamic Law," *Islamic Law and Society* 5, 3 (1998): 326–358.

[103] Muḥammad Jawād Maghniyya, for example, defines *al-marīḍ* as an illness "which leads to death, being a dreaded (*makhūfan*) ailment, so that the person expects (*yaẓunnu*) that his life is in danger" (*al-Waṣāyā wal-mawārīth ʿalā al-madhāhib al-khamsa* [Beirut: al-Maktaba al-Ahliyya, n.d.], 27).

ill, for the rules are theoretically only applied retroactively after death occurs, if it is determined that the sale or gift in question was enacted while in death-sickness.

The legally relevant factors in defining death-sickness are what Coulson calls "apparent and reasonable grounds for apprehending death,"[104] and what the Mālikī jurist al-Ṣāwī calls "circumstances in which death comes as no surprise."[105] Minor ailments, such as headache or toothache are not death-sickness, regardless of whether the person fears death and even if he or she does in fact die from the ailment. If it is not normal and reasonable to expect death from an ailment, it cannot be legally defined as death-sickness. However, something deemed life-threatening constitutes death-sickness regardless of any optimism or courage on the part of the sufferer.[106] The ailment need not be one that is inevitably fatal; it simply must be deemed likely to cause death. One must actually die from the ailment, and should a person with a legitimate death-sickness actually die of some other cause, the rules of death-sickness do not apply.[107] Finally, most jurists agree on a time frame of one year prior to the date of death as the legally effective duration of a death-sickness.[108] Recovery, regardless of the ill person's expectation or fear of death, makes any transactions during the illness valid, and even improvement in health to the point where recovery is reasonably expected, even if relapse occurs leading to death, erases the status of death-sickness from before the relapse.[109] In short, purely objective measures, including prevailing societal norms and expectations, as determined by a judge, determine whether acts on the deathbed are valid or not, and the intentions of the acting party—whether he in fact intended to skirt the rules—do not matter.[110]

---

104 N.J. Coulson, *Succession in the Muslim Family* (Cambridge: Cambridge University Press, 1971), 263.

105 *Bulghat al-Sālik* (Cairo, 1952), 2:144; in Coulson, *Succession*, 262.

106 Coulson, *Succession*, 264. He also notes that most jurists agree that "physical pain, debility or incapacity is not a necessary condition of death-sickness, except in the case of chronic diseases like tuberculosis ... Whether or not certain ailments constitute death-sickness will often be a matter of degree of their seriousness," so occasional bouts of dysentery do not usually qualify, but constant, unremitting dysentery does.

107 Ibid., 266.

108 Ibid., 265.

109 Ibid., 265–266.

110 Matters are complicated by the possibility of *muḥābāt* sales, legally valid contracts for consideration in which part of the consideration is waived; see ibid., 270–271 for examples of how the jurists treat such cases.

Still, the jurists seem to consider the objective factors likely indicants of intent in a given situation. Technicalities aside, the goal of the law here appears to be have the judge look for indications of intent to circumvent the law and to disallow transactions when such intent is discerned. However, evidence from another legal genre, that of the *fatwā* collection, suggests something akin to the opposite: rather than seeking subtle indications of intent that might justify disallowing deathbed transactions, judges may have been more inclined to favor factors that would allow them. A *fatwā* issued by the Mālikī jurist Aḥmad al-Wansharīsī (d. 914/1508) and studied by David S. Powers records a case of the heirs of a deceased man challenging a sale he made of all his property to a third party prior to his death.[111] The heirs asserted that the sale was invalid because it was an instance of *tawlīj*, a sale or donation that illegitimately circumvents the rules of inheritance. As Powers observes, the Islamic "rules of partible inheritance ... to the extent that they were applied in practice, resulted in the progressive fragmentation of wealth and capital. It is perhaps not surprising that Muslim proprietors found numerous ways to circumvent the inheritance rules and that they received important assistance in this regard from Muslim jurists." In this vein, many jurists applied the *ʿilm al-farāʾiḍ* only to "property owned by the deceased at the moment they enter their deathbed illness," and held that prior to that moment, proprietors may dispose of their properties as they saw fit.[112] Based on the evidence of al-Wansharīsī's *fatwā*, it appears that Mālikī jurists, at least, tended to hold cases of *tawlīj* to a high standard of evidence, deeming them illegal only on the basis of direct evidence, such as a confession, or overwhelming circumstantial evidence, thus aiding the cause of free disposal of property.

The rules of inheritance further stipulate that all legitimate debts, including any *zakāt* owed, must be paid out of an estate before either bequests or mandatory division to heirs. Jurists consider the possibility that a person might lie regarding a debt, falsely indicating that he or she owes a debt to thus evade the *ʿilm al-farāʾiḍ*. When a debt is

---

[111] "The Art of the Legal Opinion: al-Wansharisi on *Tawlīj*," in *Islamic Legal Interpretation: Muftis and their Fatwas*, ed. Muhammad Khalid Masud, Brinkley Messick, and David S. Powers (Cambridge, Mass.: Harvard University Press, 1996), 98–115. Powers notes that *tawlīj* originally referred to a transfer of wealth from parent to child, but came by extension to signify more generally a transaction masking a technically illegal transfer of wealth (99–100).

[112] Ibid., 99.

proven by evidence other than acknowledgment (*iqrār*) by the dying person, no questions arise regarding its legitimacy. However, if the only evidence of a debt is the acknowledgment, and an otherwise unsupported claim by the debtee, it may be challenged by the heirs whose interest the debt would harm. The Shāfiʿī *madhhab* treats all deathbed debt acknowledgments as valid and binding on the estate, while the other *madhhab*s treat such a debt as a gift that is valid only up to one-third of the net estate, after debts are paid.[113]

Addressing a related issue, Ibn Rushd notes that Mālik restricts a person's ability to delay payment of *zakāt* until death, paying *zakāt* by bequest or simply making no arrangements for how the *zakāt* should be taken from his wealth.[114] Mālik holds that leaving such an obligation until death may reflect an intent to withhold wealth from the heirs and circumvent quranic inheritance rules. Thus, Mālik holds that if the deceased made no bequest for the *zakāt*, it is not incumbent on the heirs to pay it, as it simply goes unpaid, and that if the deceased did make a bequest for *zakāt*, that amount is taken "from the third."[115] Shāfiʿī, in contrast, holds that whether the deceased bequested for his *zakāt* or simply dies owing *zakāt*, the *zakāt* is taken from the total wealth before any other bequests or inheritance are calculated.

In sum, the rules of inheritance and bequests theoretically work to prevent any avoidance of the quranic rules on the subject. On the one hand, the inspiration of inheritance and bequest law seems to be an assumption that a person, when facing death, might act to intentionally circumvent the law and devolve property according to his or her own wishes, not those of the religio-legal tradition. In such a case, a person might act in a way that is legal, but do so with the intention of achieving illegal ends, much as in the case of selling grapes

---

113 Coulson, *Succession*, 272–274; the opinion of non-Shāfiʿīs here refers to the case of acknowledging a transaction that occurred during the death-sickness. Non-Shāfiʿīs disagree over debts transacted prior to the illness; Mālikīs treat it as a gift, Ḥanafīs and Ḥanbalīs disallow such debts when the acknowledgee is an heir (one who actually succeeds to part of the estate in a given case, not simply a potential heir), unless the other heirs consent. In the case of a non-heir, these two *madhhab*s treat the acknowledgment as valid evidence of a true debt. Coulson asserts that Mālikīs are generally the most restrictive regarding deathbed acts, Shāfiʿīs the least restrictive (269–270, 273).

114 Ibn Rushd, *Bidāyat al-mujtahid*, 2:336–338; *DJP*, 2:408–410.

115 This refers to the one third of wealth that can be bequested according to quranic provisions, while the remaining two thirds of the wealth is divided up according to the quranic rules. Should the owed *zakāt* exceed that third, the heirs are not obligated to pay the excess.

to a winemaker. On the other hand, the law does not actually give attention to the expressed or implicit intentions of a person facing death. Rather, the rules simply disallow transactions of sale or gift-giving when a person is in a situation where prevailing norms dictate an expectation of death and death actually occurs from that cause.

Conclusion: Toward a Theory of Intent in Islamic Civil Law?

We are now in a position to revisit the question of how best to account, in some general and theoretical way, for the treatment of intent in Islamic civil law, particularly contracts and personal status law. As we saw in the previous chapter, several scholars have offered theoretical explanations in this regard, and indeed, more attention has been paid to intent in commercial and family law than in other areas of Islamic law. Johansen argues that Muslim jurists consider intent—in terms of basic sincerity and voluntary consent—as decisive in contract law. Thus, "contracts have to be interpreted in light of the parties' intentions (*nīya*) and purposes (*maqṣūd*). They cannot be interpreted in a formalistic way."[116] This guarantees that contracting parties are acting freely and sincerely. Johansen apparently assumes that jurists will consider intent decisive whenever possible unless doing so threatens social stability. Thus, intent would matter more in contract law where he claims social stability is not much at risk, and less in 'social' or 'symbolic' transactions, such as marriage and divorce, where social stability is prominently implicated. We saw that Johansen was correct regarding the role of intent in contract law, but only for some jurists—especially the Ḥanafīs who make up Johansen's major source of evidence. In these cases, Johansen's view is complemented by that of Schacht, who asserts that reference to intent in contracts of sales opens a loophole in the law by allowing "the possibility of evading the resulting obligation."[117] Together, Johansen and Schacht help explain one prominent tendency in contract law: the insistence on basic sincerity and the invalidation of any contract undertaking without free, intentional consent. Such insistence not only ensures that contracts are freely undertaken, but also fosters flexibility in business interactions by providing an 'intent loophole'.

---

[116] Johansen, "Valorization," 73.
[117] Schacht, *Introduction*, 117.

However, we also saw that other tendencies are evident in contract law, namely the tendency on the part of some jurists to disregard intent, in the absence of coercion, and to insist on the valid and binding nature of even an insincere offer or acceptance of contractual terms. Johansen's view rests on the notion that business transactions have little potential to affect general social relations; perhaps some jurists disagree and downplay intent so as to limit the social (and economic) damage of broken contracts. Further, Johansen and Schacht pay little attention to the matter of complex intentions—the intent that a given contract achieve some further, potentially unlawful ends beyond the immediate terms of the contract. Here, Sanhūrī's *madhhab* typology suggests an explanation that goes beyond Johansen's or Schacht's. Sanhūrī's findings, amplified by Arabi, suggest that Ḥanbalīs and Mālikīs emphasize complex intentions in contracts because doing so contributes to their wider view of *fiqh* as a broadly moral enterprise that serves to guide society. Jurists with this vision tend to look beyond the immediate legality of a contract and hold contracting parties liable for the wider implications of the act, and to restrict basic contract law accordingly. In contrast, Shāfiʿīs and Ḥanafīs tend to view the law in more narrowly legalistic terms and to focus on the immediate legality of the contractual terms, while overlooking even fairly obvious and potentially unlawful wider effects.

Sanhūrī and Arabi focus on complex intentions, but if we apply this hypothesis to basic sincerity, we see an interesting implication emerge. Ḥanafīs, to begin with, minimize the importance of complex intentions in the service of their relatively narrow view of the law. However, as Johansen rightly noted, they tend to consider basic sincerity crucial to a valid contract. Rather than being incoherent, this combination seems to produce a consistent 'liberal' view of contract law, making it relatively easy to negotiate a contract by giving contracting parties maximum leeway, first by allowing an 'intent loophole', and second by disregarding any wider implications of the contract.

Turning to the matters of personal status law, we begin by noting that intent is a very different issue in inheritance law than in marriage and divorce. Inheritance law may appear at first glance to hinge on the intent of a dying person to evade legal restriction on division of an estate. However, in the end the subjective state of intent is, at least in theory, entirely eclipsed by objective matters. In matters of inheritance, the jurists do not claim that intent is clearly expressed in outward expressions, nor do they consider intentions apart from the expressions; they simply do not include intentions per se in their assessments. Inheritance ultimately fits uneasily under the analysis of the rest of Islamic civil law, at least in terms of present concerns. Intent in inheritance law does not hinge on speech acts in the same way contracts, marriage, and divorce do, which perhaps helps explain the disjuncture.

Marriage and divorce, however, do invite analysis alongside contract law because of their many shared characteristics. On the whole, marriage is treated formalistically, with jurists of all *madhhab*s largely excluding intent from the considerations of marriage contracts. Johansen accounts for the formalism of marriage by asserting that the disregard of intent serves to maximize social stability—recall Johansen's assertion that in marital relations "the subject matter is much too explosive … to leave the parties the same range of maneuvering that they enjoy in commercial exchange," suggesting that marriages should be held together for the social good.[118] This theory is at least plausible, for it meshes with our findings and nothing in the sources disproves it. However, Johansen does not explicitly consider divorce, which, it turns out, presents a problem for his wider theory. Divorce would seem to fit Johansen's definition of social or symbolic exchange and to implicate the same issues of social relations and stability as marriage. Extending Johansen's theory would predict that intentions should matter in divorce only if reference to intentions created loopholes that allowed a person to escape a divorce procedure once it had been started—that is, if reference to intentions only mitigated *against* carrying out a divorce and thus fostered social stability. This is in fact one aspect of the treatment of intentions in divorce, as jurists widely agree that *kināya* (allusive) expressions are effective only if intended, thus creating an intention loophole. However, Islamic divorce law also displays a widespread disregard of intentions in *ṣarīḥ* (explicit) expressions, which are held binding regardless of intent, often even in cases of joking, intoxication, or other ill-considered speech. As for *kināya* expressions, the role of intent here could equally be said to make divorce easier, not more difficult, by allowing a wide range of metaphorical expression to effect a *ṭalāq* if so intended. And the other aspect of intent, complexity in terms of number, cannot downgrade an explicit indication of number, but can only increase the number effect of a *ṭalāq* pronouncement that is vague or

[118] Johansen, "Valorization," 73.

equivocal about number. Thus, intent in divorce law generally tends to work as an intensifier, making a *kināya* expression binding, or giving a single pronouncement the legal weight of a double or triple pronouncement. Johansen's theory of intent in social transactions runs into trouble here. (Meanwhile, Ibn Qudāma's explanation that *niyya* cannot be included in the terms of a marriage contract because such a contract must be witnessed and *niyya* is beyond the reach of witnesses, does not extend to contracts of sale and ultimately appears rather *ad hoc*.)

The Sanhūrī/Arabi *madhhab* typology offers a promising explanation for the treatment of intent in contract law. However, if we try to extend this analysis to personal status law we quickly run aground. We saw, for example, that Ḥanafīs tend to maximize the flexibility of contracting parties in terms of both basic sincerity and complexity. In marriage and divorce, however, Ḥanafīs tend to do just the opposite. While most jurists treat marriage formalistically, virtually all hold that coercion invalidates a marriage contract. Ḥanafīs, however, disagree and hold a coerced marriage contract valid and binding. The same pattern holds for *ṭalāq*, where Ḥanafīs, against the grain of the other *madhhab*s, hold an otherwise valid pronouncement of *ṭalāq* binding, not only in cases of jest and intoxication, but even in cases of duress. Sanhūrī and Arabi suggest that Ḥanafīs emphasize the letter of the law in service of a minimalist view of the law's scope, limiting legal interference in personal affairs. While this may hold within the confines of contract law and economic activity, it seems not to hold for social interactions. Binding coerced marriage partners to their unintended word, or dissolving a marriage based on forced or intoxicated statements hardly minimizes the impact of the law on the free workings of human social activity. Further complicating the *madhhab* typology, we see that the Ḥanbalī Ibn Qudāma, supposedly aligned with Mālikīs against the Ḥanafīs and Shāfiʿīs, agrees with the Ḥanafīs about coercion in marriage, but not in *ṭalāq*.

Messick's view helps fill in lacunae in the other theories, and may come closest to a full 'theory of intent', at least in Islamic commercial and family law, though it presents some problems of its own. He highlights a key tension between a tendency to treat intent as definitive and the difficulties of ascertaining that intent. His notion of "foundationalism" fits well with significant aspects of the texts, giving real insight into the dynamics of the jurists' treatment of intent, agency, and authority. Messick rightly observes that for many jurists—though, importantly, not all—the sincerity of speech acts in contracts of sale matters greatly. He draws the compelling conclusion that this points to a particular view of the inner self as the creative locus of a "bedrock of human authority and truth."[119] In situations where intentions are given significant weight, whether in terms of basic sincerity or wider complexity, this analysis holds. It suggests that, in the medieval Islamic legal view, human agency and authority are essentially internal, subjective elements only indirectly and imperfectly articulated in outward indicants. This meshes with Johansen's apparent assumption that reference to intent is the jurists' default preference.

One implication of Messick's foundationalism is that the key verbal utterances in commercial and family law might not fit well the category of 'performative' speech acts. Messick examines the work of the Zaydī jurist al-Ḥasan b. Aḥmad al-Jalāl (d. 1673) and his commentator Muḥammad b. Ismāʿīl al-Amīr (d. 1769), who assert that for some jurists, "wordings of contracts are a report (*khabar*) concerning what is in the self (*nafs*)."[120] This contrasts with the view of other jurists who treat the wordings of contracts as 'performative' or 'creative' (*inshāʾī*). These views correspond to a stronger and weaker commitment to foundationalism, respectively. If one conceives of the contract actually being formed or authored internally, at the moment of intent formation, the wording becomes 'informational' (*khabarī*), a report of something already done. The other tendency is to downplay intent, treating it as, at most, incidental to the moment of verbalization, which creates or performs the contract. Ibn al-Amīr observes that "the jurisprudents differ as to the status of these forms (*siyagh*); the Ḥanafīs are of the opinion that they are reports (*akhbār*), [while] the Ḥanbalīs and the Shāfiʿīs hold that they are performative acts (*inshāʾāt*), not reports."[121] So for some jurists, at least, the key speech acts of contract and family law are not true performative utterances.

Both the general notion of foundationalism and Messick's exploration of its implications for the nature of contracts and other speech

[119] Messick, "Written Identities," 45.

[120] Messick, "Indexing the Self," 174–175. Messick asserts that the general use of the perfect tense in Arabic legal texts may reflect this foundationalist understanding of words as reports of completed actions. He chooses to translate the Arabic perfect into the English past tense, so as to at least leave this question open and not "confuse the main legal issue ..., namely, whether such expressions are 'performative' or not" (157, n. 14). See also 165.

[121] Muḥammad b. Ismāʿīl al-Amīr, *Minḥat al-Ghaffār* (Ṣanʿāʾ: Majlis al-Qaḍāʾ al-Aʿlā, 1985), 1118; in Messick, "Indexing the Self," 175. Ibn al-Amīr cites in support comments by the Ḥanbalī Ibn Qayyim al-Jawziyya.

acts are compelling and help to illuminate Islamic legal understandings of intent. Where one might read the evidence somewhat differently, however, is suggested by Messick's own implicit admission that only some aspects of some texts consistently express foundationalism. Ibn al-Amīr identifies only the Ḥanafīs (and Messick extends this to some Zaydīs who also take this tack[122]) as treating contractual speech as an informational report rather than a performative utterance. As Messick notes, for the other *madhhab*s, "their foundationalism, their emphasis on anchoring legal analyses in a bedrock of intent, is less marked."[123] Thus, foundationalism is not a general characteristic of all Muslim legal treatments of intent, but is one of at least two divergent and widely represented views. Further, we see that Ibn al-Amīr and Messick's characterization of Ḥanafīs as foundationalists clashes with Sanhūrī and Arabi's presentation of Ḥanafīs (alongside of Shāfiʿīs) as downplaying intent in contracts and focusing on the immediate legality of explicit terms: "when the ultimate aim of the contracting party is not apparent either from the terms of the contract or from the prevalent usage of the object under contract, the Ḥanafīs (and Shāfiʿīs) ignore ulterior motivation, which has no legal effect on the validity of the transaction."[124] To the extent that foundationalism is a prominent feature of *fiqh*, it seems not to neatly characterize any single *madhhab*.

Messick offers another helpful, if also partial, analytical framework for understanding intent in Islamic law, one that grows out of his theory of foundationalism. He distinguishes *ṭalāq* from contracts of sale, noting that the former is a 'unilateral' declaration, whereas the latter involves a 'bilateral' interaction of 'offer and acceptance'. He uses this distinction as the basis for his explanation of the role of intentions in divorce. In Messick's view (as in Johansen's), jurists give intentions a relatively heavy weight in bilateral contracts, but formalism predominates in *ṭalāq*. He explains this by asserting that, "Supposedly uncluttered by a response from an interlocutor and the latter's intention, intentionality in unilateral acts can come closer to being directly reflected in manifest expression."[125] In contrast, "analyzing mutual consent in a situation involving at least two participants to an undertaking requires an effort

[122] Messick, "Indexing the Self," 176.
[123] Ibid.
[124] Arabi, "Intention and Method," 215.
[125] Messick, "Written Identities," 46. This analysis is closely echoed in "Indexing the Self," 177–178.

to understand dialogically constituted meaning."[126] I take this to mean that jurists prefer to consider intent, reflecting their general foundationalism, but that at times they treat intent as obvious. However, the suggestion that in a bilateral exchange the words and intentions of one party can 'clutter' the act of another raises questions about just how this occurs and just what this 'clutter' is. One could also question the implicit argument that intentions matter in bilateral contracts simply because the complexity of two persons interacting necessitates this.

Certainly Messick is correct that the unilateral act of an explicit (*ṣarīḥ*) expression of *ṭalāq* is treated formalistically. However, the jurists indicate that this is because in such cases the speaker's intentions simply do not matter—not because they are assumed to be apparent. That is, a husband's intention may not be reflected in his statement at all. He may have had the opposite intention, perhaps joking warmly with a beloved wife, yet in theory his declaration is held binding. Moreover, intentions do determine the legal effects of ambiguous (*kināya*) expressions of *ṭalāq*, and also can determine the effects of all declarations in terms of number. In short, these unilateral declarations are not free of the effects of intent. This fact actually extends Messick's foundationalism into an area of unilateral legal acts, showing that, with the prominent role they give intent in matters of divorce, many jurists hold that the authority of human speech resides in the internal self, where intentions are formed. The effect of such an extension may demonstrate the pervasiveness of foundationalism, but it challenges the utility of the unilateral/bilateral distinction. Further, this view does not account for marriage, a bilateral agreement in which meaning is constructed dialogically, yet which the jurists treat formalistically. Messick's theory is a general one, and though it helps make sense of the centrality of intent where that is evident, it alone does not account for some exceptions or contrary trends apparent in the sources.

Another prominent attempt to theorize intent in Islamic law is that of anthropologist Lawrence Rosen, whose groundbreaking work has helped call attention to the importance of the topic. Insofar as his work focuses on the application of Islamic law in contemporary Moroccan *qāḍī* courts, his task diverges significantly from my own. However, Rosen states his understanding of the role of intentions in Islamic legal thought and practice in general terms: "In the Middle East, intent and

[126] Messick, "Indexing the Self," 178.

act are thought to be so closely linked that one can read rather directly from a person's words and deeds the intent that lies within;" in short, "words and deeds are connected directly to intent; to know one is thus to know the other."[127] This view forms the basis for Rosen's various and extensive reflections on the role of intentions in Islamic law, and is, no doubt, an accurate description of the legal culture of his field site. However, it contrasts with the aforementioned scholarly analyses, all of which, in varying degrees, see Muslim jurists as treating the relationship between intent and outward expression or action as problematic.[128] Rosen's presentation borders on behaviorism: "Indeed, most Arabs do not recognize the idea of a distinct inner self that could exist apart from action, only of overt expressions that must of necessity conform to what a person must carry inside."[129] This may apply in the case of

[127] Lawrence Rosen, *The Anthropology of Justice: Law as Culture in Islamic Society* (Cambridge: Cambridge University Press, 1989), 51, 52; further, "a person's state of mind is available to others through his or her situated acts—occurrences that draw together the qualities of nature, background, and biography to make an inner state 'obvious'" (53). Along similar lines, Rosen elsewhere asserts that "The Arabic word for intent, *niya* [=*niyya*], not only means 'purpose', 'design', and 'will', but inasmuch as these features manifest themselves in direct faith *niya* also means 'simple', 'naïve', and 'sincere'. It suggests in its semantic range what informants readily acknowledge in actual use, that individuals constantly display what lies inside them when they act" ("Justice in Islamic Culture and Law," in *Perspectives on Islamic Law, Justice, and Society*, ed. R.S. Khare [Lanham, Md., and Oxford: Rowman & Littlefield, 1999], 37); and again, "in ordinary social life this means that people readily presume to know others' states of mind and do not hesitate to elicit behavior or exert pressure by characterizing words and deeds in such a way that their attendant motivations may also be adduced. In law … this means that judges usually presume they can discern intent simply from what a person has said or done and that intent can therefore remain a distinct element of legal consideration even when, in terms of formal doctrine, it does not necessarily appear as a constituent feature" (ibid.). In another text, Rosen similarly asserts that in both law and everyday life, "Moroccans believe that overt acts are directly connected to interior states, and that if you know a man's traits and ties, and the contexts in which these are revealed you will also know that person's intentional structure" ("Intentionality and the Concept of the Person," in *Criminal Justice*, ed. J. Roland Pennock and John W. Chapman [New York: New York University Press, 1985], 58). Indicating that his informants use the term *niyya* as general description of character, Rosen quotes a judge: "If a man is a bad one … he cannot hide it. It will show up in the way he acts. If you ask a lot of questions a man cannot keep his thoughts hidden: his intentions [*niya*] will be obvious" (ibid., 60). See also his "Equity and Discretion in a Modern Islamic Legal System," *Law & Society Review* 15, 2 (1980–1981): 217–245; and "Have the Arabs Changed Their Mind? Intentionality and the Discernment of Cultural Change," in *Other Intentions: Cultural Contexts and the Attribution of Inner States*, ed. Lawrence Rosen (Santa Fe: School of American Research Press, 1995), 177–200.

[128] For Messick's views of Rosen's work, see "Indexing the Self," 152, n. 2.

[129] Rosen, "Justice in Islamic Culture," 37.

inheritance law, but even in the more formalistic aspects of contract, marriage, and divorce, intent is treated less as apparent than as irrelevant. Because Rosen's theoretical framework encompasses areas of the law beyond commercial and personal status, we will return to a fuller assessment of it in each of the next two chapters.

The fact that each of these analytical approaches casts light on the topic, but in the end provides only partial illumination, indicates that no single unified theory of intentions in civil law seems emergent. The complex combination of formalism and subjectivism in *ṭalāq* alone resists theorization, and the simultaneous formalism of some aspects of *ṭalāq* and of marriage intensifies the resistance. This should not be taken as a sign of irrationality or incompetence on the part of the jurists, however. In fact, Islamic law may be the product of a certain hyper-rationality, a quest to think through the details of nearly endless possible permutations of human action and legal consequence. Certainly the jurists incorporated a wide range of concerns and a multiplicity of logics within the law. As Sanhūrī remarks,

> Islamic law is subject to two conflicting trends in relation to the cause [ulterior motive]: First it is a law with a marked objective tendency, giving weight to the expression of the will and not the will as such, i.e. prefering (*sic*) the apparent, not the latent, will ...; on the other hand, Islamic law is a law in which ethical, moral and religious factors predominate, implying the significance of motivation, as the latter is the measure of the honesty and purity of intentions.[130]

Yet these two trends, one favoring the objective, apparent, and technical, the other favoring the subjective, latent, and moral, appear not to play out with great consistency along strict *madhhab* lines, and may not always prove consistent even within a single *ouvre* or text. The approaches exemplified in the *fiqh* manuals indicate that, while the various aspects of civil law have important elements in common—for example, the centrality of speech acts and an insistence on voluntary action—one legal issue need not necessarily be treated in precisely the same way as another. In spite of commonalities, contracts of sale, for example, are different in some significant regards from contracts of marriage, and each of these from divorce. Perhaps the integrity of the Islamic legal system is rooted more in its casuistic methodology and its attention to attenuated nuances of difference in various legal areas

---

[130] Sanhūrī, *Maṣādir*, 4:52; in Arabi, "Intention and Method," 210.

than in an artificial insistence that all speech acts and all formulations of intention must have the same legal consequences, or that one must unflinchingly chose between objective/technical and subjective/moral visions of the law.

CHAPTER SIX

INTENT IN ISLAMIC PENAL LAW

Introduction

Questions of intent in cases of harmful action have long exercised the minds of lawyers, law professors, moral philosophers, and mystery novelists, generating perhaps as much imaginative casuistry as any legal topic. As Mary Douglas once observed about law in another context, "everything would be quite straightforward were it not that the legal mind has seen fit to ruling on some borderline cases."[1] Beyond confessed, cold-blooded murders and unambiguous accidents, legal systems must prepare for a range of possible—if unlikely—scenarios, including hidden motives, hired guns, and coerced killers.[2] The inaccessibility of others' intentions produces many cases where the exact nature of events is not clear, and finding the dividing line between outwardly similar, yet inwardly different, cases can prove quite difficult. Still, it seems such that distinctions must be made if justice is to be attained, or even approximated.

Islamic law has certainly produced its share of reflection on harmful and injurious intent. The standard handbooks consider offenses against persons and property (offenses generally called *jināyāt* or *jirāḥ*) and violations of the set of ordinances called the *ḥudūd*; both are penal legal matters, involving assessing culpability and assigning punishments. Islamic law establishes the boundaries of acceptable action, generating categories of acts marked by a negative imperative: these are the acts which a Muslim should not do. Transgression of these rules necessitates some counteraction to restore order: punishment, financial recompense, and/or expiation. Regarding *jināyāt* or *jirāḥ*, Muslim jurists

[1] Douglas, *Purity and Danger: An Analysis of the Concepts of Pollution and Taboo* (London: Routledge and Keegan Paul, 1966), 54.

[2] For an engaging exploration of such difficult cases of intent in Western criminal law, see Leo Katz, *Bad Acts and Guilty Minds: Conundrums of the Criminal Law* (Chicago: University of Chicago Press, 1987).

treat intent as a critical factor in defining transgressions and assigning punishments, weighing the intention of the actors, even as they insist on a form of strict liability. However, rather than give legal weight to intentions per se, as they theoretically do to some extent in ritual, contract, and family law, jurists consistently rely on indirect, objective evidence when assessing subjective states in penal situations. Further, jurists recognize limitations in their ability to know and evaluate human intentions, and some explicitly acknowledge that, because of this, they can achieve no more than a provisional form of justice.

Islamic law also includes a special class of ordinances called the *ḥudūd* (sg. *ḥadd*), the 'rights [of God]', which include fornication, consumption of intoxicants, and theft. At first look, it appears that intent does not matter at all for such offenses, for once it is determined that a *ḥadd* ordinance has been violated, certain penalties automatically ensue—for example, amputation of the hand for theft. The law seems to make no accommodations for grades of offense, such as more or less intentional. However, on closer inspection, it becomes clear that intentions do come into play, specifically in terms of acting mistakenly or in ignorance of the *ḥudūd* rules. This approach fits the pattern of treating intent as definitive of actions, recognizing that an unintentional breach of the law should not be treated in the same way as an intentional one. It also fits a larger pattern of reluctance to apply the *ḥudūd* penalties, which are also hedged about with unusually narrow definitions of action and high standards of proof.

As we move into the arena of penal matters in Islamic law, we see another significant shift in the terminology of intent. If *niyya* is the predominant and technically precise term for intent in *fiqh al-ʿibādāt*, and if a variety of terms function largely interchangeably in contracts and personal status law, the term *ʿamd* eclipses these in the case of actions for which penalties apply. Other terms appear occasionally, but *ʿamd* predominates, and it also takes on a technical meaning: it is the intent to do harm, especially bodily harm. The restricted use of the term *ʿamd* serves in effect to quarantine this type of intent to morally negative actions. In fact, when the term *niyya*—which I have argued is partly reserved for morally positive intentions—does appear in discussion of penal matters, it is employed in ways that preserve its neutrality or goodness. The jurists simply do not speak of the *niyya* to do harm.

Part 1. *Intent to Injure*

A. *Overview*

Ibn Qudāma defines *al-jirāḥ* as "any hostile act toward a person or property, but in customary usage [the term] is limited to illegal infringement of the body, while offenses against property are called *al-jināyāt*, [and these latter include] unjustified seizure of property (*ghaṣb*), robbery (*nahb*), theft (*sariqa*), fraud (*khiyāna*), and damage (*itlāf*)."[3] In what follows, I focus primarily on homicide (*qatl*)—though my analysis largely holds for bodily injuries in general.[4] Consistent with the general Islamic legal view of agency, one must be of age and of sound mind to be potentially culpable for injurious acts.[5] For offenses against persons, the Qur'ān indicates two general categories of remedy: retaliation (*qiṣāṣ*

[3] Ibn Qudāma, *al-Mughnī*, 11:443. Ibn Rushd defines the *jināyāt* as "offenses that have prescribed legal penalties," and list these as (1) offenses against the body, life or limbs, which are called *qatl* (homicide) if death results and *jurḥ* (injury) if not; (2) sexual offenses, called *zinā* (unlawful sexual intercourse) and *sifāḥ* (fornication); (3) offenses against property (*amwāl*), including *ḥirāba* (brigandage), *baghy* (trespass), and *sariqa* (theft), or *ghasb* (usurpation) if done through power of high office (*sulṭān*); (4) offenses against reputation, which are called *qadhf* (slander). He mentions a fifth category also, which he seems to set apart as not having a "prescribed legal penalty," namely making lawful what is unlawful among food and drink (*Bidāyat al-mujtahid*, 2:394–395; *DJP*, 2:478; on the last category, see *DJP*, 2:478, n. 209).

[4] Schacht notes that in cases of non-lethal bodily injury, quasi-intentional acts are treated the same as intentional acts (with retaliation or compensation), but retaliation only occurs for certain kinds of injuries (*Introduction*, 181–182). He observes that "retaliation for bodily harm is restricted to those cases in which exact equality can be assured, e.g. the loss of a hand, a foot, a tooth, &c.;" retaliation also occurs for an eye if its ability to see is lost, but not if it has been knocked out, and for a head wound that lays bare the bone (185). In all other cases, a compensation is determined for a given injury, paid by the victim himself, except for indirect/inadvertent injury, in which case the injuring party's *ʿāqila* shares the burden (181–182). "The full blood-money [i.e., equivalent to that of a homicide] is to be paid not only for homicide but for grievous bodily harm, particularly for the loss of organs which exist singly, e.g. the tongue (also for the loss of the beard and of the head of hair); half the blood-money for the loss of organs which exist in pairs, one-tenth for one finger or one toe, one-twentieth for one tooth; a detailed tariff covers most other wounds. This penalty for wounds is called *arsh*; if no percentage of the blood-money is prescribed, the so-called *ḥukma* becomes due, i.e. it is estimated by how much the bodily harm in question would reduce the value of a slave, and the corresponding blood-money must be paid" (185–186).

[5] The financial liability for *jināyāt* incurred by a slave rests on the slave's owner (Schacht, *Introduction*, 128). Slaves are punished for *ḥadd* offenses to a reduced degree—they cannot be stoned to death, and are generally subject to half the number of lashes (ibid., 177).

or *qawad*) and material/financial compensation, or 'blood money' (*diya* or *'aql*).[6] As a general rule, whenever retaliation is a potential remedy, the injured party has the option of substituting compensation or foregoing all remedy. If the facts of the case are such that retaliation is permitted, then the classic 'eye for an eye' calculus comes into effect. While the details are complex, the principle is relatively simple: for a broken tooth, a ruined eye, a severed or mangled digit or limb, etc., the injuring party is given the same injury in retaliation. As retaliation for homicide, the injuring party is killed, though jurists debate whether the form of the retaliatory killing should match that of the initial offense—drowning for drowning, for example.[7] Financial compensation for injury or death is assessed according to a scale determined by prevailing economic circumstances (classically one hundred camels or a thousand gold dinars for a free male Muslim). Compensation for injuries and homicide is a matter between the injuring and injured parties and a certain set of their social circles, referred to as the *awliyā'* (roughly, the plaintiff's kin) and the *'āqila* (those liable for compensation, roughly the defendant's kin[8]). Jurists assign a material value to a given body part, or for the whole person in the case of homicide, and payment is made by the injuring party or his *'āqila* to the injured party or his *awliyā'*. Because of the option to waive retaliation in favor of compensation or forgiveness, some have suggested that an injurious act in Islamic law "is in the nature of a private injury, more akin to a tort than a crime involving public interest or concern."[9]

In cases where bodily injury or death are caused by a person deemed capable of acting willfully, by some means other than the legitimate execution of corporal or capital punishment, the assessment of the

[6] See, for example, Qur'ān 2:178–179; 5:45.

[7] See Ibn Rushd, *Bidāyat al-mujtahid*, 2:404–405; *DJP*, 2:489–490: for Mālik and Shāfi'ī, in most cases, *qiṣāṣ* takes the form of the murder, although they disagreed over death by burning or arrow. Abū Ḥanīfa, however, held on the basis of a *ḥadīth* that all retaliatory killing must be done with a sword.

[8] See Schacht, *Introduction*, 186.

[9] Farhat J. Ziadeh, "Criminal Law," in *Oxford Encyclopedia of the Modern Islamic World* (Oxford: Oxford University Press, 1995), 1:329. However, responding to this commonplace characterization, J.N.D. Anderson has argued that "no such simple classification will suffice: instead, it is essential to view [the Islamic law of homicide] in its historical setting and detailed development," which he proceeds to do ("Homicide in Islamic Law," *Bulletin of the School of Oriental and African Studies, University of London* 13, 4 [1951]: 811–828; quote is from 811). Bernard Weiss compellingly links this issue to the patriarchal family unit and kinship ties so central to the worldview of pre-modern Islamic law (*Spirit*, 152–153); see the conclusion to this chapter, below.

intentions of the injuring party plays a central role in determining the remedy. This, of course, is not a peculiar characteristic of Islamic law, as many legal systems recognize a distinction between intentionally and accidentally causing injury or death. For example, the Anglo-American legal tradition establishes a range of types of intentional homicides, from premeditated murder, to intentional murder that is not premeditated, to justifiable homicide, all of which are intentional but which are assigned very different penalties. One theoretical alternative to weighing intentions would be a system of strict liability, in which the person causing harm is held liable for punishment and/or recompense based on the results of the act, not the intention. In such a system, a killing in cold blood or in self-defense would produce the same legal response.

The Islamic jurists' treatment of intent in injurious acts combines what appear to be incompatible approaches, by taking account of intentions while also insisting on strict liability. We might call this 'intention-based strict liability': the injuring party is in some measure strictly liable, regardless of whether the act was intentional or otherwise, but the exact nature of the liability depends on the injuring party's intentions. All Muslim jurists posit a distinction between intentional (*'amd*) and accidental (*khaṭa'*) homicide, and most add a third, intermediate category, quasi-intentional homicide (*shibh al-'amd* or *'amd al-khaṭa'*). While jurists often elaborate on this three-fold taxonomy, most retain its basic framework. Someone must be held responsible in all cases of injurious action, but whether retaliation, compensation, and/or any other remedy applies depends on the ascribed intention.[10]

However, if paying attention to intentions may appeal to a certain sense of justice, mitigating strict liability's moral equivocation, it raises the serious question of how such intentions are to be known and assessed. On this crucial matter, J.N.D. Anderson observes that

[10] In certain cases where the killer cannot be identified, the *qasāma* oath applies; Schacht summarizes this as follows: "If the killer is not known, the ancient procedure of *ḳasāma*, a kind of compurgation, takes place. If the body of a person is found who has obviously been killed, the inhabitants of the quarter, the owner of the house (and his *'āḳila*), the passengers and crew of the boat in which he is found, must swear fifty oaths that they have not killed him and do not know who has killed him; if there are not fifty of them, they must swear more than once. Should they refuse to swear, they are imprisoned until they do. They thereby become free from liability to *ḳiṣāṣ* [retaliation] but must, as *'āḳila*, pay the blood-money. If the body of a killed person is found in the main mosque, the public treasury pays his blood-money; if it is found in open country, his blood is not avenged" (*Introduction*, 184).

> one of the basic problems debated … [among] jurists concerns the nature and proof of that category of homicide designated 'deliberate' (*'amd*). The matter is one of much complexity and confusion, for often the same writer will in places assert that deliberate homicide means homicide committed with the actual intention to kill, while in other places he will state or imply that it means homicide which results from an intentional use of any weapons or means intrinsically likely to kill. Speaking generally, it may be stated that all the schools except the Mālikīs base their definitions on the principle that only cases of homicide in which the killer intended to kill and employed some means likely to have that result should be put in that category [i.e., deliberate homicide].[11]

This suggests that jurists seek some direct knowledge of the killers intent, alongside the indirect evidence of the objective form and context of the killing. "The differences," he continues,

> between the jurists (and, indeed, the real or apparent contradictions in a single book) largely arise from the varying degrees to which they consider a man's overt act as adequately establishing his inner purpose or even, in some schools, allow the act so to stand in the place of the intention that they speak indiscriminately now of the one and now of the other and in practice concern themselves with the act alone.[12]

However, while I find some passing evidence to support this view—that jurists disagree about seeing overt acts as evidence of intent—in my reading of Islamic penal law most jurists of whatever affiliation in effect abandon the quest for direct access to intentions and rely nearly exclusively on indirect evidence. As the above statements suggest, Anderson seems himself open to such a reading. He characterizes Ḥanafīs as "the most thorough-going" in taking the weapon or means used as a direct indication (*dalīl*) of intent.[13] But he also admits that although

> the Shāfiʿī and Ḥanbalī books seem more equivocal and sometimes appear to insist more strongly on the actual intention to kill: it seems, however, that in both schools the better view regards a fatal assault with a lethal weapon, or by some means which would usually prove fatal, as "deliberate" homicide, whether or not the assailant actually intended to kill.[14]

---

[11] Anderson, "Homicide," 819. While insightful and reliable, Anderson's article unfortunately provides nearly nothing in terms of reference to specific primary texts.

[12] Ibid., 820.

[13] Ibid. See, for example, Kāsānī, *Kitāb badāʾiʿ al-ṣanāʾiʿ*, 10:237.

[14] Anderson, "Homicide," 820.

Mālikīs likewise treat as deliberate any homicide done with an instrument thought intrinsically likely to kill. In fact, they do not recognize the category of quasi-intentional homicide and instead "adopt much the widest definition" of deliberate homicide, effectively shifting into this category acts in which the killer did not strictly speaking intend to kill, but committed "any unjustified assault."[15] In sum, while at times jurists may discuss the actual intent of the killer, and may suggest rather vaguely that one should investigate after the intent itself, the overwhelming weight of their concern is for objective evidence. The jurists have few illusions about ascertaining intent as a purely subjective state, but instead pragmatically seek to determine what objective criteria are indicative of certain intentions.

Three factors emerge as primary in assessing the intentional state of the actor: the type of action, the instrument or weapon used (and the normal expected use of such), and the physical and social context (and the normal expectations for behavior in such a context). The first category, type of action, is usually discussed as 'striking a blow' or some other generic type of injury-producing act. The other two categories, instrument and context, emerge as the crucial elements in assessing intentions, and socio-cultural norms are critical to such assessments. The general pattern that emerges is as follows: (1) purely intentional homicide involves striking intentionally while intending to kill. This subjective state is objectively indicated by the use of an instrument normally associated with causing injury or death, in a setting where intentional killing might be expected. (2) The intermediate case, quasi-intentional homicide, involves striking intentionally, but without the intention to kill. The subjective state is indicated by complex criteria, not universally agree-upon, mixing aspects of the two extremes—that is, purely intentional and purely accidental.[16] (3) An accidental homi-

[15] Ibid.

[16] The relationship of intention to responsibility is a vexed one in Western philosophical literature. Searle points out that knowing something will be the consequence of an action does not necessarily mean one intends that consequence (*Intentionality*, 103). A dentist, Searle observes, may know his drilling will cause pain to the patient, but it would be wrong to say the dentist intends to cause pain. If no pain resulted, we would not say he failed, but that he was mistaken (the conditions of satisfaction for his belief were not satisfied, rather than those for his intention). Searle further notes there is no necessary close connection, let alone identity, between intention and responsibility. He notes that "we hold people responsible for many things they do not intend and we do not hold them responsible for many things they do intend." Here, however, his discussion is insufficiently nuanced to be very helpful. He gives examples of a driver who

cide involves striking accidentally, and this subjective state is indicated by the use of an instrument not normally associated with causing injury or death, in a setting where intentional killing would not normally be expected. Jurists assign various remedies to each category, including some combination of retaliation, compensation, and (for some jurists) expiation (*kaffāra*). The following table displays this general pattern:

Table 1. *Basic Tripartite Assessment of Injurious Action*

Type of Action	*Instrument Norm*	*Circumstance Norm*	*Assessment of Intent*	*Remedy*
Striking a blow	Usually used to kill	Killing is normal	Intentional: intent to strike, intent to kill	Retaliation or compensation, (expiation)
Striking a blow	(Various)	(Various)	Quasi-intentional: intent to strike, no intent to kill	Compensation, (expiation)
Striking a blow	Not usually used to kill	Killing is not normal	Accidental: no intent to strike or kill	Compensation

The jurists seek to establish, through both general principle and casuistic example, the boundaries between these categories. To do so, they discuss exactly what instruments and contexts indicate each type of intention, based primarily on prevailing expectations regarding normal use of a given instrument, normal expected results of a given action, and normal behavior in a given context. They do not recognize any gradations within the category of 'intentional', such as 'with malice aforethought' or 'in the heat of the moment'.

recklessly but unintentionally runs over a child (no intention but held responsible) and someone forced to act at gunpoint (intention but not held responsible). The philosophical distinction may be valid, but whether "we hold [such] people responsible" in either a commonsensical or a legal way would clearly depend on the wider circumstances of the event. Degrees of responsibility must be distinguished in all but the strictest liability system. The latter case is simple enough—coercion clearly mitigates responsibility—but even here, degrees of coercion would have to be distinguished. In the former case, common sense and certainly most legal systems would consider a reckless or drunk driver responsible to some degree for the consequences of his or her actions, whether truly intended or not.

B. *A Closer Look*

To throw more light on the framework presented so far, we can draw on the Ḥanafī Ibn Mawdūd al-Mūṣilī, who is terse and to-the-point, and the Ḥanbalī Ibn Qudāma, who provides more colorful detail. Both are typical in displaying an intention-based strict liability approach, and a reliance on objective indicants of subjective states. Further, both employ terms other than *niyya*, especially *ʿamd*, for intent to injure. Elaborating on the basic tripartite scheme, Mūṣilī introduces the topic of homicide as follows:

> Homicide is connected to five assessments: intentional (*ʿamd*), quasi-intentional (*shibh ʿamd*), accidental (*khaṭaʾ*), that which can be assimilated to accident (*mā ujriya mujrā al-khaṭaʾ*), and indirect homicide (*al-qatl bi-sabab*). Intentional [homicide is defined as] deliberately striking (*yataʿammada al-ḍarb*) with what severs into parts, such as a sword, a spear, a flint, and fire.[17]

Intentional homicide, he notes, is a sin (*maʾtham/ithm*—discussed below), for which the legal remedy is retaliation, and this may be waved by the *awliyāʾ* in favor of compensation from the killer's property or no remedy at all. There is no other expiation for intentional homicide.[18] He names several instruments, implying that there is a general agreement that these are potentially mortal weapons. Prevailing social norms and expectations regarding a given action, not the actual subjective state of the actor, determine the assessment of the intent.

While generally in accord with Mūṣilī, Ibn Qudāma considers more potential nuances and juristic disagreements in the category of deliberate intent, such as the prospect of using an instrument the dangers of which are ambiguous:

> If the wound is a small one such as ... [when the victim] is stabbed with a needle or thorn, you [i.e., the one assessing the case] look [to examine the situation]. If [the wound] is in a [potentially] fatal place (*fī maqtalin*), like the eye, heart, torso [near the kidneys], temple, or inner ear, so that he dies, this is also intentional [homicide] because the blow by that instrument is in a fatal place, like a wound with a knife in a non-fatal place [i.e., a fatal stab with a knife in any part of the body]. If [the small wound] is in a non-fatal place, then you look; if it has

[17] Mūṣilī, *al-Ikhtiyār*, 5:22–23.
[18] Ibid., 5:24.

> reached the interior of the body, then it is like a large wound because of the increase in the severity of pain, and it can thereby lead to death, like a large [wound].[19]

Some jurists assign retaliation to these lesser instruments or acts, deeming them deliberate, while others require only compensation, treating them as quasi-intentional, depending on whether they think this act indicates a desire to kill, 'because it usually kills'. But Ibn Qudāma still does not discuss pure intent as such, but rather the objective form of the action, generating the general principle that intentional homicide can involve normally non-lethal instruments if the blow is directed at a particularly vulnerable part of the body. Ibn Qudāma leaves such a determination to the judge in an actual case.

Ibn Qudāma notes a further disagreement over what constitutes a normally lethal instrument: "killing with an item without a sharp edge (*ghayr al-muḥaddad*), such as something that should be thought likely to cause death when used in its usual manner; this is intentional homicide and necessitates retaliation also."[20] On the one hand, this category amounts to a catch-all, encompassing any blunt instrument "thought likely to cause death when used in its usual manner." On the other hand, some jurists, including Abū Ḥanīfa, consider this category of killing to be quasi-intentional, and not licensing retaliation, because the Prophet said "Verily in the [category of] quasi-intentional homicide is killing by lash, rod, and stone."[21] Ibn Qudāma counters by citing the Qur'ān (17:33): "And if anyone is killed wrongfully (*maẓlūman*), We have given his heir authority," implying that any 'wrongful' killing leads to the victim's kin having the right to retaliate.[22] He says that acts in this category, using a non-sharpened but normally lethal instrument, count as 'wrongful', and thus retaliation applies. Trumping an explicit *ḥadīth* with a more general Qur'ān verse, Ibn Qudāma leaves room for debate over lashes, stones, and rods.

He also considers other ways that the category of intentional homicide might be clouded. The first is what we might call 'intervening intent'. Discussing suffocation and strangulation, throwing someone

19 Ibn Qudāma, *al-Mughnī*, 11:446.
20 Ibid., 11:447.
21 Ibid.
22 Ibn Qudāma also cites Qur'ān 2:178.

from a height, drowning, and casting into a well, he notes that "this is all intentional, for each usually causes death."[23] Similarly, forcing someone into close proximity with a dangerous animal is also intentional homicide, although Shāfiʿī dissents, asserting that lions and snakes and the like normally flee from people.[24] Depriving a person of food or drink is also potentially intentional homicide: "if the duration is such that one would usually die, there is retaliation [that is, the homicide is intentional], and if one would not usually die [but does], this is quasi-intentional."[25] Again, expectations for normal cause-and-effect relations are used to assess the intention. However, Ibn Qudāma asserts that "If a person is thrown into shallow water which he is able to get out of, and he chooses to delay and then dies from this, there is no retaliation or blood money assessed, because the actions [of the person who did the throwing] did not cause death."[26] That is, the intentional actions of the 'victim' can change the nature of the situation: if the 'victim' freely chooses to act in such a way that causes his death, this is not held against anyone else. However, he gives no indication of how to determine if this happens.

Poisoning provokes a disagreement along similar lines. Poisoning is widely deemed intentional if the poison used is typically fatal. According to one opinion attributed to Shāfiʿī, he reportedly disagrees, saying "eating [the poison] is voluntary, and this is like one person holding up a knife and the other person stabbing himself with it."[27] Shāfiʿī considers the injured party to have acted freely, thus mitigating the harmful intention of the person supplying the poison. This differs from the example of a person choosing to remain in water after being thrown there, for there is no explicit indication that Shāfiʿī's opinion hinges on the victim's knowing about the poison and choosing to ingest it. This is a highly restrictive, formalistic approach to intentions, taking into

[23] Ibn Qudāma, *al-Mughnī*, 11:449–450. He adds that another opinion distinguishes between acts which are of a longer duration and thus more likely to death, which are deemed intentional, and acts which are of a shorter duration and thus less likely to cause death, which are deemed quasi-intentional.

[24] Ibid., 11:450–452.

[25] Ibid., 11:453.

[26] Ibid., 11:450–451. Note here that there is no mention of whether the initial throwing was done with the intention of killing. In any case, if the person dies as a result of this action, but the person killed intervenes, so to speak, with his choice to remain in the water, the intention to kill is disrupted.

[27] Ibid., 11:453.

account only the most immediate intention-in-action, and disregarding the wider scope of intended consequences. Shāfiʿī breaks the action into several parts, namely 'adding of poison to the food' and 'causing the victim to eat', and he holds the poisoner liable only for the former, refusing to consider the compound intentional action of 'poisoning the victim'.[28] As we saw in the previous chapters, dividing an action into component parts is an effective strategy for limiting the importance of intentions, as this allows the intentions in a given component to be isolated from the rest of the action.

Ibn Qudāma discusses "that which indirectly causes death by some means that usually causes death" (*yatasabbab ilā qatlihi bi-mā yaqtulu ghāliban*).[29] Beginning with the case of a person coerced into killing, Ibn Qudāma says the coercer and coerced share the liability for retaliation, while Abū Ḥanīfa and Muḥammad al-Shaybānī hold only the coercer liable "because the coerced is an instrument of the coercer." Similarly, Ibn Rushd notes that the Mālikīs do not excuse a person under coercion, analogizing him to a person starving to death, who is not considered justified in killing another person and eating him to survive.[30] Still others hold only the coerced liable, since he does the actual killing, or hold neither liable, since each is insulated from full responsibility for the act.[31] In short, there is no consensus on coercion. As for other indirect homicides, Ibn Qudāma holds a person liable for retaliation for testifying falsely in a case that leads to corporal

[28] Shāfiʿī cites a *ḥadīth*, which may explain why this only applies to poisoning: the *ḥadīth* singles out acts of poisoning, but may not apply in other cases. Further, this echoes Shāfiʿī's treatment of intentions in contracts (discussed in chapter 4 above), where he also breaks the complex intentional action into constituents, and limits the actor's liability to the narrowest scope.

[29] Ibn Qudāma, *al-Mughnī*, 11:455.

[30] Ibn Rushd, *Bidāyat al-mujtahid*, 2:396; *DJP*, 2:480.

[31] Ibn Qudāma indicates that "There are four subsets of this [type]: One, a person coerces someone to kill another …, then both the coercer and the coerced share the liability for retaliation. This is Mālik's opinion. Abū Ḥanīfa and Muḥammad [al-Shaybānī] say there is retaliation only incumbent on the coercer because the coerced is an instrument of the coercer … Zufar says the direct actor (*al-mubāshir* [the coerced]) is liable [for retaliation], not the coercer, for the direct actor is the cause. Shāfiʿī holds the coercer liable, and notes that the coerced [may be held liable or not]. Abū Yūsuf says neither is liable, because the coercer did not directly cause the death, like one who digs a well [and someone falls into it]; and the coerced is exempted, for it is as if he was thrown against a person [the victim]. We [Ibn Qudāma and the Ḥanbalīs] hold the coercer liable, for he indirectly causes the death" (*al-Mughnī*, 11:455–456).

or capital punishment,[32] and also a judge who delivers a corporal or capital sentence while knowing of the falsity of the evidence.[33]

Turning to quasi-intentional homicide (*shibh al-ʿamd*), Mūṣilī defines this as "striking in a way that does not sever into parts, as with a stone, a stick, or a hand." This is also a sin, but for this there is no retaliation, only compensation (from the *ʿāqila*) and expiation (*kaffāra*).[34] For Mūṣilī, the objective form indicates an intention to strike, but not to kill, because the instrument used is something normally used to strike but not normally associated with causing severe injury or death. For his part, Ibn Qudāma remarks that in *shibh al-ʿamd* the injuring party "intends (*qaṣada*) to strike without killing. This may be called '*ʿamd al-khaṭa*'' (intentional accident) or '*khaṭa' al-ʿamd*' (accidental intention) because of the combination of intention and accident in it, for the person intends (*ʿamada*) the act, but commits an error in killing."[35] Here again the issues are observable indicants, not actual states of mind. If death results from a justifiable act, such as disciplining, or even an aggressive act not done in a manner that usually causes death, this is quasi-intentional. Ibn Qudāma notes that some Mālikīs consider such a homicide intentional and assign retaliation for it, claiming that "the Qur'ān only mentions intention and accident, and whoever adds a third category, adds to the [Qur'ān]. Homicide resulting from an intentional action is intentional."[36] However, Ibn Qudāma cites a *ḥadīth*, providing a textual source to counter the Mālikī argument: "Verily in the [category of] quasi-intentional homicide (*ʿamd al-khaṭa'*) is killing by lash, rod, and stone, and [the compensation is] one hundred camels."[37] Ibn Qudāma makes no mention of expiation (*kaffāra*) for either intentional or quasi-intentional homicide, nor does he follow Mūṣilī in invoking the terminology of sin.

---

[32] Ibn Qudāma notes that Shāfiʿī holds such a witness liable for retaliation; Abū Ḥanīfa does not, saying that such a witness is like one who digs a well that another falls into (ibid., 11:456). The Ḥanafī Mūṣilī, as seen above, calls this 'indirect homicide' (*al-qatl bi-sabab*), and he holds the person liable for compensation.

[33] Ibn Qudāma, *al-Mughnī*, 11:456–457.

[34] Mūṣilī, *al-Ikhtiyār*, 5:24. See also Ibn Qudāma, *al-Mughnī*, 11:463: "There is no retaliation for this, though there is compensation owed by the *ʿāqila* according to most jurists." The compensation here is the 'heavier' amount, classically measured in terms of the specific types of camels required.

[35] Ibn Qudāma, *al-Mughnī*, 11:462–463, emphasis added.

[36] Ibid.

[37] Ibid. See also 11:447: this is the same *ḥadīth* that Abu Ḥanīfa cited in regard to Ibn Qudāma's second subset of intentional homicide (see n. 21 above).

Regarding the third category, accidental homicide, jurists often make a basic distinction between "accident in the intention" and "accident in the act." The former is often represented by the example of a person who is hunting but mistakenly strikes a person while thinking he is game, or when one kills an opponent in battle, not realizing he is a Muslim (basically cases of mistaken identity); the latter occurs, for example, when one shoots at a target but hits a man he had no intent to hit.[38] For accidental homicide there is no retaliation, but there is compensation and expiation, although accidental homicide is not a sin. Here, the act is done without any intention to either strike or kill the victim, although the basic act of striking out at something is intentional. Ibn Qudāma approaches purely accidental homicide by identifying the two subsets of such acts noted above: first, cases in which one "performs an action in which one does not want (*lā yurīdu*) to strike a deadly blow, but does, such as when one shoots at prey or at a target, but strikes a person and kills him."[39] For this there is compensation and expiation, but no retaliation. The second subset involves intentionally killing in battle or outside of the Islamic lands (*fī dār al-ḥarb*), thinking that the victim is not a Muslim, but in fact he is a Muslim; "this is as if [the game] one were hunting proved to be human."[40] For this there is expiation, but no retaliation or compensation.[41] In effect, these two cases are linked in that the intentional action has unintended consequences. Ibn Qudāma explicitly analogizes the second case to the first by likening the non-Muslim to a beast of prey. This differs from quasi-intentional homicide, where there is intent to strike a person but not to kill, while in these examples of purely accidental homicide, there is no intention to strike a person.

As for 'that which can be assimilated to accident', Mūṣilī notes that "this is like a sleeping person rolling over and killing another person."[42] While this is very similar to purely accidental homicide, a sleeping person has no real capacity for agency. (This clarifies the nature of 'accidental' acts, highlighting the fact that in an accident, the intended act of an agent goes awry.) Still, the principle holds that someone must be held responsible, and the penalty is identical to that of purely

[38] See, for example, Mūṣilī, *al-Ikhtiyār*, 5:25. See also Schacht, *Introduction*, 182; and Anderson, "Homicide," 821.

[39] Ibn Qudāma, *al-Mughnī*, 11:464.

[40] Ibid., 11:465; and see 11:465–473.

[41] Ibid., 11:465. In support he cites Qur'ān 4:92.

[42] Mūṣilī, *al-Ikhtiyār*, 5:26. See also Ibn Qudāma, *al-Mughnī*, 11:445.

accidental injurious action: there is no retaliation (or sin), but there is compensation and expiation.

The final category, 'indirect homicide' (*al-qatl bi-sabab*), is also represented through casuistic example: when someone is digging a well and "places a stone where it does not belong so that it is overlooked and someone perishes thereby."[43] For this, there is compensation, but no sin and no retaliation, and unlike accidental acts and 'that which is equivalent to accidental', there is no expiation. In this case as well, there is no intention to strike or harm the victim, and the action is one not normally associated with causing injury. Thus, here too, there is little difference from purely accidental homicide, although the remedy in this case is less still than in the case of accident, for there is no expiation—and, significantly, this is the only case of homicide where the person causing the death can inherit from the deceased.[44] Still, a form of strict liability is applied, so that the injuring party, in spite of lacking any intent to injure, is liable for compensation.

C. *Intent, Sin, and Expiation*

To better understand the nature of injurious actions and the intentional aspects of them, Mūṣilī's presentation of homicide may be represented as follows:

---

[43] Mūṣilī, *al-Ikhtiyār*, 5:26; he also notes that this assessment extends to the case where someone falls in the well and dies—but in that case there is expiation. See also Ibn Qudāma, *al-Mughnī*, 11.445. Schacht notes that "indirect causation (*tasbīb*) creates liability only if the act in question was unauthorized," and that "the sphere of authorized acts is very extensive": for example, if the act occurs on one's own property, or with the permission of the property owner, or on land which the actor is a joint owner (including some public land), there is no liability (*Introduction*, 182–183).

[44] "In all of these cases except *al-qatl bi-sabab* there is no inheritance"—that is, for the injuring party, if he or she stands to inherit otherwise (Mūṣilī, *al-Ikhtiyār*, 5:26). The jurists discuss whether a person who kills another can inherit from his or her victim. Some hold that a killer can never inherit from his victim, while others make a distinction between intentional and accidental killing, allowing inheritance in the latter case but not the former (unless that intentional killing was an obligatory or excusable act, as in the case of an executioner inheriting from a rightfully executed person) (see Ibn Rushd, *Bidāyat al-mujtahid*, 2:360; *DJP*, 2:436). Mūṣilī notes: "If someone falls into the well and dies of suffocation or starvation, the [owner of the well] is liable for an expiation of freeing a Muslim slave, or, if he cannot, then fasting for two consecutive months" (5:26).

Table 2. *Mūṣilī's Assessment of Homicide*

Assessment	*Retaliation*	*Compensation*	*Expiation*	*Sin*
Intentional	Yes (if no compensation)	Yes (if no retaliation)	No	Yes
Quasi-intentional	No	Yes	Yes	Yes
Accidental	No	Yes	Yes	No
Assimilated to Accidental	No	Yes	Yes	No
Indirect	No	Yes	No	No

Retaliation is only an option for intentional injury, while compensation is either an option (for intentional injury) or required (in all other cases). Expiation is not assigned for intentional injury or for the least intentional act, *al-qatl bi-sabab*, but is required in all other cases.[45] Intentional and quasi-intentional acts are the only sins. This table demonstrates that a form of strict liability consistently holds: compensation is required in every case, except where it may be preempted by the more severe retaliation—if an injurious action occurs, someone must be held responsible for compensating the victim and/or his/her kin. However, intentions determine what other remedies or penalties apply.

The category of 'sin' (*ithm*) discussed by Mūṣilī, but not by all jurists, is primarily a soteriological concern: such an act is held against a person by God, and potentially has consequences on judgment day.[46] However, the category of sin has no direct legal consequences, no effect on the worldly punishment assessed by a jurist. Mūṣilī deems only intentional and quasi-intentional homicide sins, while Ibn Qudāma does not employ this terminology. The matter of expiation or atonement (*kaffāra*) has both religious or soteriological and worldly, legal aspects. Only Mūṣilī's affiliation, the Ḥanafī *madhhab*, totally discounts the possibility of *kaffāra* for intentional homicide, and only the Shāfiʿī *madhhab*

[45] However, according to Zuḥaylī, the Ḥanafīs are alone in not assigning *kaffāra* for indirect or inadvertent homicide; all others treat this with the same punishments as purely accidental homicide (*al-Fiqh al-islāmī wa-adillatuhu*, 6:328). Further, Zuḥaylī notes that only Ḥanafīs allow the killer to inherit from the victim in indirect homicide.

[46] Mūṣilī's modern commentator, Maḥmūd Abū Daqīqa, asserts that jurists agree that intentional homicide is a sin, based on Qur'ān 4:93: "Whoever intentionally kills a believer, his punishment is an eternity in hell, and the anger and curse of God is upon him"; and based on a *ḥadīth*: "God built up man, and cursed is the one who tears him down" (*al-Ikhtiyār*, 5:23).

assigns non-negotiable expiation. The other two *madhhab*s hold that if the victim's kin opt for retaliation (or forgiveness), this accomplishes the expiation of the sin of the injuring party, and thus they assign no other expiation.[47] For quasi-intentional homicide, jurists typically assign *kaffāra* in addition to the payment of compensation, and do not allow retaliation.[48] *Kaffāra* is applied by most jurists for accidental homicide.[49] Thus, quasi-intentional and accidental homicide differ only in that the former may be a sin.

Etymologically, the term *kaffāra* refers to covering a thing or person so that it is hidden from view.[50] The term appears in the Qur'ān, including in reference to acts of propitiatory redemption or pardon.[51] As used in *fiqh*, *kaffāra* is often mentioned in connection with sin (*ithm*, as above, or *dhanb*), and is an act which removes sin from—or, truer to the term's etymology, eclipses sin in—one's soteriological record.[52] *Kaffāra* is only done as reparation after the fact, not as a preventive measure, and jurists employ the term primarily with connotations of punishment distinct from the quranic emphasis on propitiation. Generally, *kaffāra* in *fiqh* is of three types: emancipating a slave or slaves, fasting, or feeding or clothing the needy; for homicide, the preferred *kaffāra* is emancipation of a slave.[53]

Given that *kaffāra* potentially functions as soteriological reparation for sin, Mūṣilī's assessment of homicide is surprising in at least two ways. First, *kaffāra* is not assigned for intentional homicide, in spite of the act's status as a sin. Thus, intentional homicide apparently cannot be undone in the eyes of God—a position, as noted, unique to the Ḥanafī *madhhab*. Second, *kaffāra* is assigned for both accidental homi-

---

[47] Zuḥaylī, *al-Fiqh al-islāmī wa adillatuhu*, 6:261–263.

[48] Ibid., 6:327.

[49] Ibid., 6:329–330.

[50] J. Chelhod, "Kaffāra," in *Encyclopaedia of Islam*, new ed.

[51] Ibid.; see Qur'ān, 5:89, 95.

[52] Muḥammad Rawwās Qal'ajī, *Mawsū'at fiqh Zayd b. Thābit wa-Abī Hurayra* (Beirut: Dār al-Nafā'is, 1993), 1:167; 2:219–221. See also Rafīq al-'Ajm, *Mawsū'at muṣṭalaḥāt uṣul al-fiqh 'inda al-muslimīn* (Beirut: Maktabat Lubnān Nāshirūn, 1998), 2:1229; he notes that *niyya* is one of the requirements for a valid *kaffāra*, and that the term carries connotations of *'ibāda*, and "the *'ibādāt* remove sins"; further, he observes that, like the *ḥudūd*, acts of *kaffāra* are decreed by God, and do not have rational explanations. Chelhod ("Kaffāra") notes that in the Qur'ān "fault and expiation are regarded in a material sense [i.e., fault as a thing to be covered over by expiation], the moral content developing rather later."

[53] Chelhod, "Kaffāra." *Kaffāra* for significant errors or omissions in performance of the *ḥajj* is a blood sacrifice.

cide and that which is treated as its equivalent, in spite of the fact that neither act is called a sin. In this view, *kaffāra* seems to lose its soteriological significance, perhaps serving instead as a means of worldly, social atonement—a concrete sign of repentance for the sake of regaining the good graces of one's fellow Muslims. Only for quasi-intentional homicide is *kaffāra* possibly an expiation of sin. The other *madhhab*s call intentional homicide a sin and assign *kaffāra*—although, according to Mālikīs and Ḥanbalīs, if retaliation or forgiveness is applied by the victim's kin, this accomplishes expiation for the sin of the killer. All the *madhhab*s call quasi-intentional homicide a sin and assign *kaffāra*, while none calls accidental homicide a sin, yet each assigns *kaffāra*. No *madhhab* calls indirect homicide a sin, and all but Ḥanafīs assign *kaffāra*.[54] This rather confusing set of patterns and anomalies reflects a complex mix of logics shaping the law, some more literalist and others more focused on broad ideas of morality.[55] For present purposes, it is enough to note that intent is not related to sin, nor is sin is related to expiation in a uniform and easily predictable way among Muslim jurists.

D. *Ibn Rushd on the Provisional Nature of Juristic Assessments*

Thus far, we have seen that Muslim jurists consider intent to be a crucial, definitive aspect of injurious actions, but that they assess intentions based on purely objective criteria. Clearly, the jurists see significant limits to the accessibility of others' intentions. Despite these limitations, however, *fiqh* texts do not advocate that one shy away from making judgments. They neither insist on direct knowledge of others' subjective states, nor do they call for suspending judgement in the absence of such knowledge. Instead, they display a certain modest attitude toward the meaning of their judgments, implicitly viewing them through a theological lens. *Fiqh* manuals are not overtly theological or metaphysical works, and the jurists do not offer much commentary on the afterlife. However, some texts display a strong sense of the provisionality of the justice they offer, a sense that their legal assessments are only one component of justice, and that divine judgement in the afterlife completes

---

[54] See Mūṣilī, *al-Ikhtiyār*, 5:23–24; Zuḥaylī, *al-Fiqh al-islāmī wa-adillatuhu*, 6:261–263; Schacht, *Introduction*, 181.

[55] The Islamic legal treatment of sin and expiation is the topic of my article in preparation, building on work first presented in my paper, "Offending God and Man: Crime, Sin, and Expiation in Islamic Law," presented at the 2004 Annual Meeting of the American Academy of Religion.

the equation. Regarding intentions in injurious actions, some jurists explicitly assert, and others imply, that these are only fully known and directly judged by God, and that human judgments are only indirect, a kind of best guess within human limits.

We previously saw suggestions of such a view in the comments of Shīrāzī regarding explicit statements of *ṭalāq*. While taking the common position that such statements are held binding even in cases where the husband claims to have misspoken or to have been merely joking, Shīrāzī places this approach in a wider context that includes divine oversight. Although the court holds a man accountable for the manifest meaning of his expression, Shīrāzī observes, God will recognize his true intention (*yudayyanu fīmā baynahu wa-bayna Allāh taʿālā li-annahu yaḥtamilu mā yudʿīhi*).[56] It is as if Shīrāzī is put off by the obvious potential for injustice in the formalism of this aspect of family law and is comforted by the recognition that any such miscarriage will ultimately be rectified in the afterlife.[57]

An even stronger and more sustained presentation of similar sentiments comes from the Andalusian Mālikī jurist Ibn Rushd. In discussing the basic three-fold classification of injurious intent, he notes that some jurists uphold the validity of the middle category, quasi-intentional acts, while others, most prominently Mālik, do not.[58] Ibn Rushd adds a remarkable explanation of the nature of intentions and the role they play in legal assessments:

> Those who deny that there is [such a thing as] quasi-intentional homicide assert that there is no middle ground between mistake and intention, between intending the killing and not intending it [using forms of

[56] Shīrāzī, *al-Muhadhdhab*, 4:292. See also Nawawī, *al-Majmūʿ*, 18:239–241; and Baber Johansen, "Die Sündige, Gesunde Amme. Moral und Gesetzliche Bestimmung (*Ḥukm*) im Islamischen Recht," in *Contingency in a Sacred Law: Legal and Ethical Norms in the Muslim* Fiqh (Leiden: Brill, 1999), 183.

[57] Such concerns over the law becoming an instrument of injustice help generate numerous stories of reluctance on the part of legal experts to serve as judges (*qāḍīs*), applying the law on behalf of the state. See N.J. Coulson, "Doctrine and Practice in Islamic Law: One Aspect of the Problem," *Bulletin of the School of Oriental and African Studies* 18, 2 (1956): 211–226.

[58] Ibn Rushd, *Bidāyat al-mujtahid*, 2:397, *DJP*, 2:481. Ibn Rushd, an adherent of the Mālikī *madhhab*, here seems to endorse the opinion of Shāfiʿī, accepting *shibh al-ʿamd* as a legitimate legal category, over the opinion of Mālik who, as noted above, denies the validity of the category. However, Ibn Rushd, in this section of the text at least, is more concerned to describe disagreements among jurists than to endorse any one opinion, and offers no definitive resolution to the matter of whether quasi-intentional homicide is a legitimate category.

> *qaṣada*]. The argument of those who uphold the middle category is that *no one knows intentions* (*al-niyyāt*) *but God Almighty, but the assessment* (*ḥukm*) *is to be assigned [by humans] on the basis of what is apparent* (*bi-mā ẓahara*).[59]

Ibn Rushd immediately reiterates this point:

> When a person intends (*qaṣada*) to strike a specific person with an instrument that does not usually kill, the assessment vacillates between intentional (*ʿamd*) and mistaken (*khaṭaʾ*), but this is *for our [human] purposes only* (*fī ḥaqqinā*) *and not in the reckoning of the Lord Himself, God, the Exalted.*[60]

And again, Ibn Rushd makes a similar assertion when noting that Mālik does not accuse a father of intentional homicide if he kills his own son, unless the killing is done in stealth (*ghīla*), "but [Mālik] considers the perpetrator of [killing in stealth] to have intended the homicide (*qaṣada al-qatl*) on the basis of predominant probability (*ghalabat al-ẓann*) and the strength of the accusation, for *no one knows intentions* (*al-niyyāt*) *but God Almighty*."[61]

These passages demonstrate two significant points. First, Ibn Rushd recognizes two realms of justice, human and divine. Humans are responsible for a practical, provisional level of justice, making judgments on "the basis of what is apparent," while final and absolute judgment must be left to God in the hereafter. R. Brunschvig observes in Islamic law "the desire to establish, in a humane fashion, what is most probable by regulated means rather than to pursue the strict truth, the certain knowledge of which belongs only to God."[62] Intentions can only be judged with certainty by God, but humans are responsible for doing their best to assess intentions so that the legal system can function to at least approximate true justice. In the first two passages, Ibn Rushd attributes this view to those who employ the 'middle category' of quasi-intentional homicide (i.e., the majority, excluding the Mālikīs), suggesting that intentional and accidental cases rest unambiguously on objective indicants, and only assessments of the gray area in between involve ambiguity and provisionality. However, his comment on Mālik's view of a father killing a son implies that, in any case where a jurist is unsure of true intentions, he should judge based on the best objective evidence available, assured that God will ultimately judge the true

59 Ibid., 2:397, *DJP*, 2:481, emphasis added.
60 Ibid., emphasis added.
61 Ibid., 2:401; *DJP*, 2:486, emphasis added.
62 R. Brunschvig, "Bayyina," in *Encyclopaedia of Islam*, new ed.; cited in Wakin, *Documents in Islamic Law*, 6.

intentions. Especially in this more general formulation, Ibn Rushd depicts juristic assessment as inherently provisional, as one element in a calculus of justice to be completed by divine judgment. Such a position also has the rhetorical effect of warning Muslims that while they may get away with an evil act in this world (if the objective evidence masks their true motives and fools their human judges), they will not fool God.

Second, in this passage we see the term *niyya* used in relation to injurious acts (i.e., "no one knows intentions [*al-niyyāt*] but God Almighty"). This is an unusual occurrence, for the vast majority of references among the jurists to subjective states and intentions in cases of harmful actions use other terms. Mūṣilī and Ibn Qudāma do not refer to *niyya*, relying primarily on *ʿamd*. Even for Ibn Rushd this is an isolated occurrence (this is the sole use of the term *niyya* in Ibn Rushd's chapter on injurious actions). While it would be difficult to draw firm conclusions from this slight evidence, we can say that Ibn Rushd seems to confirm our suspicions. Ibn Rushd here seems to treat *niyya* as a general term or meta-term for intentions, while treating *ʿamd* as a technical term for specific types of homicidal intentions. One could argue that Ibn Rushd's use of the term *niyya* here supports my contention that *niyya* carries positive connotations, for within the sentence in question, *niyya* is the direct object of God's act of knowing (*al-niyyāt lā yaṭliʿu ʿalayhā illā Allāh*). This not only generates an allusion to the oft-cited *ḥadīth* ('Actions are defined by intentions' [*innamā al-aʿmāl bil-niyyāt*]), but also rhetorically isolates God from the negative connotations of *ʿamd*. Human evil is a product of human will, and God has no truck with evil intent. Ibn Rushd apparently strategically deploys the terms *niyya* and *ʿamd* to preserve a moral distinction.

Part 2. *The* Ḥudūd

Islamic penal law encompasses a second general category beyond *jināyāt* or *jirāḥ*. The *ḥudūd* (sg. *ḥadd*) are a distinct sub-category of the *muʿāmalāt*; they are '*ḥaqq Allāh*', the 'claim of God' or 'right of God'. The term *ḥadd* literally means 'limit', and implicit—and sometimes explicit—in the legal usage is the phrase '*ḥudūd Allāh*', meaning 'the limits of God [placed on human conduct]'.[63] This is a set of offenses and atten-

[63] See Qalʿajī, *Mawsūʿat fiqh Zayd b. Thābit*, 1:109.

dant penalties derived more or less directly from the Qur'ān or *ḥadīth*: apostasy (*ridda*), treason or rebellion (*baghy*), unlawful sexual intercourse (*zinā*), slander (*qadhf*, meaning unsubstantiated accusation of *zinā*), theft (*sariqa*), highway robbery or brigandage (*ḥirāba* or *qaṭʿ al-ṭarīq*), and drinking wine (*shurb al-khamr*).[64] While grave, the *ḥudūd* are not necessarily the most serious offenses—homicide, for example, is not among them. The *ḥudūd* are simply those offenses considered to be assigned a clear penalty by the *sharīʿa* and thus on which there is no latitude in the penalty. The penalties for *ḥudūd* offenses are generally corporal (e.g., amputation and flogging), and, in certain cases, capital.[65]

Because the *ḥudūd* are considered to have been assigned specific punishments in the Qur'ān and *ḥadīth*, they are not open to modification at judicial discretion; if the evidence establishes that the act occurred, a given penalty automatically ensues.[66] Thus the *ḥudūd* are based on a principle of strict liability, as neither intentions nor circumstances are taken into account in assigning penalties—if a *ḥadd* ordinance is violated, the set penalty applies.[67] (If an act is deemed not to violate the *ḥudūd*, but a judge considers it a lesser violation, he may apply a discretionary [*taʿzīr*] punishment of lesser severity.) Strictly within the category of the *ḥudūd*, there is no gradation of the liability based on intentions or circumstances, as is the case for injurious acts—although a violation of the *ḥudūd* must be voluntary, and coercion removes liability for the *ḥadd*.[68] It seems to be assumed that a violation of the *ḥudūd* restrictions is necessarily an intentional act. Two significant exceptions

---

[64] See Aly Aly Mansour, "*Hudud* Crimes," in *The Islamic Criminal Justice System*, ed. M. Cherif Bassiouni (London, Rome, and New York: Oceana, 1982), 197–200.

[65] For some cases of *zinā*, the penalty is death by stoning; for highway robbery with homicide, death by crucifixion or sword; for theft (and highway robbery without homicide), severing of the hand and/or foot; for most other cases, flogging with differing numbers of lashes (Schacht, *Introduction*, 175). Apostasy and rebellion are punished by death, usually in the form of beheading with a sword.

[66] While these are discussed to varying degrees in the Qur'ān, jurists extrapolated extensively from the relatively terse quranic passages taken as proof texts for the *ḥudūd*.

[67] Circumstances may be weighed in determining if a given act counts as a *ḥadd* violation; theft, for example is defined both by the value of the property taken and the circumstances of the taker. A pauper is given greater leeway than someone with adequate means, and his taking a limited amount is not 'theft'. However, this enters into the basic definition of theft, akin to the circumstance of marriage making intercourse lawful; once a theft has occurred, the penalty applies.

[68] Schacht, *Introduction*, 176.

to the general disregard for intentions, however, are the matters of mistaken action and action done in ignorance of the law.

Regarding the former, some jurists consider the possibility that one would perform an action with the intention of doing one (permitted) action, but in fact would mistakenly do another (prohibited) action. In these cases an act that is outwardly identical to a *ḥadd* offense is differentiated solely by the subjective intent of the actor. While accidental sexual intercourse may sound implausible, this is exactly the example Ibn Qudāma considers:

> If a woman other than one's wife is presented to him as his wife, and it is said to him, "this is your wife," and he has sex with her believing her to be his wife (*yaʿtaqiduhā zawjatahu*), there is no *ḥadd* applied to him. I do not know of any [juristic] disagreement on this. If it is not said to him, "this is your wife," or he finds a woman in his bed and supposes her (*ẓannahā*) to be his wife or his slave-girl and he has sex with her, or he summons his wife or slave-girl and some other woman comes and he presumes that she is the one he summoned and has sex with her, or some such situation occurs, and he is unaware (*li-ʿamāhu*, lit. 'blind'), there is no *ḥadd* applied to him. This is the opinion of Shāfiʿī.[69]

Ibn Qudāma presents two possibilities. In the first case, a third party presents a woman to a man and indicates verbally or otherwise that she is the man's wife, and the man has sex with her in the mistaken belief that she is his wife. Jurists agree that this is no *ḥadd* offense. Though Ibn Qudāma does not say so explicitly, this case might be assimilated to a case of coercion. In the second case, there is no third-party intervention, but the man finds a woman in his bed, where norms would indicate that she is likely his wife, or he calls for his wife or slave-girl, and another woman comes to him and he has sex with her in the mistaken belief that she is lawful to him. Again, Ibn Qudāma does not assign the *ḥadd* penalty. He further generalizes his opinion by saying "if some such situation occurs," opening the example to wider applicability. Thus the matter hinges on ignorance of the true situation, and any analogous situation of ignorance regarding the identity of the sexual partner would apparently excuse the offense. However, not all jurists agree on the second general situation, where no third party creates the mistaken impression:

[69] Ibn Qudāma, *al-Mughnī*, 12:344. See also Shīrāzī: "If a man finds a woman in his bed and presumes her (*ẓannahā*) to be his [sexually licit slave] or his wife and he has sex with her, there is no *ḥadd* upon him, for he is excused according to his claim of uncertainty (*al-shubha*)" (*al-Muhadhdhab*, 5:381).

> Abū Ḥanīfa holds that the *ḥadd* must be applied to him [in this second case], because [the man] had sex in a situation without legal right (*fī maḥall lā milk lahu fīhi*). We [i.e., Ibn Qudāma/Ḥanbalīs] hold that if he had sex believing it to be permitted, this is excused, for it is like someone saying to him, "this is your wife" [i.e., the first instance above, upon which all jurists agree that there is no *ḥadd*], because the *ḥudūd* are averted by uncertainties (*li-anna al-ḥudūd tudra'u bil-shubuhāt*), and this is the most likely [of the rulings].[70]

For Abū Ḥanīfa, the second case produces guilt because, regardless of his intentions, he violated the rules of sexual intercourse and the context does not excuse this violation. Ibn Qudāma disagrees (siding with Shāfiʿī), equating this with the first case.

In a third permutation of this situation, reversing the basic structure of the previous two cases, however, the *ḥadd* does apply:

> As for a man who summons a *muḥarrama* [i.e., a woman with whom sex is forbidden], and someone else responds, and he has sex with her assuming her to be the one he summoned, the *ḥadd* applies to him, whether the one he summoned was among those about whom there is doubt [regarding the legality of having sex], like a slave-girl owned in common with others (*al-jāriya al-mushtaraka*), or not, because there is no excuse in this.[71]

Here the actual act—sex with a permitted woman—is not unlawful, but the intended act is, and so the *ḥadd* penalty applies. The intention, indicated objectively by his calling for a forbidden woman, defines the act. Thus, Ibn Qudāma is consistent in holding a person accountable for his intentions, whether to act legally or illegally, based on the objective indicants of that intention. Note, however, that he gives no account of how one would prove guilt in such a case. The objective act of summoning a forbidden partner indicates unlawful intent, but it seems the man would have to confess that he failed to noticed the mistake before engaging in sex and never changed his intent, for the only thing wrong

[70] Ibn Qudāma, *al-Mughnī*, 12:344. See also the Ḥanafī Mūṣilī: "If a woman [other than one lawful to him] is presented to a man [as lawful to him], and he has sex with her, the *ḥadd* does not apply, but he does owe her a *mahr*. If a man finds a woman [other than one lawful to him] in his bed and has sex with her, the *ḥadd* applies" (*al-Ikhtiyār*, 4:91). This confirms Ibn Qudāma's indication that Abū Ḥanīfa applies the *ḥadd* when no third party intervenes, when the man can be held responsible for ascertaining the identity of the person in his bed.

[71] Ibn Qudāma, *al-Mughnī*, 12:344–345. Ibn Qudāma adds here that mistakenly killing a person, thinking him to be a son or slave, does not excuse the act, and it is treated as the intentional killing of a non-relative. For a detailed discussion of the case of a father killing his son, see Ibn Rushd, *Bidāyat al-mujtahid*, 2:400–401; *DJP*, 2:485–486.

with the actual action would be his intent. This passage, it seems, carries more rhetorical weight regarding the seriousness of the *ḥudūd* than it does literalist conviction. All in all, appeal to intent seems to lessen the likelihood of the *ḥudūd* penalties being applied.

The final exception to the rule of disregarding intent in *ḥadd* cases involves ignorance of the law:

> There is no *ḥadd* applied to one who does not know that fornication is forbidden. ʿUmar said this, as did ʿUthmān and ʿAlī. *There is no ḥadd except regarding what one has knowledge of* (*lā ḥadda illā ʿalā man ʿalimahu*). This is the opinion of most men of learning.[72]

Ibn Qudāma goes on to assert that if it seems plausible that a person is genuinely ignorant of the law prohibiting *zinā* or intoxication, "if the prohibition is not obvious to him" (*lā yakhfā ʿalayhi*), the *ḥadd* is lifted, since there are many aspects of the law that are "obscure to those without learning [in the law]" (*yakhfā ʿalā ghayr ahl al-ʿilm*). However, the *ḥadd* does apply if the law should be obvious, "as in the case of a Muslim intoxicated while among a group of Muslims." Ibn Qudāma only explicitly applies this principle to potential cases of *zinā* and intoxication, and many other jurists do not explicitly consider ignorance of the law to be a mitigating factor in the *ḥudūd*. Still, this presents a potentially problematic legal principle: the law only applies to those who have knowledge of the law. In effect, a person must knowingly and intentionally break the law, at least in the case of these *ḥudūd*, or no offense occurs. This is not the approach taken in non-*ḥudūd* situations, where the law is consistently depicted as applying to all Muslims regardless of their knowledge of its details.[73] Further, Ibn Qudāma's declaration of this principle differs considerably from the examples which lead up to it. In those examples, the man is mistaken about the identity of his sexual partner, and the issue is how this mistake comes about—there is no suggestion that the man is ignorant of the law pro-

---

[72] Ibn Qudāma, *al-Mughnī*, 12:345, emphasis added; cf. 12:343 where Ibn Qudāma indicates that, according to some jurists, if a man does not know of conditions that would make his marriage to a woman illegal (e.g., she is currently married), he is not liable for the *ḥadd* punishment for *zinā*. See also Shīrāzī, *al-Muhadhdhab*, 5:379. On a slightly different matter, Shīrāzī notes that if a man has sex with a corpse, either this violates the *ḥadd* against *zinā*, "because he penetrates a forbidden opening, without doubt about the matter (*wa-lā shubha lahu fīhi*)," or the *ḥadd* penalty is not applied because "he did not intend (*lā yaqṣidu*) so there is no *ḥadd* upon him" (5:387).

[73] This also calls to mind a larger issue, the 'before revelation complex' studied by A. Kevin Reinhart, *Before Revelation: The Boundaries of Muslim Moral Thought* (Albany: State University of New York Press, 1995).

hibiting certain sexual unions. Further, in the examples given, objective factors figure prominently, such as the existence of a third party making misleading indications, or the location of the act in a context where certain expectations normally prevail. However, in the more general declaration, it is the person's knowledge and intention per se that determine the status of the act. Thus, the expansion of the cases into a general absolution on account of ignorance seems a considerable stretch indeed.

I would suggest that it is not accidental that this remarkable allowance for ignorance as an excuse occurs only for the *ḥudūd*, for it is consonant with a prevalent attitude in the texts, a reluctance to apply the *ḥudūd* penalties. As noted above, an offense against the *ḥudūd* ordinances automatically triggers a penalty. However, several elements of the law mitigate against reaching this point. As Schacht observes, "There is a strong tendency to restrict the *ḥadd* punishments as much as possible, except the *ḥadd* for false accusation of unlawful intercourse, but this in turn serves to restrict the applicability of the *ḥadd* for unlawful intercourse itself."[74]

The several means of restricting the application of the *ḥadd* penalties include narrowly defining the acts. Theft presents the clearest case of this: the theft must be by stealth—which excludes open robbery and snatching unawares (e.g., pickpocketing)—of a certain minimum value (classically, ten *dirhams*), of an object lawfully subject to ownership, actually removed from the custody of the owner.[75] Also a given act is weighed for *shubha*, 'resemblance' to a lawful act—if such a resemblance can be established, the *ḥadd* is avoided.[76] Further, jurists treat duress, widely conceived, as a mitigating factor—unlawful intercourse

[74] Schacht, *Introduction*, 176–177. He adds that "whereas in other matters there exists, to a certain extent, the religious duty of giving evidence, in lawsuits concerning offenses punishable by *ḥadd* it is considered more meritorious to cover them up than to give evidence on them, and the oath is disregarded as an element of proof" (198).

[75] Ibid., 179–180. Catching a thief in the act eliminates *ḥadd*, and for some jurists, so does the case of a thief handing the stolen goods to an accomplice outside the house, such as through a window.

[76] For unlawful intercourse (*zinā*), for example, *shubha* can remove the *ḥadd*, as when the marriage is not formally valid but the husband thought it was valid, or if the marriage took place during the *ʿidda* (waiting period during which a woman may not remarry) after a divorce, but the husband was unaware of the situation or the waiting period, for technical reasons, was longer than the husband thought, and similar such technical definitions of valid circumstances for intercourse that a husband may have unwittingly breached; jurists even debate the applicability of *ḥadd* in cases of prostitution and homosexuality (ibid., 178). Note, however, that a discretionary (*taʿzīr*) punishment may be imposed when the *ḥadd* is not fully incurred (ibid., 175).

and drinking wine, for example, must be shown to have been voluntary. If several offenses against the same *ḥadd* ordinance occur, they are punished by a single application of the penalty, and the statute of limitations, so to speak, for *ḥadd* offenses is rather short, usually one month, and in the case of drinking wine, usually only the time the drunkenness or smell of wine persists.[77] Repentance (*tawba*) by an offender can, in some cases, remove the *ḥadd*—if a thief returns the stolen goods or a highway robber repents, the *ḥadd* is removed, if the repentance takes place before the penalty is completed.[78] Perhaps most importantly, the standards of evidence in *ḥadd* cases are very high, limited to a confession (easily withdrawn) or eyewitness testimony (four of them in the case of *zinā*).[79] As noted, if the *ḥadd* is avoided, a judge may still apply a *taʿzīr* penalty, usually limited to a degree significantly less than the *ḥadd*.[80]

So much, then, for first impressions. At first glance intentions seem to play no role in the *ḥudūd*, as these offenses are punished rather harshly whenever found, theoretically with no attention to intentions or circumstances. However, on closer look, circumstances matter considerably in determining whether or not what looks like a breach of the *ḥudūd* really counts. Strict liability for the *ḥudūd* is mitigated by the tendency to define the offenses out of existence, or at least into a less serious cate-

---

[77] Ibid., 176–177. Technically, the act is punishable beyond this time limit, but the *qāḍī* no longer accepts evidence, unless there is justification for the delay.

[78] Ibid., 176. In such cases, property damage is treated as a non-*ḥadd* offense; however, repentance has no effect in cases of bodily injury or homicide (ibid., 177–178).

[79] Schacht summarizes the various aspects of evidence law in the *ḥudūd*: "In contrast with the acknowledgement concerning other matters, the confession of an offense involving a *ḥadd* can be withdrawn (*rujūʿ*); it is even recommended that the *ḳāḍī* should suggest this possibility to a person who has confessed, except in the case of false accusation of unlawful intercourse; and particularly high demands are made of the witnesses as regards their number, their qualifications, and the content of their statements. These demands are most severe with regard to evidence on unlawful intercourse;... in this case four male witnesses are required instead of the normal two, and they must testify as eyewitnesses not merely to the act of intercourse but to 'unlawful intercourse' (*zinā*) as such; correspondingly, a confession of unlawful intercourse, in order to bring about the *ḥadd* punishment, must be made on four separate occasions [although in other cases a single confession is sufficient]. A further safeguard lies in the fact that an accusation of unlawful intercourse which is dismissed constitutes *ḳadhf* which itself is punishable by *ḥadd*; if one of the four required witnesses turns out to be a slave or to be otherwise disqualified from giving valid evidence, or if there are discrepancies between their respective depositions, or if one of them retracts (*rujūʿ*) his evidence, all are, in principle, liable to the *ḥadd* for *ḳadhf*" (ibid., 177). See also Ibn Qudāma, *al-Mughnī*, 12:354, 379.

[80] For example, the *ḥadd* penalty for *zinā* is stoning to death in some cases, 100 lashes in others. Mūṣilī limits the *taʿzīr* for *zinā* to between three and 39 lashes (*al-Ikhtiyār*, 4:92; Mūṣilī also applies this *taʿzīr* penalty for cases of bestiality).

gory. Further, in some cases, the intention to act in accordance with the law outweighs the actual unlawful act: a mistake or ignorance here does not lead to punishment, and intentions produce a potential loophole in the law. Conversely, however, intending to breach the law, but unintentionally failing to do so does not exempt one from a *ḥadd* punishment. The rhetorical seriousness of the *ḥudūd* is thus preserved, though imagining someone being held liable for such an illicit intent stretches the bounds of the credible.

Conclusion

I noted above the negative imperative governing this sphere of Islamic law: *jināyāt/jirāḥ* and the *ḥudūd* are acts a Muslim should not commit, and the law stipulates the penalties for those who do. In this context we have seen that jurists strongly favor the term *ʿamd* to refer to intentions, rather than *niyya*, which dominates ritual law and is prevalent in civil law. The eclipsing of the term *niyya* in these contexts by other terms, especially *ʿamd* in the context of injurious action, and *irāda* and *qaṣd* more generally, implies that *niyya* is a particular kind of intention, an intention to do good, or at least to act in morally neutral ways. The term is thus insulated from the negative moral implications of injurious and offensive actions. One apparent exception, Ibn Rushd's use of *niyya* in his assertion that "no one knows intentions but God Almighty" can actually be seen as fitting this pattern and even strengthening the positive moral connotations of *niyya*. Likewise, *ʿamd* is a particular kind of intention—the intention to do harm. *Niyya* and *ʿamd* serve as bookend terms for the moral range of human intentions.

Looking at intentions in the context of injurious actions tells us some specific things about both intentions and Islamic penal law. Combining strict liability with some reference to intentions preserves the benefit of a strict liability system, that someone must be held accountable for an injurious action. While this may sound odd to anyone inclined to think that 'accidents will happen', this strict liability perhaps fills the role many modern societies fill with private insurance systems and public disaster aid. Even for a purely accidental injury or homicide, the injured party is compensated by the injuring party (and his *ʿāqila*) for the damage, thus distributing some of the cost of the damage over a wider segment of society. In this way, strict liability may contribute to social stability, especially in a smaller-scale, pre-modern society. Muslims often argue, with some historical evidence in their favor, that by limiting retaliation in clearly defined ways, the Islamic approach to injurious actions greatly improved on the pre-Islamic free-for-all of cyclical revenge. Going further, Bernard Weiss helpfully places the Islamic approach to homicide in the sociological context of the patriarchal family and kinship ties that were so central to the worldview informing Islamic law:

> Homicide does not belong within the domain of criminal law, strictly speaking; it is not an offence against society as such calling for public prosecution. Rather, it belongs under the rubric of a *lex talionis* in which the family unit—or, more precisely, the *ʿāqila*, which comprises certain male agnates—is the primary actor; it is an offence against the family, and the family must decide how to deal with it … Within the setting of patriarchal family life as envisioned by the Muslim jurists, the talio operates as a highly effective deterrent to homicide and as a means of preserving life. Every individual, including the one inclined to take the life of another, is part of a tightly knit extended family unit. The murderer therefore does not act alone but rather represents his family in an act inimical to another family, for the victim too represents a family. All human life is embedded in the web of kinship … When one kills without cause, one therefore is as much accountable to one's own family, which incurs responsibility for appropriate action, as to the family of the victim. Therein lies the deterrent force of the talio within a society founded on ties of kinship.[81]

So Islamic homicide law both deters and spreads the cost of harmful actions, doubly serving to strengthen and, if necessary, repair the pervasive 'web of kinship'.

Weighing intentions alongside the strict liability approach has the benefit of making the system more just and better able to distinguish among acts that have the same result but differing motivations, adjusting the penalty to fit a more nuanced definition of the offense. Above, I used the example of a cold-blooded killing versus killing in self-defense; without reference to intentions, strict liability would treat these exactly the same. The Muslim jurists instead assess offenses on a graded scale of intentions, so that while they still treat self-defense or pure accident as requiring compensation to the injured party, they significantly reduce the penalty from the retaliation allowed against a cold-blooded killer.

That the jurists recognize significant limits to the accessibility of others' intentions results in a reliance on objective indicants of sub-

[81] Weiss, *Spirit*, 152–153. See also n. 9 above.

jective states and, for some at least, a profound sense of the provisionality of earthly justice in a context seen to include divine justice in the afterlife. Jurists consistently assess injurious intentions according to type of action, means, and circumstance, measuring a given case against culturally-defined expectations of normal behavior and cause-and-effect relations. However, the jurists neither consider their judgments in such cases airtight and infallible, nor do they shy away from making them, despite the admitted limitations. Rather, as we have seen, they implicitly, and sometimes explicitly, view their judgments as only part of the system of justice. They recognize their judgments as provisional, a sort of 'best guess' in imperfect circumstances circumscribed by human limitations. The equation is completed by the justice meted out in the afterlife by an omniscient and omnipotent God. The expectation of divine justice pervades not only the Qur'ān, but virtually all aspects of Islamic religious life, and here we see one of the specific implications of this worldview.

On the level of scholarly theories of intent in Islamic law, the sphere of penal law may bring together two seemingly disparate approaches, those of Rosen and Messick. Rosen sees Muslim jurists (indeed Muslims and Arabs in general) as being perfectly comfortable reading intent through its outward actions and signs. Messick, in seemingly stark contrast, stresses the foundationalism of the jurists, the tendency to see agency and authority rooted in the inner self and only obliquely and secondarily reflected in the outer manifestations of words and actions. I suggested above that Rosen's views, however well they describe moderns Moroccan courts, fit rather poorly the theoretical treatment of intent in contract and personal status law. However, it seems they work better in describing penal law. The jurists here expend little energy in the pursuit of intentions per se, relying almost exclusively on objective actions, especially means, context, and the prevailing norms of interpretation. Moreover, Rosen does not assert that intentions do not exist, or that they do not matter at all to jurists, only that they are thought of as transparently revealed in outward indicants. This seems not a bad approximation of the approach to intent found in laws regarding injurious actions. However, Messick's foundationalism is also in evidence, as is especially borne out in Ibn Rushd's comments about the provisionality of worldly justice given the difficulties of ascertaining the intent that is definitive of actions. This view suggests that intentions may not be thought of as perfectly aligned with actions, but rather as operating at some remove, and with significant authority—the act itself may almost serve as a 'report' of the more real, or at least more morally significant, occurrence at the level of intent. The reliance on outward indicants would then seem to be more of a pragmatic capitulation to problematic limits than an unwavering trust. Perhaps we see a range of views that stretches to include both Rosen's near-behaviorism and Messick's foundationalism, rather than simply one or the other.

CHAPTER SEVEN

CONCLUSION

"Actions are defined by intentions, and to every person what he intends." So holds the Prophet's dictum. However, as we have seen, intentions are treated differently in differing legal contexts, and in a few cases, actions are decidedly not defined by intentions. In the ritual sphere, formulation of intention is a discrete step in the ritual actions; 'proper intention', alongside proper movement and proper utterance, helps to constitute the *ʿibādāt*. In the civil sphere, intentions matter primarily in terms of the basic sincerity and potential complexity of performative speech acts. In this sphere especially, however, not all acts rest on intentions. In penal law, we find intentions strongly emphasized as determinative of punishment, coupled with a recognition that access to intentions is necessarily indirect and partial. Prevailing norms and expectations regarding behavior and material circumstances serve as indicants of inner states, and the texts display a sense of the concomitant provisionality of juristic assessments.

These differences are reflected in the diversity of language jurists use when discussing intentions. In ritual law, the term *niyya* dominates to the point of near exclusivity. Jurists give the term a technical meaning specific to this legal context; *niyya* is the intention to perform the positively-valued, required (or recommended) acts of obedient worship. In *fiqh al-ʿibādāt*, *niyya* does at times carry some general, non-technical connotations, but it largely carries the meaning of a specifically 'ritualized' form of intention. In civil law, which concerns acts with generally neutral moral connotations, jurists again use the term *niyya*, but it effectively becomes a different term than it is in ritual law, losing the technical ritual implications. *Niyya* here is also intermixed with other terms, especially *qaṣd* and *irāda*, which are treated as synonymous and generic referents to intent. Finally, in penal law, the intentions behind negatively valued forbidden acts are couched primarily in terms of *ʿamd*, and *niyya* is avoided almost altogether. Thus, *niyya* emerges as an intention to do good or neutral acts, while *ʿamd* emerges as malicious intent.

This range of terminology points to a broader issue. While the English term 'intent' serves reasonably well as an umbrella for the whole range of Islamic legal terms and concepts under consideration here, this usage should not obscure the complexity of the Arabic Islamic legal discourse of intent. Muslim jurists make many distinctions among types of intent, distinctions which are at times rather vague and inconsistent, and at others quite fine and elegant. One is reminded of the commonplace observations that Eskimos have a remarkable multiplicity of words for 'snow', or that Arabs have the same for 'camel'. Such sayings may be accurate or otherwise, and no doubt can mislead us about these languages and cultures, and about language and culture in general. But there is perhaps some kernel of truth in suggesting that the development of a complex and variegated terminology referring to a range of interrelated concepts indicates some degree of special, heightened concern for those concepts.[1] At any rate, if intent is a complicated concept in Western thought, it is certainly no less so in Islamic law.

As for Western scholarly efforts to analyze Muslim legal approaches to intent, Brinkley Messick's notion of 'culturally specific foundationalism' has probably fared the best in light of my findings. Other theoretical and analytical frameworks, such as those of Johansen and Rosen, provide insight into various aspects of the jurists' treatment of intentions, but Messick's, if not universally applicable, works best at the level of macrocosmic generalization. This "foundationalism … locates the site of meaning generation internally, within the heart or spirit, and beyond direct observation … at a crucial remove from the lived sign world of language."[2] Islamic law is pervaded by a sense that humans have an interior dimension that is not readily observed, and further, that this dimension is often the locus of human agency and authority. Islamic law is manifestly concerned with defining and classifying actions, and the jurists consistently see intentions as crucial to making actions what they are. We have seen that there are significant exceptions to this foundationalism, as the jurists sometimes pointedly disregard intentions in assessing a given action. In such cases, meaning and authority are treated as residing in the *ẓāhir*, the readily observed indicants of gesture and speech.[3] These cases do not constitute the prover-

[1] I am grateful to an anonymous reader at Brill for suggesting the potential relevance of these ideas.

[2] Messick, "Written Identities," 46; objective actions, including speech acts and language, are epiphenomenal to the "deeper, or prior 'language' of human intentions." Messick adds that "the limit case here, I suggest, is the divine word, in which, by definition, there is no separation of intentionality and expression."

[3] And, as we have seen, Rosen's argument that Muslims consider intentions to be

bial 'exceptions that prove the rule', but rather point out the limits of foundationalism as a descriptive and explanatory rubric. Still, recognizing the pervasiveness and implications of foundationalism is invaluable in making better sense of many aspects of intent in Islamic law, and, in turn of Islamic legal discourse in general.

With our general survey and analysis behind us, we can now recount some if its major findings. In ritual law, jurists often use *niyya* as a technical term referring to an element in the formal constitution of ritual. Medieval *fiqh al-ʿibādāt* depicts and prescribes acts in formalistic terms, indicating what should be done with the body and what utterances should be made in order to achieve the proper form of divinely ordained obedient worship. *Niyya*, perhaps surprisingly, is used in ways that consistently fit this formalism, rather than providing some free-floating subjective counterpart or antidote to it. *Niyya* is what one does with the mind while making certain ritualized bodily movements and verbal utterances. Seen in this light, any putative mind-body duality is overshadowed by the inclusion of the mind in the ritual, as the mind is treated as part of the body. The legal texts do not indicate a capacity or mental mode such as 'will' that is separate from, and which directs, the *niyya*. Rather, one simply intends, formulates *niyya*, and this is the inner self in a ritual mode. There is nothing 'further inside' than *niyya*, no 'self' standing back while the mind/body performs the acts of ritual. As Humphrey and Laidlaw help illuminate, the jurists recognized that the outward movements could be done correctly without *niyya*, but just as an *ʿibāda* done without the proper bodily movement is invalid, so too is it invalid without the proper mental movement, *niyya*.

This emphasis on a subjective component in ritual points toward the possibility that the *ʿibādāt* involve an inner self not strictly limited to a focused mind, but perhaps including what one might call a 'spirit'. However, the Western scholars who pursue this interpretation push too far in this direction and abandon without justification the technical formalism of *fiqh al-ʿibādāt*. Some Muslims in the medieval period, of course, also pushed in this direction: as we saw, Ṣūfīs such as al-Ghazālī pressed away from the technical formalism, treating *niyya* as something perhaps akin to the 'spiritual' side of ritual. Later documents of popular piety, such as the devotional manuals studied by Constance Padwick,

transparent and easily read through outward indicants does not fill in the gap left by Messick's foundationalism, for the jurists in these cases tend not consider intentions apparent but irrelevant.

likewise take *niyya* into this territory. However, this is a major difference in interpretation from the formalism that predominates medieval *fiqh* treatments of ritual intent. It must be left to future studies to explore the details of how intentions in general, and *niyya* in particular, are understood in Ṣūfism and Muslim popular piety; how this relates to medieval *fiqh* manuals; whether these understandings might reflect Hellenistic, Jewish, or Christian influence; and whether these Ṣūfī and popular views eclipsed the more formalistic legal understanding in actual practice and in later formulations of the law.

While *niyya* in ritual law displays numerous qualities specific to that legal sphere, the role of intent in helping give actions their specific, legally recognized identity overlaps significantly with the understanding of intention in the other spheres of Islamic positive law. That is, while there is a specifically ritual form of intention distinct from intention in the other spheres, the separation is not absolute. In both civil and penal law, jurists consistently treat intention as the mental directedness and the formation of purpose that gives actions their identity and thus defines their location in the legal taxonomy. While civil law focuses on the intentions behind speech acts, and penal law on the intentions behind injurious bodily acts, jurists consider intentions in both cases—when they do consider them—to be a definitive element of the act. Intentions in these cases need not be addressed with an imperative, as in the ritual case of insisting that a ritual actor intend his actions, but rather are assumed to pervade human activity.

In civil law, it remains to be better understood just why intentions matter in some, but not all, cases. In addition to further exploring the reasons for formalism in marriage and some aspects of divorce—testing and perhaps modifying Johansen's sociological approach—future work might fruitfully address the *madhhab* differences suggested by Sanhūrī in regard to contract law. It may be that jurists strategically emphasize or deemphasize intentions in the service of wider visions of the nature and role of law. The Ḥanafī/Shāfiʿī deemphasizing of intentions in contract law may not reflect a general tendency to downplay intentions, but rather a tendency to minimize the role of law in everyday life. Sanhūrī's views to the contrary notwithstanding, downplaying intentions in contracts may give contracting parties greater flexibility to act without having to worry about the broader social and moral consequences of their actions, since this approach attributes fewer legal implications to a given contract. If this Ḥanafī/Shāfiʿī pair can be shown to consistently emphasize intentions to a higher degree than the Mālikī/Ḥanbalī pair in marriage or divorce, for example, this might indicate a desire to give participants in those transactions greater legal flexibility by giving them the option of evading or modifying legal obligations. Further, it remains to be seen whether these patterns extend not only to other areas of civil law, but to the ritual and penal spheres of law. While I have not systematically explored this possibility, my preliminary impression is that, for reasons yet to be explained, *madhhab* differences in general are more pronounced in civil law than in either ritual or penal law. Moreover, it appears that Ḥanafīs, for one, cannot be characterized as simply emphasizing or deemphasizing intentions, for while Arabi and Sanhūrī see them as largely overlooking intent in contracts, Messick presents them as the most foundationalist of the *madhhab*s.

This inquiry into *madhhab* patterns might build not only on the work of Sanhūrī and Arabi, but on that of N.J. Coulson as well. Coulson argues that the reason early Islamic documents portray many legal scholars as reluctant to accept appointments as *qāḍīs* was that they feared "the awe-inspiring responsibility of applying their beliefs as rules of law."[4] Whether or not this explanation is entirely accurate or complete, Coulson also suggests that this reluctance follows *madhhab* lines: those who tend to abhor the office of *qāḍī*, he asserts, are "those who were religious idealists rather than practical lawyers,… [and] who preferred to conceive of the *Sharīʿa* as a code of moral duties rather than enforceable legal rules. Such was, in essence, the spirit of the traditionists."[5] These traditionists, the *ahl al-ḥadīth*, of course, are the Mālikīs (and presumably, though Coulson does not explicitly mention them, the Ḥanbalīs). Coulson ascribes the opposite spirit to the Ḥanafīs, who "are traditionally regarded as concerned primarily with the letter of the law rather than with its underlying moral or religious significance."[6]

Relevant data might emerge from closer inspection of the nature and use of pragmatic, but quasi-legal, textual genres such as the *ḥiyal*, *shurūṭ/wathā'iq*, *maḥāḍir*, and *sijillāt*. These materials served pragmatic ends, and, as Schacht observes of the *ḥiyal*, "they enabled persons who would otherwise have had no choice but to act against the provisions of the sacred Law, to arrive at the desired result while actually conforming

[4] Coulson, "Doctrine and Practice," 220.
[5] Ibid., 225–226.
[6] Ibid., 226.

to the letter of the law."[7] Wakin finds that Ḥanafīs tend to be the most practical or pragmatic in their approach to the law, and the most likely to employ such strategems; however, she also notes that Ḥanbalīs, though less inclined in this direction, employ them as well.[8] Building on the work of Schacht and Wakin, one could explore the contours of these *madhhab* patterns, and ask whether the employment of such quasi-legal devices corresponds to any patterns of strategic emphasis and deemphasis of intentions.

In penal law, further study might address the implications of the provisionality of juristic assessments that emerges implicitly, and at times explicitly, in this legal sphere. When a jurist of the stature of Ibn Rushd asserts that "no one knows intentions but God Almighty, but the assessment is to be assigned [by humans] on the basis of what is apparent," he makes clear that at least some jurists explicitly recognize that the limits to human access to others' intentions potentially limits human justice.[9] Though evident in other legal spheres, this attitude is most apparent in penal law, perhaps because it is there that the stakes are highest, since a mistaken judgment could lead to misapplied corporal or even capital penalties. But one could ask whether this provisional view of assessments pervades all Islamic positive law, and what effects this view might have in terms of both the normative construction of the law and the historical application of it. This line of inquiry might have comparative dimensions as well, for it may be a common feature of religio-legal traditions that jurists and judges must acknowledge a sovereign and omniscient authority beyond their own, though the specific impact of such an acknowledgement cannot easily be predicted.

---

[7] Schacht, "Ḥiyal"; Schacht continues: "For instance, the Ḳur'ān prohibits interest, and this religious prohibition was strong enough to make popular opinion unwilling to transgress it openly and directly, while at the same time there was an imperative demand for the giving and taking of interest in commercial life. In order to satisfy this need, and at the same time to observe the letter of the religious prohibition, a number of devices were developed. One, very popular, device consisted of a double sale (*bayʿatān fī bayʿa*), of which there are many variants. For instance, the (prospective) debtor sells to the (prospective) creditor a slave for cash, and immediately buys the slave back from him for a greater amount payable at a future date; this amounts to a loan with the slave as security, and the difference between the two prices represents the interest; the transaction is called *mukh̲āṭara* … or, more commonly, *ʿīna*."

[8] Wakin, *Documents in Islamic Law*, 10–13, and 13, n. 5.

[9] Ibn Rushd, *Bidāyat al-mujtahid*, 2:397; *DJP*, 2:481.

For all spheres of law, historical and anthropological work such as that done by Rosen raises questions regarding whether the law in actual practice reflects the normative views found in the textual sources. As previously noted, Rosen finds that, in contemporary Morocco, *qāḍīs* believe that they directly access human interiors through outward signs. This suggests a potential departure from the view espoused in medieval *fiqh* manuals that often intentions may not correspond closely to act, gesture, or speech, and thus are at times altogether irrelevant and at others can only be assessed partially and provisionally based on decidedly indirect evidence. Rosen's findings present an opportunity to explore when, how, and why this departure occurred, and just how these Moroccan *qāḍīs* understand the medieval texts. Similar questions could be asked about ritual law where, for example, one wonders whether Muslims in various times and places prefer to verbalize their *niyya* before prayer, what verbal formulas they might employ, and just what they understand themselves to be doing when 'formulating *niyya*'. In civil law, one could ask how a given Muslim society treats the intentions behind a divorce, how they claim to have access to a husband's intention that a pronouncement of *ṭalāq* count as two rather than one or three, how long they give a man to declare his intentions, and whether reference to intentions actually makes divorce more or less easy and likely.

Two other prominent examples of the potential for anthropological work to clarify the treatment of intentions in Islamic law are the writings of Messick and John Bowen. In addition to exploring doctrinal treatments of intent, Messick has worked extensively in post-Ottoman Yemen, where he identifies a shift toward greater reliance on written documents as legal evidence and records. Running "counter to the thrust of the doctrinal *fiqh* on the matter, which envisions only oral forms of evidence," but in accord with the Ottoman *Majalla*, Imām Yaḥyā (d. 1948) allowed Yemeni courts to recognize certain written records, such as property documents and some documentation of bilateral contracts.[10] Accompanying this shift, however, Messick observes a tendency to maintain "doctrinal reservations concerning the evidential status of written instruments."[11] He notes that

> the problematizing of such writings by jurists is crucial to understand, since it informs us about the cultural parameters of the local analytic

[10] Messick, "Written Identities," 47–48.

[11] Ibid., 49.

> system. Behind these ordinary written legal documents is a system of thought grounded first in intent and, second, in human presences and the related authority of the spoken word. The jurists' cautious, even suspicious, treatment of such writings were associated not just with the very real threat of forgery but also with other circumstances of the late manuscript era just prior to the rise of print culture and the nation-state. In this era, writings had yet to be secured by either the new authority of printed forms, or, more important, by the backing of a state that would license notaries and lawyers and record and archive their written instruments.[12]

On this view, Yemeni legal culture in the twentieth century was undergoing a shift away from a reliance on the spoken word, a reliance on known persons who embody their relationships and reputations, and who provide in their speech the best available access to the realm of authoritative generation of truth—namely, human intentions. Messick observes Yemeni courts, in what appears to be a classic example of Weberian rationalization (with its attendant ambiguous and ambivalent effects), relying increasingly on writing in place of speech and human personal presence. The Yemeni jurists' ambivalence toward writing is a reluctance to give up what is perceived as the clearest window on the authoritative inner self.

John Bowen has studied a remarkable dispute in the Gayo region of Indonesia in the 1980s over whether to make a verbal pronouncement of intent to worship. This dispute pits 'modernists' (or the 'young group'), those endorsing religious reform inspired by teachings from the Middle East, especially the Egyptian Muḥammad 'Abduh, against 'traditionalists' (or the 'old group') who affirm "long-standing religious practices and the authority of prominent religious scholars of the past."[13] These groups debated various religio-legal (especially *'ibādāt*) matters, such as the details of bodily movements in *ṣalāt*. But, as Bowen observes, "no debate occasioned as much hurt and discord as that concerning the statement of intent to worship":

> Many Gayo (and other Muslims), just before beginning to worship (proclaiming *Allahu akbar*), state to themselves their intent to worship, usually reciting a one-sentence formula (in Gayo, Indonesian, or, for the more learned, Arabic), such as: "I worship at daybreak with two cycles on account of God, may He be exalted." Those who do pronounce the formula consider it to be an aid to worship; most modernists see it as an

[12] Ibid.

[13] John R. Bowen, "Modern Intentions," 159.

> illegitimate addition to the actions dictated by scripture. The opening pronouncement "I worship" in Arabic is "*ushalli*," and the dispute has been called the "*ushalli* controversy."[14]

Rather than a simple debate over doctrinal minutiae, this Gayo controversy emerges in Bowen's analysis as a case study in "how the emphasis on intent can be used as a foundation for a sweeping modernist critique of ritual practices."[15] This was a dispute over modes of religio-legal authority, as well as over the very nature of Islamic ritual practice:

> In modernist usage … "intent" is intended to define the subjective component of a more narrow view of religion and ritual. Against older notions of ritual as a wide field of powerful *communication*, modernists assert a conception of ritual as the tightly defined range of ways in which an individual can fulfill God's commands, and thus as *obedience* … If ritual is primarily about communicating with God, then anything that serves to clear the way and the mind must be in God's service and thus properly part of worship. If, however, ritual is primarily about obeying God's commands, then two objections to the *ushalli* follow. First,… scripture does not explicitly order worshippers to pronounce the *ushalli*,… Secondly,… adding the *ushalli* to the prescribed ritual pattern implies that intent is not already part of every ritual act, that it is something extraneous to religious action … Because you must perform all your religious acts with the correct intent (in order to serve God), intent should suffuse all acts.[16]

Traditionalists are wedded to the *ushalli* because they see worship as communicative, and the *ushalli* initiates the communication. Modernists assert that they need not pronounce their intent because they "express the intent to worship by preparing for worship: by walking to the mosque, by performing ablutions, and so forth, even before we begin to worship." Moreover, as Bowen paraphrases this position, "if one's subjective formation of intent defines and constitutes an act as a religious act of a particular nature, then the notion that one can have an action apart from intent is false and misleading." No statement of intent is needed because, in short, "actions have built-in intentions."[17] Signif-

---

[14] Ibid., 159–160.

[15] Ibid., 164. Bowen adds that "the practice of saying the *ushalli* came to index one's acceptance of a larger package of positions." This package included such established Gayo practices as adding a separate session of worship after Friday congregational services, adding a separate section to morning prayers, and delivering recitation to (or on the behalf of) the recently deceased (161).

[16] Ibid., 164, emphasis in original.

[17] Ibid., 164–165.

icantly, then, while the modernists seek to eliminate local 'innovations' from pure Islamic worship, they themselves appear to depart markedly from the medieval normative texts that prescribe a non-verbal formulation of intent (*niyya*) as part of prayer. Bowen's study suggests that there is still much work to be done exploring how medieval Islamic law relates to later Islamic doctrine and practice.

Some of the issues raised in my study could also be traced through later manifestations of Islamic law. It is noteworthy that the second article of the 1869 Ottoman civil law code, the *Majalla*, holds that "Decisive in contracts is intentions and meanings, not wordings and forms."[18] Thus, in spite of being largely based on Ḥanafī sources, the *Majalla* prescribes a decidedly subjectivist or foundationalist view of contract law. According to Arabi, one of Sanhūrī's primary motives in excavating the medieval Muslim jurists' treatment of intentions in contract law is "an ardent desire to revive Muslim legal thought through underlining its essential affinity to modern norms of law."[19] Especially in the French jurisprudence so influential in colonial and post-colonial Egypt, Sanhūrī finds echoes of a strand of thought present in medieval *fiqh*, namely the Ḥanbalī/Mālikī tendency to place a great deal of weight on the intentions of contracting parties. In short, Sanhūrī recognizes that modern French law looks for evidence of intentions in such cases, and that some interpretations of Islamic law not only resonate with this approach, but might contribute usefully to the overall modernization of Islamic law. Commenting on law in modern Islamic contexts, Johansen observes that

> Neither in marriage nor in any other field of social exchange do the law codes of Muslim countries keep the binding force of the pronounced formula independently of the intention, the knowledge, the will of the parties concerned. As far as consent and duress are concerned, modern Muslim law has decidedly abolished the formalistic dimension of social exchange and with it one of the procedural aspects that most clearly distinguished the social from commercial exchange.[20]

There appears to be a decisive tendency among modernizers to employ various methods—foremost among them a 'mix and match' approach

---

[18] This translation is taken from Messick, "Written Identities," 45. Another translation renders the previous article "An act is judged in accordance with its object" (*The Medjellè or Ottoman Civil Law*, trans. W.E. Grigsby [Cyprus: Herbert E. Clarke, 1895], 3). See also Arabi, "Intention and Method," 211, n. 29.

[19] Arabi, "Intention and Method," 221.

[20] Johansen, "Valorization," 99.

to legal rules rather than the traditional consistent adherence to a single *madhhab*—to emphasize the role of intentions in civil law, apparently based on the perception (questionable though it may be) that such emphasis will add useful flexibility to the law.

If the pre-modern treatment of intentions in commercial law has some potential implications for modern legal reform efforts, so might the treatment of intentions in other spheres of the law. In particular, the tendency of pre-modern jurists to rely on means and contexts as evidence of intent in penal matters might come under review as Muslims seek to apply Islamic law in the contemporary world. If, as Messick points out, medieval Muslim courts did not employ legal psychology to any significant extent, perhaps this is open to change.[21] The prospect of employing new forms of expert testimony, including phsychologists, psychiatrists, and other modern medical personnel, could induce changes in the legal understanding of 'criminal intent'. The openness of Muslim legal reformers of whatever stripe to such new understandings of the nature of the self and its availability for scrutiny remains to be seen. The exact parameters of a properly Islamic legal psychology have, to my knowledge, yet to emerge—no doubt in part because many of the contortions Islamic law has been subjected to in the colonial and post-colonial periods have yet to be resolved. Indeed, it should be noted that the general Islamic legal approach to bodily injury and homicide, embedded as it is in pre-modern notions of social and political order, might necessarily undergo significant revisions—to unpredictable effect—if Islamic law is ever more widely applied by modern nation-states.

This study makes clear that no single explanation for the treatment of intentions in Islamic positive law has yet emerged, and moreover, that such a sweeping, all-inclusive theory is not likely to emerge in the future. Various scholars, as we have seen, offer insightful analyses of limited areas of law, but no overarching, unifying thesis has surfaced. This fact is itself significant, for Islamic law is the product and expression of a multiplicity of factors. The form and content of Islamic law was influenced by other legal and religious traditions. The emergence of a systematic, widely agreed-upon system of legal reasoning, *uṣūl al-fiqh*, created hierarchies of justification for various opinions. Practices of learning and transmitting texts through a combination of orality, mem-

[21] Messick, "Indexing the Self," 177.

ory, and informal notebooks, especially in the formative period, introduced opportunity for change and expansion of the law, while even after the shift to a more stable written form of recording, the casuistic methods of the medieval period continued to allow jurists to change the law to suit new ideas and socio-historical circumstances. Medieval *fiqh* manuals record a range of opinions on many topics, rather than a single consensus view, but do not systematically recount the myriad influences and logics that led to the range of opinion. In the end, then, explanations of Islamic law tend to work best either at the microcosmic level of isolated issues and sources, or at a macrocosmic level of general patterns and trends. The former type tend to explain only limited aspects of the law and fall apart when expanded too far, while the latter tend toward vagueness, blurring the numerous distinctions present in the texts.

We might finally return to the idea of foundationalism, which, if we have seen its limits, nonetheless sparks some of the most provocative suggestions about not only intent, but also the very nature of Islamic law. Messick notes that "given the assumed gap between forms of expression and intention, legal analyses amount to attempts to erect bridges from the accessible to the inaccessible."[22] Further,

> Like the divinity, the source of authority in human intentions is,... in Bakhtin's terms, "located in a distanced zone." Ultimately, neither knowledge of God Almighty nor of the interiors of others' intentionalities are fully attainable by humans, but these sources of authoritative meaning, these locales of truth, remained the identified goals of interpretive effort. Meaning conceived of as constituted in "a distanced zone" activated and motivated a distinctive semiotics, a legal science of manifest signs integral to an interminable, yet always incomplete and also always contested human pursuit of understanding.[23]

In this view, the jurists must strive for "knowledge of God Almighty," and for an understanding of the implications this knowledge has for human action. Simultaneously, they must strive for knowledge of human interiors and how these might be reflected in actions and language. In both cases, full and certain knowledge is assumed to be impossible, and yet this impossibility does nothing to mitigate the imperative to seek.

---

[22] Ibid., 178. Cf. "Written Identities," 46.

[23] Messick, "Written Identities," 46–47, citing M.M. Bakhtin, *The Dialogic Imagination* (Austin: University of Texas Press, 1981), no page number given. Cf. Messick, "Indexing the Self," 177–178.

This study has been an effort to gain a more specific understanding of the nature and role of intentions in Islamic positive law, including ritual, civil, and penal law, and including cases, such as inheritance, marriage, and some aspects of divorce, where intent is given little or no role at all. The complexity and diversity of the medieval jurists' treatments of intent, and my ultimate inability to provide a single unifying theory of intent in Islamic law, should, in the end, be neither surprising nor especially troubling. As Oussama Arabi has observed, "Perhaps more than any other discourses in Islam, legal discourse carries the historical memory of a cultural identity marked by the spirit of tolerance."[24] The jurists tolerated diversity among themselves and uncertainty about many crucial aspects of their vaunted enterprise. Their treatment of intent is just one of many specific cases demonstrating that Islamic law, rather than being a simple—or even complex—list of rules, has always been a living entity committed to tolerance, pluralism, and an ongoing quest for the best answers to crucial questions.

---

[24] Arabi, "Contract Stipulations," 30.

BIBLIOGRAPHY

Primary Sources

ʿAlī, ʿAbdullah Yūsuf, trans. *The Meaning of the Holy Qur'ān*. Brentwood, Md.: Amana, 1991.

Al-Bayjūrī, Ibrāhīm b. Muḥammad. *Ḥāshiyat al-shaykh Ibrāhīm al-Bayjūrī ʿalā sharḥ al-ʿalāmat Ibn al-Qāsim al-Ghazzī ʿalā matn al-shaykh Abī Shujāʿ*. Beirut: Dār al-Kutub al-ʿIlmiyya, 1994.

Al-Bukhārī, Abū ʿAbd Allāh Muḥammad b. Ismāʿīl. *Ṣaḥīḥ al-Bukhārī*. N.p.: Dār Iḥyāʾ al-Kutub al-ʿArabiyya, n.d.

Al-Ghazālī, Abū Ḥāmid. *Iḥyāʾ ʿulūm al-dīn*. Cairo: Lajnat Nashr al-Thaqāfa al-Islāmiyya, 1938.

——. *The Mysteries of Worship in Islam: Iḥyāʾ ʿulūm al-dīn, Book 4*. Translated by Elliot Calverley. Lahore: Sh. Muḥammad Asraf, 1977.

——. *Al-Wajīz*. Beirut: Dār al-Maʿrifa, 1979.

Grigsby, W.E., trans. *The Medjellè or Ottoman Civil Law*. Cyprus: Herbert E. Clarke, 1895.

Ibn Abī al-Dam, Ibrāhīm b. ʿAbd Allāh. *Kitāb adab al-qaḍāʾ*. Edited by Muḥammad Muṣṭafā al-Zuḥaylī. Damascus: Dār al-Fikr, and Beirut: Dār al-Fikr al-Muʿāṣir, 1982.

Ibn Abī Shayba, Abū Bakr ʿAbd Allāh b. Muḥammad b. Ibrāhīm b. ʿUthmān. *Al-Kitāb al-muṣannaf*. Hayderabad: Maṭbaʿat al-ʿUlūm al-Sharqiyya, 1967.

Ibn Khaldūn. *The Muqaddimah: An Introduction to History*. Translated by Franz Rozenthal. London: Routledge and Kegan Paul, 1967.

Ibn Naqīb al-Miṣrī, Aḥmad. *ʿUmdat al-sālik wa-ʿuddat al-nāsik*. Edited and translated by Nūḥ Ḥā Mīm Keller, *Reliance of the Traveller: A Classic Manual of Islamic Sacred Law*. Beltsville, Md.: Ammana, 1994.

Ibn Qudāma, Muwaffaq al-Dīn ʿAbd Allāh b. Aḥmad. *Al-Mughnī*. Edited by ʿAbd Allāh b. ʿAbd al-Muḥsin al-Turkī and ʿAbd al-Fatāḥ Muḥammad al-Ḥilū. Cairo: Hajir, 1992.

Ibn Rushd, Abū al-Walīd Muḥammad b. Aḥmad al-Qurṭubī. *Bidāyat al-mujtahid wa-nihāyat al-muqtaṣid*. Beirut: Dār al-Kutub al-ʿIlmiyya, 1988.

——. *The Distinguished Jurist's Primer: A Translation of "Bidāyat al-Mujtahid."* Translated by Imran Ahsan Khan Nyazee. Reading: Garnet, 1994.

Ibn Taymiyya, Aḥmad. *Majmūʿ al-fatāwā*. Riyāḍ: Maṭābiʿ al-Riyāḍ, 1381–1386 H.

Al-Kāsānī, Abū Bakr b. Masʿūd. *Kitāb badāʾiʿ al-ṣanāʾiʿ fī tartīb al-sharāʾiʿ*. Beirut: Dār al-Kitāb al-ʿArabī, 1974.

Al-Makkī, Abū Ṭālib Muḥammad b. ʿAlī. *Qūt al-qulūb fī muʿāmalat al-maḥbūb wa-waṣf ṭarīq al-murīd ilā maqām al-tawḥīd*. Cairo: Muṣṭafā al-Bābī al-Ḥalabī, 1961.

Mālik b. Anas. *Al-Muwaṭṭa'*. Edited by Muḥammad Fuwād 'Abd al-Bāqī. N.p.: Dār Iḥyā' al-Kutub al-'Arabiyya, n.d.

——. *Al-Muwaṭṭa*. Translated by 'A'isha 'Abdarahman at-Tarjumana and Ya'qub Johnson. N.p.: Diwan Press, 1982.

Al-Marghīnānī, 'Alī b. Abī Bakr. *The Hedaya, or Guide: A Commentary on the Mussulman Laws*. Translated by Charles Hamilton. Lahore: Premier, 1870.

——. *Al-Hidāya, sharḥ bidāyat al-mubtadī*. Cairo: Maktabat Muṣṭafā al-Bābī al-Ḥalabī wa-Awlāduhu, 1975.

Al-Māwardī, Abū al-Ḥasan 'Alī b. Muḥammad b. Ḥabīb. *Adab al-qāḍī*. Baghdad: Maṭba'at al-Irshād, 1971.

——. *Al-Aḥkām al-sulṭāniyya wal-wilāyāt al-dīniyya*. Edited by Khālid 'Abd al-Laṭīf al-Sab' al-'Alamī. Beirut: Dār al-Kitāb al-'Arabī, 1994.

——. *Al-Ḥawī al-kabīr fī fiqh al-imām al-Shāfi'ī*. Beirut: Dār al-Kutub al-'Ilmiyya, 1994.

al-Mūṣilī, 'Abd Allāh b. Maḥmūd b. Mawdūd. *Al-Ikhtiyār li-ta'līl al-mukhtār*. Edited by Maḥmūd Abū Daqīqa. Beirut: Dār al-Kutub al-'Ilmiyya, n.d.

Muslim, Abū al-Ḥusayn. *Ṣaḥīḥ Muslim*. Beirut: Dār Iḥyā' al-Turāth al-'Arabī, n.d.

Al-Nawawī, Abū Zakariyyā Muḥyī al-Dīn b. Sharaf. *Rawḍat al-ṭālibīn*. N.p.: Al-Maktab al-Islāmī lil-Ṭabā'a wal-Nashr, 196–.

——. *Gardens of the Righteous: Riyadh al-Salahin of Imam Nawawi*. Translated by Muhammad Zafrullah Khan. London: Curzon, 1974.

——. *Riyāḍ al-ṣalāḥīn*. Beirut: Dār Maktabat al-Ḥayāt, 1979.

——. *Kitāb al-majmū': sharḥ al-muhadhdhab lil-Shīrāzī*. Cairo: Dār Iḥyā' al-Turāth al-'Arabī, 1995.

Al-Qarāfī, Aḥmad b. Idrīs. *Al-Umniyya fī idrāk al-niyya*. Beirut: Dār al-Kutub al-'Ilmiyya, 1984.

——. *Al-Iḥkām fī tamyīz al-fatāwā 'an al-aḥkām wa-taṣarrufāt al-qādī wal-imām*. Aleppo: Maktabat al-Maṭbū'āt al-Islamiyya, 1967. Reprint, Beirut: Dār al-Nashā'ir al-Islamiyya, 1995.

Al-Qayrawanī, 'Abd Allāh b. Abī Zayd. *Risāla*. Edited and translated (French) by Kawthar 'Abd al-Sallām al-Buhayrī. Cairo: Dār al-Kitāb al-Miṣrī, and Beirut: Dār al-Kitāb al-Lubnānī, n.d.

Al-Rāfi'ī, Sālim 'Abd al-Ghanī. *Mukhtaṣar al-majmū' sharḥ al-muhadhdhab*. Jadda: Maktabat al-Sawādī lil-Tawzī', 1995.

Al-Sarakhsī, Abū Bakr Muḥammad b. Ahmad. *Kitāb al-mabsūt*. Beirut: Dār al-Ma'rifa, n.d.

Al-Shāfi'ī, Muḥammad b. Idrīs. *Al-Risāla*. Edited by Aḥmad Muḥammad Shākir. Beirut: Dār al-Fikr, n.d.

——. *Al-Umm*. Beirut: Dār al-Fikr, 1990.

——. *Al-Shāfi'ī's Risāla: Treatise on the Foundations of Islamic Jurisprudence*. Translated by Majid Khadduri. Johns Hopkins, 1961. Reprint, Cambridge: Islamic Texts Society, 1997.

Al-Sha'rānī, Abū al-Mawāhib 'Abd al-Wahhāb b. Aḥmad b. 'Alī. *Al-Mīzān al-kubrā*. Cairo: Maktabat Muṣṭafā al-Bābī al-Ḥalabī wa-Awlāduhu, 1940.

Al-Shawkānī, Muḥammad b. 'Alī. *Kitāb al-sayl al-jarrār*. Damascus: Dār al-Fikr, 1984.

Shayzarī, ʿAbd al-Raḥman b. Naṣr. *The Book of the Islamic Market Inspector.* Translated by Ronald Paul Buckley. Oxford: Oxford University Press, 2000.
Al-Shīrāzī, Abū Isḥāq. *Al-Muhadhdhab fī fiqh al-imām al-Shāfiʿī.* Edited by Muḥammad al-Zuḥaylī. Damascus: Dār al-Qalm, 1996.
Al-Ṭabarī, Abū Jaʿfar Muḥammad b. Jarīr. *Jāmiʿ al-bayān ʿan taʾwīl āy al-Qurʾān.* Cairo, Maktabat Muṣṭafā al-Bābī al-Ḥalabī wa-Awlāduhu, 1954–1968.

Secondary Sources

Al-ʿAjm, Rafīq. *Mawsūʿat muṣṭalaḥāt uṣul al-fiqh ʿinda al-muslimīn.* Beirut: Maktabat Lubnān Nāshirūn, 1998.
Alishan, Leonardo P. "Beyond the Law: The Experience of Some Persian Ṣūfī Poets—A Response to Mahmoud Ayoub." In *Religion and Law: Biblical-Judaic and Islamic Perspectives,* ed. Edwin B. Firmage, Bernard G. Weiss, and John W. Welch, 231–241. Winona Lake: Eisenbrauns, 1990.
Amerdoz, H.F. "The Office of the Kadi in the Ahkam Sultaniyya of Mawardi." *Journal of the Royal Asiatic Society* (1910): 761–796.
Anderson, J.N.D. "Homicide in Islamic Law." *Bulletin of the School of Oriental and African Studies, University of London* 13, 4 (1951): 811–828.
Ansari, Zafar Ishaq. "Islamic Juristic Terminology Before Šāfiʿī: A Semantic Analysis with Special Reference to Kūfa." *Arabica* 19, 3 (1972): 255–300.
Anscombe, G.E.M. *Intention,* 2d ed. Oxford: Basil Blackwell, 1963.
Arabi, Oussama. "Intention and Method in Sanhūrī's *Fiqh*: Cause as Ulterior Motive." *Islamic Law and Society* 4, 2 (1997): 200–223.
——. "Contract Stipulations (*Shurūṭ*) in Islamic Law: The Ottoman *Majalla* and Ibn Taymiyya." *International Journal of Middle East Studies* 30, 1 (1998): 29–50.
Arberry, A.J., trans. *The Koran Interpreted.* New York: Macmillan, 1955.
Asad, Talal. *Genealogies of Religion.* Baltimore: Johns Hopkins University Press, 1993.
Al-Ashqar, ʿUmar Sulaymān. *Maqāṣid al-mukallafīn fīmā yutaʿabbadu bihi li-rabb al-ʿālamīn, aw, "al-Niyyāt fī al-ʿibādāt."* ʿAmmān: Dār al-Nafāʾis, and Kuwait City: Maktabat al-Falāḥ, 1991.
Austin, J.L. *How to Do Things with Words.* Cambridge, Mass.: Harvard University Press, 1962.
Ayoub, Mahmoud. "Law and Grace in Islam: Ṣūfī Attitudes toward the Sharīʿa." In *Religion and Law: Biblical-Judaic and Islamic Perspectives,* ed. Edwin B. Firmage, Bernard G. Weiss, and John W. Welch, 221–229. Winona Lake: Eisenbrauns, 1990.
Bahnasī, Muḥammad ʿAbd al-Raʾūf. *Al-Niyya fī al-sharīʿa al-islāmiyya.* Cairo: Dār al-Qawmiyya al-ʿArabiyya lil-Ṭibāʿa, n.d.
Bakhtiar, Laleh. *Encyclopedia of Islamic Law: A Compendium of the Major Schools.* N.p.: ABC International Group, 1996.
Bassiouni, M. Cherif, ed. *The Islamic Criminal Justice System.* London, Rome, and New York: Oceana, 1982.

Bell, Catherine. "Ritualization of Texts and Textualisation of Ritual in the Codification of Taoist Liturgy." *History of Religions* 27, 4 (1988): 366–392.

———. *Ritual Theory, Ritual Practice*. Oxford: Oxford University Press, 1992.

———. *Ritual: Perspectives and Dimensions*. Oxford: Oxford University Press, 1997.

Bell, R. *Introduction to the Qur'ān*. Revised and enlarged by M.W. Watt. Edinburgh: Edinburgh University Press, 1970.

Berman, Harold J. *Law and Revolution: The Formation of the Western Legal Tradition*. Cambridge, Mass.: Harvard University Press, 1983.

Bernand, M. "Mu'āmalāt." *Encyclopaedia of Islam*, new ed. Leiden: Brill, 1960–.

Boecker, Hans Jochen. *Law and the Administration of Justice in the Old Testament and Ancient East*. Translated by Jeremy Moiser. London: S.P.C.K., 1980.

Bourdieu, Pierre. *Outline of a Theory of Practice*. Translated by Richard Nice. New York: Cambridge University Press, 1977.

Bousquet, G.-H. "'Ibādāt." *Encyclopaedia of Islam*, new ed. Leiden: Brill, 1960–.

Bowen, John R. "*Salāt* in Indonesia: The Social Meanings of an Islamic Ritual." *Man: The Journal of the Royal Anthropological Institute* 24 (1989): 600–619.

———. *Muslims Through Discourse: Religion and Ritual in Gayo Society*. Princeton: Princeton University Press, 1993.

———. "Modern Intentions: Reshaping Subjectivities in an Indonesian Muslim Society." In *Islam in an Era of Nation-States*, ed. Robert W. Hefner and Patricia Horvatich, 157–181. Honolulu: University of Hawai'i Press, 1997.

———. "Qur'ān, Justice, Gender: Internal Debates in Indonesian Islamic Jurisprudence." *History of Religions* 38, 1 (August 1998): 52–78.

Brown, Daniel W. *Rethinking Tradition in Modern Islamic Thought*. Cambridge: Cambridge University Press, 1996.

Brunschvig, R. "Bayyina." *Encyclopaedia of Islam*, new ed. Leiden: Brill, 1960–.

Bulliet, Richard. *Islam: The View from the Edge*. New York: Columbia University Press, 1994.

Calder, Norman. *Studies in Early Islamic Jurisprudence*. Oxford: Clarendon, 1993.

———. "Sharī'a." *Encyclopaedia of Islam*, new ed. Leiden: Brill, 1960–.

Chaumont, E. "Al-Shīrāzī, al-Shaykh al-Imām Abū Isḥāḳ Ibrāhīm b. 'Alī b. Yūsuf al-Fīrūzābādī." *Encyclopaedia of Islam*, new ed. Leiden: Brill, 1960–.

Chelhod, J. "Kaffāra." *Encyclopaedia of Islam*, new ed. Leiden: Brill, 1960–.

Christmas, Simon. "Intensionality." *Routledge Encyclopedia of Philosophy*. London and New York: Routledge, 1988.

Cook, Michael. *Commanding Right and Forbidding Wrong in Islamic Thought*. Cambridge: Cambridge University Press, 2000.

Coulson, N.J. "Doctrine and Practice in Islamic Law: One Aspect of the Problem." *Bulletin of the School of Oriental and African Studies* 18, 2 (1956): 211–226.

———. *A History of Islamic Law*. Edinburgh: Edinburgh University Press, 1964.

———. *Succession in the Muslim Family*. Cambridge: Cambridge University Press, 1971.

Cragg, Kenneth, ed. and trans. *Readings in the Qur'ān*. London: Collins, 1988.

Crane, Tim. "Intentionality." *Routledge Encyclopedia of Philosophy*. London and New York: Routledge, 1988.

Crone, Patricia. "Jāhilī and Jewish Law: The Qasāma." *Jerusalem Studies in Arabic and Islam* 4 (1984): 153–201.

———. *Roman, Provincial and Islamic Law: The Origins of the Islamic Patronate.* Cambridge: Cambridge University Press, 1987.

Crone, Patricia, and Michael Cook. *Hagarism: The Making of the Islamic World.* Cambridge: Cambridge University Press, 1977.

Denny, Frederick M. "Islamic Ritual: Perspectives and Theories." In *Approaches to Islam in Religious Studies*, ed. Richard C. Martin, 63–77. Tucson: University of Arizona Press, 1985.

———. "Ethical Dimensions of Islamic Ritual Law." In *Religion and Law: Biblical-Judaic and Islamic Perspectives*, ed. Edwin B. Firmage, Bernard G. Weiss, and John W. Welch, 199–210. Winona Lake: Eisenbrauns, 1990.

———. *An Introduction to Islam*, 2d ed. New York: Macmillan, 1994.

Diamond, Cora and Jenny Teichman, eds. *Intention and Intentionality: Essays in Honor of G.E.M. Anscombe.* Ithaca: Cornell University Press, 1979.

DiMatteo, Larry A. *Contract Theory: The Evolution of Contractual Intent.* East Lansing: Michigan State University Press, 1998.

Donaldson, Dwight M. *Studies in Muslim Ethics.* London: S.P.C.K., 1953.

Douglas, Mary. *Purity and Danger: An Analysis of the Concepts of Pollution and Taboo.* London: Routledge and Keegan Paul, 1966.

———. *Natural Symbols: Explorations in Cosmology.* London: Barrie and Jenkins, 1973.

Dunn, Robert. "Intention." *Routledge Encyclopedia of Philosophy.* London and New York: Routledge, 1988.

Dutton, Yasin. "The Introduction to Ibn Rushd's Bidāyat al-Mujtahid." *Islamic Law and Society* 1, 2 (1994): 188–205.

Eilberg-Schwartz, Howard. *The Human Will in Judaism: The Mishnah's Philosophy of Intention.* Atlanta: Scholars Press, 1986.

Encyclopaedia of Islam, new ed. Leiden: Brill, 1960–.

Enelow, H.G. "Kawwana: The Struggle for Inwardness in Judaism." In *Studies in Jewish Literature*, 82–107. Berlin: Georg Riemer, 1913.

Esposito, John L. *Women in Muslim Family Law.* Syracuse: Syracuse University Press, 1982.

Fadel, Mohammad. "Adjudication in the Mālikī *Madhhab*: A Study of Legal Process in Medieval Islamic Law." Ph.D. diss., University of Chicago, 1995.

Fierro, Maribel. "The Legal Policies of the Almohad Caliphs and Ibn Rushd's Bidāyat al-Mujtahid." *Journal of Islamic Studies* 10, 3 (1999): 226–248.

Forte, David F. "Lost, Strayed, or Stolen: Chattel Recovery in Islamic Law." In *Islamic Law and Jurisprudence: Studies in Honor of Farhat J. Ziadeh*, ed. Nicholas Heer, 97–115. Seattle and London: University of Washington Press, 1990.

Frank, Richard M. *Al-Ghazali and the Ash'arite School.* Durham: Duke University Press, 1994.

Fuller, Lon L. *The Morality of Law*, rev. ed. New Haven and London: Yale University Press, 1969.

Gardet, L. "'Ilm al-Kalām," "Ḳalb." *Encyclopaedia of Islam*, new ed. Leiden: Brill, 1960–.

Gätje, Helmut. *The Qur'ān and Its Exegesis*. Translated and edited by Alford T. Welch. Oxford: Oneworld, 1971.

Geertz, Clifford. *The Interpretation of Cultures: Essays in Interpretive Anthropology*. New York: Basic Books, 1973.

——. *Local Knowledge: Further Essays in Interpretive Anthropology*. New York: Basic Books, 1983.

Gibb, H.A.R. *Mohammedanism*. Oxford: Oxford University Press, 1970.

Giffen, Lois A. "Another Perspective on Ethics in Islamic Law and Ritual: A Response to Frederick Denny." In *Religion and Law: Biblical-Judaic and Islamic Perspectives*, ed. Edwin B. Firmage, Bernard G. Weiss, and John W. Welch, 211–220. Winona Lake: Eisenbrauns, 1990.

Glassé, Cyril. *The Concise Encyclopedia of Islam*. San Francisco: Harper & Row, 1989.

Goldziher, Ignaz. *Introduction to Islamic Theology and Law*. Translated by Andras Hamori and Ruth Hamori. Princeton: Princeton University Press, 1981. Originally published as *Vorlesungen über den Islam*. Heidelberg, 1910.

Goldziher, Ignaz (revised by Joseph Schacht). "Fiḳh." *Encyclopaedia of Islam*, new ed. Leiden: Brill, 1960–.

Grimes, Ronald L. *Readings in Ritual Studies*. Upper Saddle River, N.J.: Prentice Hall, 1996.

Halberstam, Joshua. "Supererogation in Jewish Halakhah and Islamic Sharī'a." In *Studies in Islamic and Judaic Traditions*, ed. William M. Brinner and Stephen D. Ricks, 85–98. Atlanta: Scholars Press, 1986.

Hallaq, Wael B. "Was the Gate of Ijtihād Closed?" *International Journal of Middle East Studies* 16 (1984): 3–41.

——. "Legal Reasoning in Islamic Law and the Common Law: Logic and Method." *Cleveland State Law Review* 34 (1985–1986): 79–96.

——. "On the Authoritativeness of Sunnī Consensus." *International Journal of Middle East Studies* 18 (1986): 427–454.

——. "Non-Analogical Arguments in Sunnī Juridical *Qiyās*." *Arabica* 36, 3 (1989): 286–306.

——. "On Inductive Corroboration, Probability, and Certainty in Sunnī Legal Thought." In *Islamic Law and jurisprudence: Studies in Honor of Farhat J. Ziadeh*, ed. Nicholas Heer, 3–31. Seattle and London: University of Washington Press, 1990.

——. "Was al-Shafi'i the Master Architect of Islamic Jurisprudence?" *International Journal of Middle East Studies* 25 (1993): 587–605.

——. "Logic, Formal Arguments and Formalization of Arguments in Sunnī Legal Thought." *Arabica* 37 (1990): 315–358. Reprinted in *Law and Legal Theory in Classical and Medieval Islam*. Hampshire, U.K.: Variorum, 1994.

——. "The Use and Abuse of Evidence: The Question of Provincial and Roman Influences on Early Islamic Law." *Journal of the American Oriental Society* 110 (1989): 1–36. Reprinted in *Law and Legal Theory in Classical and Medieval Islam*. Hampshire, U.K.: Variorum, 1994.

——. "*Uṣūl al-Fiqh*: Beyond Tradition." *Journal of Islamic Studies* 3 (1992): 172–202. Reprinted in *Law and Legal Theory in Classical and Medieval Islam*. Hampshire, U.K.: Variorum, 1994.

——. "From *Fatwās* to *Furūʿ*: Growth and Change in Islamic Substantive Law." *Islamic Law and Society* 1, 1 (1994): 29–65.
——. "Ifta' and Ijtihad in Sunni Legal Theory: A Developmental Account." In *Islamic Legal Interpretation: Muftis and their Fatwas*, ed. Muhammad Khalid Masud, Brinkley Messick, and David S. Powers, 33–43. Cambridge, Mass.: Harvard University Press, 1996.
——. *A History of Islamic Legal Theories: An Introduction to Sunnī* Uṣūl al-Fiqh. Cambridge: Cambridge University Press, 1997.
——. *Authority, Continuity, and Change in Islamic Law*. Cambridge: Cambridge University Press, 2001.
——. *The Origins and Evolution of Islamic Law*. Cambridge: Cambridge University Press, 2005.
Hart, H.L.A. *The Concept of Law*, 2d ed. Oxford: Oxford University Press, 1994.
Hawting, Gerald. "An Ascetic Vow and an Unseemly Oath?: *Īlā'* and *Ẓihār* in Muslim Law." *Bulletin of the School of Oriental and African Studies* 57 (1994): 113–125.
Heffening, W. "Zum Aufbau der Islamischen Rechtswerke." In *Studien zur Geschichte und Kultur des Nahen und Fernen Ostens*, ed. W. Heffening and W. Kirfel, 101–118. Leiden: Brill, 1935.
Higger, Michael. "Intention in Talmudic Law." Ph.D. diss., Columbia University, 1927.
Hodgson, Marshall G.S. *The Venture of Islam*. Chicago and London: University of Chicago Press, 1974.
Hollis, Martin. "Reason and Ritual." In *Rationality*, ed. Bryan R. Wilson, 221–239. Oxford: Basil Blackwell, 1970.
Hooker, M.B. "Sharīʿa." *Encyclopaedia of Islam*, new ed. Leiden: Brill, 1960–.
Horii, Satoe. "Reconsideration of Legal Devices (*Ḥiyal*) in Islamic Jurisprudence: The Ḥanafīs and Their 'Exits' (*Makhārij*)." *Islamic Law and Society* 9, 3 (2002): 312–357.
Hornsby, Jennifer. "Action." *Routledge Encyclopedia of Philosophy*. London and New York: Routledge, 1988.
Hourani, G.F. "The Basis of Authority of Consensus in Sunnite Islam." *Studia Islamica* 21 (1964): 13–60.
——. "Ethical Presuppositions of the Qur'ān." *The Muslim World* 70, 1 (January 1980): 1–28.
——. *Reason and Tradition in Islamic Ethics*. New York: Cambridge University Press, 1985.
Humphrey, Caroline and James Laidlaw. *The Archetypal Actions of Ritual: A Theory of Ritual Illustrated by the Jain Rite of Worship*. Oxford: Oxford University Press, 1994.
Humphreys, R. Stephen. *Islamic History: A Framework for Inquiry*, rev. ed. Princeton: Princeton University Press, 1991.
Hurvitz, Nimrod. "Schools of Law and Historical Context: Re-examining the Formation of the Ḥanbalī *Madhhab*." *Islamic Law and Society* 7, 1 (2000): 37–64.
Jackson, Bernard S. "Legalism and Spirituality: Historical, Philosophical, and Semiotic Notes on Legislators, Adjudicators, and Subjects." In *Religion and*

Law: Biblical-Judaic and Islamic Perspectives, ed. Edwin B. Firmage, Bernard G. Weiss, and John W. Welch, 243–261. Winona Lake: Eisenbrauns, 1990.

Jackson, Sherman A. "From Prophetic Actions to Constitutional Theory: A Novel Chapter in Medieval Muslim Jurisprudence." *International Journal of Middle East Studies* 25 (1993): 71–90.

——. *Islamic Law and the State.* Leiden: Brill, 1996.

——. "The Alchemy of Domination? Some Ash'arite Responses to Mu'tazilite Ethics." *International Journal of Middle East Studies* 31 (1999): 185–201.

Al-Jazīrī, 'Abd al-Raḥman. *Kitāb al-fiqh 'alā al-madhāhib al-arba'a.* Cairo: Al-Maktaba al-Tijāriyya al-Kubrā, n.d.

Jennings, Theodore. "On Ritual Knowledge." *Journal of Religion* 62, 2 (1982): 111–127.

Johansen, Baber. "Casuistry: Between Legal Concept and Social Praxis." *Islamic Law and Society* 2, 2 (1995): 135–156.

——. "The Valorization of the Human Body in Muslim Sunni Law." In *Law and Society in Islam*, Devin J. Stewart, Baber Johansen, and Amy Singer, 71–112. Princeton: Markus Wiener, 1996.

——. "Die Sündige, Gesunde Amme. Moral und Gesetzliche Bestimmung (*Ḥukm*) im Islamischen Recht." In *Contingency in a Sacred Law: Legal and Ethical Norms in the Muslim* Fiqh. Leiden: Brill, 1999.

Kadushin, Max. *Worship and Ethics: A Study in Rabbinic Judaism.* Evanston: Northwestern University Press, 1964.

Al-Kafawī, Abū al-Baqā' Ayyūb b. Mūsā al-Ḥusaynī. *Al-Kulliyāt.* N.p.: Wizārat al-Thaqāfa wal-Irshād al-Qawmī, 1974.

Kamali, Mohammad Hashim. *Principles of Islamic Jurisprudence*, rev. ed. Cambridge: Islamic Texts Society, 1991.

Kassis, Hanna E. *A Concordance of the Qur'an.* Berkeley: University of California Press, 1983.

Katz, Leo. *Bad Acts and Guilty Minds: Conundrums of the Criminal Law.* Chicago: University of Chicago Press, 1987.

Katz, Marion Holmes. *Body of Text: The Emergence of the Sunnī Law of Ritual Purity.* Albany: State University of New York Press, 2002.

——. "The Problem of Abortion in Classical Sunni *Fiqh*." In *Islamic Ethics of Life: Abortion, War, and Euthanasia*, ed. J. Brockopp, 25–50. Columbia: University of South Carolina Press, 2003.

Kennedy, Hugh. *The Prophet and the Age of the Caliphates.* London and New York: Longman, 1986.

Khadduri, Majid, and Herbert J. Liebesny, eds. *Law in the Middle East*, Vol. I: *Origin and Development of Islamic Law.* Washington, D.C.: The Middle East Institute, 1955.

Kimber, Richard. "The Qur'ānic Law of Inheritance." *Islamic Law and Society* 5, 3 (1998): 291–325.

Kugler, Itzhak. *Direct and Oblique Intention in the Criminal Law: An Inquiry into Degrees of Blameworthiness.* Burlington: Ashgate, 2002.

Lane, Edward William. *An Arabic-English Lexicon.* London: William and Norgate, 1863. Reprint, Beirut: Librairie du Liban, 1968.

Leiser, G. "Notes on the Madrasa in Medieval Islamic Society." *Muslim World* 76 (1986): 16–23.

Liebesny, Herbert J. *The Law of the Near & Middle East: Readings, Cases, & Materials*. Albany: State University of New York Press, 1975.

Linant de Bellefonds, Y. *Traité de Droit Musulman Comparé*. Paris: Mouton, 1965–1973.

Lippman, Matthew, Sean McConville, and Mordechai Yerushalmi. *Islamic Criminal Law and Procedure*. New York: Praeger, 1988.

MacDonald, D.B. "Fiṭra." *Encyclopaedia of Islam*, new ed. Leiden: Brill, 1960–.

Maghen, Ze'ev. "Much Ado about Wuḍū'." *Der Islam* 76 (1999): 205–252.

Maghniyya, Muḥammad Jawād. *Al-Waṣāyā wal-mawārīth 'alā al-madhāhib al-khamsa*. Beirut: Al-Maktaba al-Ahliyya, n.d.

———. *Fiqh al-imām Ja'far al-Ṣādiq*. Beirut: Dār al-'Ilm lil-Malāyīn, 1965.

Makdisi, George. "The Juridical Theology of Shāfi'ī: Origins and Significance of *Uṣūl al-Fiqh*." *Studia Islamica* 59 (1984): 5–47.

———. *The Rise of Humanism in Classical Islam and the Christian West, with Special Reference to Scholasticism*. Edinburgh: Edinburgh University Press, 1990.

———. "Ibn Taymīya: A Ṣūfi of the Qādiriya Order." *American Journal of Arabic Studies* 1 (1974): 118–129. Reprinted in *Religion, Law and Learning in Classical Islam*. Hampshire, U.K.: Variorum, 1991.

Mansour, Aly Aly. "*Hudud* Crimes." In *The Islamic Criminal Justice System*, ed. M. Cherif Bassiouni, 195–201. London, Rome, and New York: Oceana, 1982.

Margoliouth, D.S. "Omar's Instructions to the Kadi." *Journal of the Royal Asiatic Society of Great Britain and Ireland* (1910): 307–326.

Marshall, James. *Intention in Law and Society*. New York: Funk & Wagnalls, 1968.

Massignon, Louis. "The Juridical Consequences of the Doctrines of al-Hallāj." In *Studies on Islam*, trans. and ed. M.L. Swartz, 140–163. New York: Oxford University Press, 1981.

———. *Essay on the Origins of the Technical Language of Islamic Mysticism*. Translated by Benjamin Clark. Notre Dame: University of Notre Dame Press, 1997.

Masud, Muhammad Khalid, Brinkley Messick, and David S. Powers, eds. *Islamic Legal Interpretation: Muftis and their Fatwas*. Cambridge, Mass.: Harvard University Press, 1996.

Mayer, Ann. "The Sharī'ah: A Methodology or a Body of Substantive Rules?" In *Islamic Law and Jurisprudence: Studies in Honor of Farhat J. Ziadeh*, ed. Nicholas Heer, 177–198. Seattle and London: University of Washington Press, 1990.

McCutcheon, Russell T. "Writing a History of God: 'Just the Same Game Wherever You Go.'" In *Critics Not Caretakers: Redescribing the Public Study of Religion*, 43–55. Albany: State University of New York Press, 2001.

McNeill, William H. and Marilyn Robinson Waldman, eds. *The Islamic World*. Chicago: University of Chicago Press, 1983.

Melchert, Christopher. *The Formation of the Sunni Schools of Law, 9th–10th Centuries C.E.* Leiden: Brill, 1997.

———. "How Ḥanafism Came to Originate in Kufa and Traditionalism in Medina." *Islamic Law and Society* 6, 3 (1999): 318–347.

Mele, Alfred R. "Recent Work on Intentional Action." *American Philosophical Quarterly* 25, 3 (1992): 199–217.

Meron, Yaakov. "L'accommodation de la Répudiation Musulmane." *Revue Internationale de Droit Comparé* 478, 4 (1995): 921–933.

Messick, Brinkley. *The Calligraphic State*. Berkeley: University of California Press, 1993.

——. "Written Identities: Legal Subjects in an Islamic State." *History of Religions* 38, 1 (August 1998): 25–51.

——. "Indexing the Self: Intent and Expression in Islamic Legal Acts." *Islamic Law and Society* 8, 2 (2001): 151–178.

Moosa, Ibrahim "Allegory of the Rule (*Ḥukm*): Law as Simulacrum in Islam?" *History of Religions* 38, 1 (August 1998): 1–24.

Murad, Hasan Qasim. "*Jabr* and *Qadar* in Early Islam: A Reappraisal of their Political and Religious Implication." In *Islamic Studies Presented to Charles J. Adams*, ed. Wael B. Hallaq and Donald P. Little, 117–132. Leiden: Brill, 1991.

Murphy, Jeffrie G. and Jules L. Coleman. *Philosophy of Law: An Introduction to Jurisprudence*, rev. ed. Boulder, San Francisco, and London: Westview, 1990.

Naffine, N., R. Owens, and J. Williams, eds. *Intention in Law and Philosophy*. Burlington: Ashgate, 2001.

Neusner, Jacob. "Ritual Without Myth: The Use of Legal Materials for the Study of Religions." *Religion* 5, 2 (1975): 91–100.

Niazi, Liaquat Ali Khan. *Islamic Law of Tort*. Lahore: Diyal Singh Trust Library, 1988.

Osborn, Robert Durie. *Islam under the Khalīfs of Baghdād*. London: Seeley, Jackson, & Halliday, 1878.

Padwick, Constance E. *Muslim Devotions: A Study of Prayer-Manuals in Common Use*. London: S.P.C.K., 1961.

Patai, Raphael. *Ignaz Goldziher and His Oriental Diary: A Translation and Psychological Portrait*. Detroit: Wayne State University Press, 1987.

Pedersen, J. (revised by Y. Linant de Bellefonds). "Ḳasam." *Encyclopaedia of Islam*, new ed. Leiden: Brill, 1960–.

Powers, David S. *Studies in Qur'an and* Ḥadīth: *The Formation of the Islamic Law of Inheritance*. Berkeley: University of California Press, 1986.

——. "On Bequests in Early Islam." *Journal of Near Eastern Studies* 48, 3 (1989): 185–200.

——. "The Art of the Legal Opinion: al-Wansharisi on *Tawlīj*." In *Islamic Legal Interpretation: Muftis and their Fatwas.*, ed. Muhammad Khalid Masud, Brinkley Messick, and David S. Powers, 98–115. Cambridge, Mass.: Harvard University Press, 1996.

——. "The Art of the Judicial Opinion: On *Tawlīj* in Fifteenth-Century Tunis." *Islamic Law and Society* 5, 3 (1998): 359–381.

Powers, Paul R. "Interiors, Intentions, and the 'Spirituality' of Islamic Ritual Practice." *Journal of the American Academy of Religion* 72, 2 (2004): 426–454.

Qalʿajī, Muḥammad Rawwās. *Mawsūʿat fiqh Zayd b. Thābit wa-Abī Hurayra*. Beirut: Dār al-Nafāʾis, 1993.

———. *Mawsūʿat fiqh al-Ṭabarī wa-Ḥammād b. Abī Sulaymān*. Beirut: Dār al-Nafāʾis, 1994.

Rahman, Falzur. "The Status of the Individual in Islam." In *The Status of the Individual East and West*, ed. Charles A. Moore and Aldyth V. Morris, 217–225. Honolulu: University of Hawai'i Press, 1968.

———. "Law and Ethics in Islam." In *Ethics in Islam*, ed. Richard G. Hovannisian, 3–15. Malibu: Undena, 1985.

Rappaport, Roy A. "The Obvious Aspects of Ritual." In *Readings in Ritual Studies*, ed. Ronald M. Grimes, 427–440. Upper Saddle River, N.J.: Prentice Hall, 1996.

Rebstock, Ulrich. "A Qāḍī's Errors." *Islamic Law and Society* 6, 1 (1999): 1–37.

Reinhart, A. Kevin. "Islamic Law as Islamic Ethics." *The Journal of Religious Ethics* 11, 2 (1983): 186–203.

———. "Impurity/No Danger." *History of Religions* 30, 1 (1990): 1–24.

———. "Transcendence and Social Practice: *Muftīs* and *Qāḍīs* as Religious Interpreters." *Annales Islamologiques* 27 (1993): 5–28.

———. *Before Revelation: The Boundaries of Muslim Moral Thought*. Albany: State University of New York Press, 1995.

———. "When Women Went to Mosques: al-Aydini on the Duration of Assessments." In *Islamic Legal Interpretation: Muftis and their Fatwas*, ed. Muhammad Khalid Masud, Brinkley Messick, and David S. Powers, 116–128. Cambridge, Mass.: Harvard University Press, 1996.

Robinson, Daniel N. *Wild Beasts and Idle Humors: The Insanity Defense from Antiquity to the Present*. Cambridge, Mass.: Harvard University Press, 1996.

Rorty, Amelie Oksenberg. "Understanding Others." In *Other Intentions: Cultural Contexts and the Attribution of Inner States*, ed. Lawrence Rosen, 203–223. Santa Fe: School of American Research Press, 1995.

Rosen, Lawrence. "Equity and Discretion in a Modern Islamic Legal System." *Law & Society Review* 15, 2 (1980–1981): 217–245.

———. "Intentionality and the Concept of the Person." In *Criminal Justice*, ed. J. Roland Pennock and John W. Chapman, 52–77. New York: New York University Press, 1985.

———. *The Anthropology of Justice: Law as Culture in Islamic Society*. Cambridge: Cambridge University Press, 1989.

———. "Have the Arabs Changed Their Mind? Intentionality and the Discernment of Cultural Change." In *Other Intentions: Cultural Contexts and the Attribution of Inner States*, ed. Lawrence Rosen, 177–200. Santa Fe: School of American Research Press, 1995.

———. "Justice in Islamic Culture and Law." In *Perspectives on Islamic Law, Justice, and Society*, ed. R.S. Khare, 33–52. Lanham, Md., and Oxford: Rowman & Littlefield, 1999.

Sachedina, Abdulaziz. "The Ideal and Real in Islamic Law." In *Perspectives on Islamic Law, Justice, and Society*, ed. R.S. Khare, 15–31. Lanham, Md., and Oxford: Rowman & Littlefield, 1999.

———. "Woman, Half-the-Man? Crisis of Male Epistemology in Islamic Jurisprudence." In *Perspectives on Islamic Law, Justice, and Society*, ed. R.S. Khare, 145–160. Lanham, Md., and Oxford: Rowman & Littlefield, 1999.

Said, Edward. *Orientalism*. New York: Vantage, 1979.

Schacht, Joseph. *The Origins of Muhammadan Jurisprudence*. Oxford: Oxford University Press, 1950.

——. *An Introduction to Islamic Law*. Oxford: Clarendon, 1964.

——. "Bayʿ," "Fiḳh," "Ḥiyal," "Mīrāth," "Nikāḥ." *Encyclopaedia of Islam*, new ed. Leiden: Brill, 1960–.

Schacht, Joseph, and A. Layish. "Ṭalāḳ." *Encyclopaedia of Islam*, new ed. Leiden: Brill, 1960–.

Scholem, Gershom G. "The Concept of Kavvanah in the Early Kabbalah." Translated by Noah J. Jacobs. In *Studies in Jewish Thought: An Anthology of German Jewish Scholarship*, ed. Alfred Jospe, 162–180. Detroit: Wayne State University Press, 1981.

Searle, John R. *Speech Acts: An Essay in the Philosophy of Language*. Cambridge: Cambridge University Press, 1969.

——. *Expression and Meaning: Studies in the Theory of Speech Acts*. Cambridge: Cambridge University Press, 1979.

——. *Intentionality: An Essay in the Philosophy of Mind*. Cambridge: Cambridge University Press, 1983.

——. *The Rediscovery of the Mind*. Cambridge, Mass.: MIT Press, 1992.

——. *Mind, Language, and Society: Philosophy in the Real World*. New York: Basic, 1998.

Sells, Michael. *Early Islamic Mysticism*. New York: Paulist Press, 1996.

Siddiqui, Mona. "Law and the Desire for Social Control: An Insight into the Hanafi Concept of *Kafa'a* with Reference to the Fatawa ʿAlamgiri (1664–1672)." In *Feminism and Islam: Legal and Literary Perspectives*, ed. Mai Yamani and Andrew Allen, 49–68. New York: New York University Press, 1996.

——. "The Defective Marriage in Classical Hanafi Law: Issues of Form and Validity." In *Studies in Islamic and Middle Eastern Texts and Traditions, In Memory of Norman Calder*, ed. G.R. Hawting, J.A. Mojaddedi, and A. Samely, 271–286. Oxford: Oxford University Press, 2000.

Simmons, A. John. "Fault, Objectivity, and Classical Islamic Justice." In *Perspectives on Islamic Law, Justice, and Society*, ed. R.S. Khare, 53–61. Lanham, Md., and Oxford: Rowman & Littlefield, 1999.

Smith, J.M. Powis. *The Origin and History of Hebrew Law*. Chicago: University of Chicago Press, 1960.

Smith, Jane H., and Yvonne Y. Haddad. *The Islamic Understanding of Death and Resurrection*. Albany: State University of New York Press, 1981.

Smith, Jonathan Z. *Imagining Religion: From Babylon to Jonestown*. Chicago: University of Chicago Press, 1982.

——. *To Take Place: Toward Theory in Ritual*. Chicago: University of Chicago Press, 1987.

Spectorsky, Susan A. *Chapters on Marriage and Divorce: Responses of Ibn Ḥanbal and Ibn Rāhwayh*. Austin: University of Texas Press, 1993.

Staal, Frits. "The Meaninglessness of Ritual." *Numen* 26 (1979): 2–22.

Al-Tahānawī, Muḥammad ʿAlī b. ʿAlī b. Muḥammad. *Kashshāf iṣṭilāḥāt al-funūn*. Beirut: Dār al-Kutub al-ʿIlmiyya, 1998.

Tahir-ul-Qadri, Muhammad. *Islamic Penal System and Philosophy*. Lahore: Minhaj-ul-Qur'an Publications, 1995.

Tambiah, S.J. *Culture, Thought, and Social Action: An Anthropological Perspective*. Cambridge, Mass.: Harvard University Press, 1985.

——. *Magic, Science, Religion, and the Scope of Rationality*. Cambridge: Cambridge University Press, 1990.

Taylor, Charles. *Sources of the Self: The Making of the Modern Identity*. Cambridge, Mass.: Harvard University Press, 1989.

Thomas, Owen C. "Interiority and Christian Spirituality." *Journal of Religion* 80, 1 (2000): 41–60.

Tisdall, William St. Clair. *The Religion of the Crescent*. 3rd ed. London: Society for Promoting Christian Knowledge, 1910.

Turner, Victor. *The Ritual Process: Structure and Anti-Structure*. Ithaca: Cornell University Press, 1969.

Tyan, Emile. "Judicial Organization." In *Law in the Middle East*, Vol. I: *Origin and Development of Islamic Law*, ed. Majid Khadduri and Herbert J. Liebesny, 236–278. Washington, D.C.: Middle East Institute, 1955.

Vogel, Frank Edward. "Islamic Law and Legal System: Studies of Saudi Arabia." Ph.D. diss., Harvard University, 1993.

von Grunebaum, Gustave E. *Muhammadan Festivals*. New York: Schuman, 1951. Reprint, London: Curzon, 1992.

Waines, David. *An Introduction to Islam*. Cambridge: Cambridge University Press, 1995.

Wakin, Jeanette A. *The Function of Documents in Islamic Law*. Albany: State University of New York Press, 1972.

——. "Interpretation of the Divine Command in the Jurisprudence of Muwaffaq al-Dīn Ibn Qudāmah." In *Islamic Law and Jurisprudence: Studies in Honor of Farhat J. Ziadeh*, ed. Nicholas Heer, 33–52. Seattle and London: University of Washington Press, 1990.

Weiss, Bernard. "Covenant and Law in Islam." In *Religion and Law: Biblical-Judaic and Islamic Perspectives*, ed. Edwin B. Firmage, Bernard G. Weiss, and John W. Welch, 49–83. Winona Lake: Eisenbrauns, 1990.

——. "Exotericism and Objectivity in Islamic Jurisprudence." In *Islamic Law and Jurisprudence: Studies in Honor of Farhat J. Ziadeh*, ed. Nicholas Heer, 53–71. Seattle and London: University of Washington Press, 1990.

——. "Law in Islam and in the West: Some Comparative Observations." In *Islamic Studies Presented to Charles J. Adams*, ed. Wael B. Hallaq and Donald P. Little, 239–254. Leiden: Brill, 1991.

——. *The Search for God's Law*. Salt Lake City: University of Utah Press, 1992.

——. "Ibn Taymiyya on Leadership in the Ritual Prayer." In *Islamic Legal Interpretation: Muftis and their Fatwas*, ed. Muhammad Khalid Masud, Brinkley Messick, and David S. Powers, 63–71. Cambridge, Mass.: Harvard University Press, 1996.

——. *The Spirit of Islamic Law*. Athens and London: University of Georgia Press, 1998.

Wensinck, A.J. "De Intentie in Recht, Ethiek en Mystiek der Semietische

Volken." *Verslagen en Mededeelingen der Koninklijke Akademie van Wetenschappen* 5, 4 (1920): 109–140.

———. *Concordance et indices de la tradition musulmane*. Leiden: Brill, 1936–1988.

———. "Niyya." *Encyclopaedia of Islam*, new ed. Leiden: Brill, 1960–.

Wheeler, Brannon M. *Applying the Canon in Islam: The Authorization and Maintenance of Interpretive Reasoning in Ḥanafī Scholarship*. Albany: State University of New York Press, 1996.

Wright, W. *A Grammar of the Arabic Language*. 3rd ed. Cambridge: Cambridge University Press, 1967. Reprinted 1991.

X, Malcolm (with Alex Haley). *The Autobiography of Malcolm X*. New York: Ballantine, 1965.

Yanagihashi, Hiroyuki. "The Doctrinal Development of '*Maraḍ al-Mawt*' in the Formative Period of Islamic Law." *Islamic Law and Society* 5, 3 (1998): 326–358.

Ziadeh, Farhat J. "*Adab al-Qāḍī* and the Protection of Rights at Court." In *Studies in Islamic and Judaic Traditions*, ed. William M. Brinner and Stephen D. Ricks, 143–150. Atlanta: Scholars, 1986.

———. "Integrity (*'Adālah*) in Classical Islamic Law." In *Islamic Law and Jurisprudence: Studies in Honor of Farhat J. Ziadeh*, ed. Nicholas Heer, 73–93. Seattle and London: University of Washington Press, 1990.

———. "Criminal Law." *Oxford Encyclopedia of the Modern Islamic World*. Oxford: Oxford University Press, 1995.

Al-Zuhaylī, Wahbah. *Al-Fiqh al-islāmī wa-adillatuhu*. Beirut: Dār al-Fikr, 1989.

Zysow, Aron. "The Economy of Certainty: An Introduction to the Typology of Islamic Legal Theory." Ph.D. diss., Harvard University, 1984.

INDEX

To increase the utility of this index, citations of frequently utilized primary sources, authors, jurists, and schools of Islamic law are limited to explicit and substantive discussions and do not include all references to evidence taken from a given source.

In classifying entries, no account is taken of the letter *ʿayn*, the *hamza*, or the Arabic definite article *al-*.

www.ingramcontent.com/pod-product-compliance
Lightning Source LLC
LaVergne TN
LVHW102227300926
849160LV00005B/51